JEKKA MCVICAR

NEW BOOK OF

Herbs

DK PUBLISHING

LONDON, NEW YORK, MUNICH,
MELBOURNE, DELHI

Editor	Bella Pringle
Design & art direction	Robin Rout
Managing editor	Anna Kruger
Managing art editor	Lee Griffiths
Senior art editor	Alison Lotinga
DTP design	Louise Waller
Picture research	Melanie Watson
Production controller	Mandy Inness
Jacket design	Nicola Powling

First American Edition, 2002

00 01 02 03 04 05 10 9 8 7 6 5 4 3 2 1

Published in the United States by
DK Publishing, Inc.
375 Hudson Street
New York, New York 10014

A Cataloging in Publication record is available
from the Library of Congress.
ISBN 0-7894-89422

Color reproduction by GRB Editrice Slr. Italy
Printed and bound in Spain by Artes Gráficas
Toledo S.A.U.
D.L. TO: 1333-2000

See our complete product line at

www.dk.com

63517

Author's note
Herbs contain natural medicinal properties and should be
treated with respect. This book is not intended as a
medical reference book, but as a source of information.
Do not take any herbal remedies if you are undergoing any
other course of medical treatment without seeking
professional advice. Before trying herbal remedies, the
reader is recommended to sample a small quantity first to
establish whether there is any adverse or allergic reaction.
The reader is advised not to attempt self-treatment for
serious or long-term problems without consulting a
qualified medicinal herbalist. Neither the author nor the
publisher can be held responsible for any adverse reactions
to the recipes, recommendations, and instructions
contained herein, and the use of any herb or derivative is
entirely at the reader's own risk.

In Loving Memory of William

Contents

Introduction

What is an Herb?

The answer to the apparently simple question "What is an herb?" is not as straightforward as you might think. A botanist would say that an herb is a plant that dies down to the ground in winter and the British Royal Horticultural Society's definition of an herb, according to its *Dictionary of Gardening*, is "a plant of which the stem dies to the ground at the end of the season." These definitions seem to me to be rather too narrow, considering that some plants I class as herbs, like bay (*Laurus nobilis*), are evergreen, and so I prefer the explanation of an herb given in the Oxford English Dictionary, where the term "herb" is "applied to plants of which the leaves or stem and leaves are used for medicine, or for their scent or flavor."

Top row left Foxglove (*Digitalis purpurea*) is a traditional medicinal herb that has been used since the eighteeth century to treat heart conditions.

Top row center Lady's mantle (*Alchemilla xanthocholra* syn. *vulgaris*) is both a culinary and medicinal herb. Young leaves are used in salads, and medicinally it is used to alleviate menopausal discomfort.

Top row right Narrow-leaved sage (*Salvia lavendulifolia*) leaves have a strong aromatic flavor in casseroles and stews. It is also good for making an herbal infusion to help the memory.

Middle row left Sweet Annie (*Artemisia annua*) is an important medicinal herb that is used in the treatment of malaria.

Middle row center This informal, aromatic herb garden combines culinary and medicinal herbs with herbaceous perennials.

Middle row right Feverfew (*Tanacetum parthenium*) is a renowned remedy for certain types of migraine.

Bottom row left Borage (*Borago officinalis*) attracts bees and other pollinating insects to the garden, and the seeds are high in polyunsaturated fats.

Bottom row center Golden lemon balm (*Melissa officinalis* 'All Gold') has lemon-scented leaves that can be added to salads or made into an infusion to relieve tiredness and tension.

Bottom row right Purple basil (*Ocimum basilicum* 'Red Rubin') has highly aromatic leaves that are good eaten raw in salads or added to pasta sauces.

The properties of herbs

Herbs have a history that is steeped in myth and magic, and there is much bogus information regarding their potency and properties. But if we put aside the superstitions attached to herbs and concentrate on the many medicinal and culinary benefits they have brought us over the past 1,500 years, we can but conclude that they are the most extraordinarily diverse and useful plants. Herbs come in all shapes, sizes, textures, and perfumes, and they can be incorporated into any size of garden or container. You may think of a particular herb like sweet basil (*Ocimum basilicum*) as a delicious cooking herb, only to discover its value in the garden as a companion plant for deterring pests from tomato plants or its ability to act as a fly repellent when planted in pots for the home. The same applies to an herb like chamomile (*Chaemomelum nobile*), which is wonderful in beauty products for lightening hair, but is also a healing herb to relieve insomnia when drunk as a tisane.

The future for herbs

Research into the properties of herbs and how people around the world use these plants is now high on most people's agenda, and I am aware of an herb revival at a time when we are more knowledgeable about the damaging effects of our lifestyles on our bodies and the environment. I think that there is a new respect for herbs, and that they have a vital part to play in a healthier approach to modern living.

Why grow herbs organically?

"The organic approach to gardening and farming recognises that the whole environment in which plants grow is much more than the sum of its individual parts, and that all living things are inter-related and inter-dependent" Henry Doubleday Research Association.

Organic methods and principles respect the environment and work in harmony with nature's cycles. Good organic gardeners build up the sustainability of the soil by feeding it with organic waste that has been recycled from the home or garden. This encourages the microbes in the soil to break down the recycled waste into food for the plants. The plants in turn will flourish, and attract beneficial insects for pollination. Seeds are produced, fall to the ground, and in turn grow into new plants for the following season. As life is a cycle, so is the garden.

Benefits of organic herbs

Herbs are one of the most beneficial groups of plants to have in the organic garden. Grown without pesticides and chemical fertilizers, organic herbs attract many beneficial insects, bees, birds and butterflies to the garden and vegetable plot, achieving a high level of pollination and increased yields. So by growing your herbs organically you not only create a beautiful garden that is teeming with wildlife, but also increase the productivity and the health of the plants you grow. You can enjoy picking and using delicious fresh herbs in cooking without the worry of introducing pesticides into your diet. Personally, I prefer to eat organic herbs because I think that they taste better. Herbs grown in the sun, rain, and soil – instead of being grown on a large scale under artificial lights – contain more nutrients as all these environmental elements help boost the natural oil content in the plants. When used in cooking, the organic herbs often go further because they have a more intense flavor and a lower water content. For common ailments, too, organic preparations are less likely than conventional medicines to cause adverse reactions, and many are gentle enough to treat small children and pets. You can also make your own herbal cleaning products for the home that are free from synthetic pollutants.

The best way forward

The organic approach to farming was practised widely until after World War II when mechanisation, a growing population and the demand for more intensive production and cheaper food increased. However, with the recent BSE (bovine spongiform encephalopathy) scare in Britain and the wider concern about genetically modified (GM) food, we are becoming more aware of the consequences of intensive farming. Organic systems, for me, represent the best way forward. They work in harmony with nature, not against it, and growing herbs organically will help to keep our environment as well as our gardens, safe, enjoyable and healthy places to be.

Balancing the ecosystem

Beneficial plants When choosing herbs for your garden, consider what the plant can contribute to the garden. For example chamomile (*Chamaemelum nobile*) as well as making a soothing cup of herb tea will repel flying insects when planted next to onions, and improve their crop yield. A chamomile infusion can also be sprayed on seedlings to prevent "damping off" or place leaves on the compost heap to help speed up the process (see page 37).

Companion planting When planted next to other species certain herbs will deter pests or have a healing effect. Plant basil next to tomatoes and this will inhibit aphids because the pest prefers basil to tomatoes. Or plant yarrow (*Achillea millefolium*) near an ailing shrub or tree and the herb will help the plant rebuild its natural disease resistance.

Attracting birds Birds eat pests and insects, so to encourage birds into the garden, plant seed-bearing herbs to give them a supply of food for the winter. For example, evening primrose (*Oenothera biennis*) attracts all members of the tit family and elecampane (*Inula helenium*) the finch family.

Bees and butterflies Both are good pollinators so plant herbs to attract them. Borage (*Borago officinalis*) with runner beans helps increase the yield. Korean angelica (*Angelica gigas*) is a beneficial late-season nectar plant, so consider growing it in the garden.

Managing herbs the natural way

The art of good organic management is constant vigilance. I regularly tour my farm on the look-out for signs of pests or disease. If I see anything, I can act quickly before the problem spreads, either by introducing a predator to control an infestation of pests, or by cutting back the plant if it is diseased. Another organic but time-consuming method is to remove or squash any pests as you see them. When I first started the farm, the ecosystem was out of balance (as your garden will be in its first year without chemicals), and I had to mount slug patrols at night. If you have previously used slug pellets, pay special attention to that area where you laid pellets because they are designed to draw slugs to them. If collecting up slugs is not working, introduce the parasitic nematode (*Phasmarhabditis hermaphrodita*); however, this only works well at temperatures above 40°F (5°C) on moist soil. To control insects like aphids, try growing a

Spring   **Summer**

Remove moss and weeds

In spring, remove moss and weeds from wintered container plants. This will prevent the weeds from taking over the pot and stop them from taking all the nutrients from the substrate. Also it allows the wind and rain to get to the plant, which makes a stronger specimen.

Fertilize pot-grown herbs

In spring, after clearing off all the winter debris and roughing up the surface of the substrate, add a small amount of organic fertilizer to the surface, then lightly cover with new substrate. Feeding at this time of year will encourage the plant to put on new growth.

Control pests

From spring, start controlling pests. Pick off any that you see, and look under the canopy of shrubs to see if there are any slugs. Check containers for vine weevil damage, and repot, removing all contaminated soil. Check the glasshouse or conservatory for aphids or red spider mite, introducing predators if required to control the problem.

Cut back flowers

In summer, cut back herbs to prolong the harvesting season. This is a good idea for soft-leaved herbs like lovage, chives, mint, and lemon balm. After cutting back, give the herbs a liquid feed with comfrey (see page 39), which will encourage rapid new growth to produce a second crop of leaves.

companion plant like buddleia mint to attract hoverfly, whose larvae will then eat greenfly. Alternatively, collect ladybugs and introduce them into the infested area. A diseased plant will drop its leaves on the soil, so cut out infested or damaged parts of the plant to inhibit the spread of disease. Act quickly, especially in the case of rust, which infects herb plants like mint, tarragon, and chives. Once the rust spores are in the soil, it is difficult to get rid of them organically (see page 194). In fall and spring, check the weather forecast for frost. Use horticultural fleece to cover and protect established tender plants and newly emerging seedlings. Before feeding the soil in the fall or spring with well-rotted manure, pick up a handful of soil and smell it. If there is only a faint aroma, the soil is deficient and needs a generous manure feed. Above all else, try to enjoy the work and do not try to fight against nature – go with it.

Fall   Winter

Cut back established plants
In early fall cut back established plants to regain shape. Evergreen herbs like thyme, lavender, and lavender cotton benefit from being cut back, not only to stop them from becoming woody and shapeless, but also to protect them from being split apart by adverse weather conditions. It also encourages light new growth for winter protection.

Lift tender plants
In the fall, lift tender plants to protect them from frost. Small herbs like scented pelargoniums (shown here) are well worth lifting. Cut them back quite hard, pot up using a loam-based substrate, water in, then place the container in a frostfree environment. The plants will then need minimal watering until the following spring.

Feed established plants
In the fall, feed established plants in the garden. Use either well-rotted manure or well-rotted compost, and dig it in around the established plants, avoiding areas of soft growth. By doing this in the fall, the feed will slowly nourish the soil and at the same time give the roots added protection.

Protect exposed plants
In winter, protect large tender and exposed plants in the garden. Tender plants that have become too large for moving may need extra protection from inclement weather. Horticultural fleece is ideal. It is light, so will not damage the plant, and it is permeable so the plant can breathe. On warm days, remove the fleece to allow better air circulation, especially if it has become wet.

The Garden

Your garden environment

The key to a successful organic herb garden is to work with nature, and remember that every garden has a unique set of growing conditions that distinguish it from any other, which goes some way to explaining why a neighbor may be able to grow certain plants that you have tried to grow with little success. Perhaps your garden is sheltered by the house and the soil does not get much rain. Or it could be exposed to a prevailing wind that makes the soil drier than the garden next door. Before you plan a new herb garden or re-design an existing one, it is a good idea to familiarize yourself with the site and note down environmental factors that may influence the herbs you select. Also, the native trees, shrubs, and weeds that are growing well in the garden or its immediate

surroundings offer clues to your soil type. The presence of horsetail and comfrey are signs of a damp, heavy soil, while shrubs like rhododendrons and azaleas indicate acid soil, and beech trees chalky soil. Herb gardens, particularly those that feature Mediterranean culinary herbs like sage, need plenty of sunshine to thrive. Note the position of the sun in relation to the growing beds in the garden. Where does the sun rise, and how does it move across the garden during the course of the day? Which areas of the garden are in permanent shade, and is there anything you can do to improve the situation? Perhaps a shadow is being cast by a large tree that needs pruning.

Planning a new herb garden

If your proposed herb garden site has been neglected for years, or you are starting a new garden from scratch in a field site – as I did – try to find old maps of the area to give you some background information on what has gone before so you will have some knowledge about what you can grow there. When I looked at an old detailed survey map of my area, I found that the site was formerly called "clay fields," so I knew from the outset that I would have to work with heavy clay soil and have to find herbs that could adapt to these conditions, or else work hard to improve the soil. Find out as much as you can before you start, and you will have all you need to plan a thriving herb garden.

Soil analysis

The easiest way to analyze your soil is to pick up a handful, and ask yourself the following questions. Does it fall through your fingers or does it form a solid lump? Does it have a sweet, warm, earthy smell? Or, is the soil poor with no odor or even a slightly sour smell? A healthy soil is teeming with life, and it should have worm channels, which indicate that the soil is aerated and not compacted. Good plant growth is dependent not only on the nutrient content of the soil, but also on its structure. Sandy soil is often low in nutrients because the rain washes them away. Clay soil can be rich in plant food, but heavy and waterlogged, so plant roots find it difficult to establish a foothold. Use bulky organic matter to improve soil structure, to help sandy soil retain water, to aerate clay soil, and generally to produce healthier herb crops.

Soil condition

Checking the pH The pH of the soil refers to its acidity or alkalinity. It is a vital factor in the plant's ability to obtain all types of plant foods and essential chemicals via its root system. For example, an alkaline soil can produce stunted plants with yellowing leaves because minerals like iron cannot be absorbed. At a neutral pH of 7, most of the essential chemicals and plant foods become available, producing healthy plants.

Soil testing To test your soil, buy a soil testing kit from a garden center. The majority of amateur soil-testing kits are very simple and rely on color rather than the numerical pH scale. Acid soils turn the indicator orange, neutral turns it green, and alkaline dark green.

Improving soil structure

• All soil improvers can be added as a mulch or dug into the top 6in (15cm) which is the main feeding area for the plant roots.

• Use a wooden plank from which to dig. Do not stand or walk on the soil, since compacted soil has little air, which makes it difficult for the roots to penetrate.

• Dig only when necessary, because overdigging can destroy soil structure.

• Keep the soil covered with a mulch to maintain soil structure.

• Do not overfertilize. If you do, the plant will produce lots of lush top growth, but no flowers, and therefore no fruit. Also lush growth encourages pests.

Basic soil types

Soil can vary from acid (pH 3.5) to alkaline (pH 8.5). Most herbs will tolerate a range of 6.5–7.5 pH, which is fairly neutral. Here, I am holding a clay soil in my right hand – the soil particles stick together – and a good quality loam soil in my left hand. The four basic soil types and their properties are outlined below. They are all suitable for growing herbs.

Clay (pH 6.5) This soil has tiny particles that stick together when wet, making the soil heavy and difficult for roots to penetrate. When it is dry, it sets hard. Even though it can be rich in nutrients, improve its structure by working in well-rotted leaf mold to enable young plants to establish themselves.

Chalk (pH 8.5) This soil is light and has lumps of flint or chalk. It drains well and is often shallow in depth. It has a high pH, making it alkaline. Increase nutrients with compost, but it is harder to reduce alkalinity. Many herbs tolerate chalk, but for root depth and moisture it may be easier to grow them in raised beds.

Loam (5.5–8.5 pH) This is often considered the optimum soil for herb growing. There are various types of loam. A sandy loam is the best for growing Mediterranean herbs, but herbs like soapwort, comfrey, angelica, valerian, Joe Pye weed, queen-of-the-meadow, and loosestrife grow best in moist to marshy loam.

Sand (4.5 pH) This soil feels gritty. It is free draining, so plant nutrients are washed away. One advantage is that is warms up quickly in spring, so sowing and planting can start early. To help retain moisture, feed in winter with leaf mold and well-rotted manure.

Which Soil

• = favorite soil   • = other suitable soils

Plant	SAND	CLAY	CHALK	LOAM
Achillea ageratum *English mace*	•		•	•
Achillea millefolium *Yarrow*	•	•	•	•
Agastache foeniculum *Anise hyssop*	•		•	•
Alchemilla xanthochlora *Lady's mantle*	•	•	•	•
Allium cepa Proliferum Group *Tree onion*	•		•	•
Allium fistulosum *Welsh onion*	•		•	•
Allium sativum *Garlic*	•		•	•
Allium schoenoprasum *Chives*	•		•	•
Allium tuberosum *Garlic chives*	•		•	•
Allium ursinum *Wild garlic*	•		•	•
Aloe vera *Aloe*	•			
Aloysia triphylla *Lemon verbena*	•		•	•
Angelica archangelica *Angelica*		•		•
Angelica gigas *Korean angelica*	•	•		•
Anethum graveolens *Dill*	•		•	•
Anthriscus cerefolium *Chervil*	•		•	•
Armoracia rusticana *Horseradish*	•		•	•
Arnica chamissonis *Arnica*	•		•	•
Artemisia annua *Sweet Annie*	•		•	•
Artemisia abrotanum *Southernwood*	•		•	•
Artemisia absinthium *Wormwood*	•		•	•
Artemisia dracunculus *French tarragon*	•		•	•
Artemisia vulgaris *Mugwort*	•		•	•
Borago officinalis *Borage*	•		•	•
Borago pygmaea *Prostrate borage*	•		•	•
Buxus sempervirens *Box*	•		•	
Buxus sempervirens 'Latifolia Maculata' *Golden box*	•		•	
Calendula officinalis *Pot marigold*	•		•	
Calomeria amaranthoides *Incense plant*	•		•	•
Carum carvi *Caraway*	•		•	•
Cedronella canariensis *Balm of Gilead*	•		•	•
Centaurea cyanus *Bachelor's buttons*	•		•	
Centella asiatica *Gotu kola*	•		•	•
Chamaemelum nobile *Roman chamomile*	•		•	•
Chamaemelum nobile 'Treneague' *Lawn chamomile*	•		•	•
Chamaemelum nobile 'Flore Pleno' *Double-flowered chamomile*	•		•	•
Chenopodium bonus-henricus *Goosefoot*	•		•	•
Chenopodium giganteum *Tree spinach*	•		•	•
Cichorium intybus *Chicory*	•		•	•
Coriandrum sativum *Coriander (cilantro)*	•		•	•
Crithmum maritimum *Sea fennel*				•
Cymbopogon citratus *Lemon grass*	•		•	
Cynara cardunculus *Cardoon*				•
Digitalis purpurea *Foxglove*		•	•	
Diplotaxis muralis *Wild rocket*	•			
Echinacea purpurea *Purple coneflower*	•			
Echinacea angustifolia *Narrow-leaved echinacea*	•			
Echinacea pallida *Echinacea*	•			
Elettaria cardamomum *Cardamom*	•			
Eriocephalus africanus *Wild rosemary*	•			
Eupatorium purpureum *Joe Pye weed*	•	•	•	•
Filipendula ulmaria *Queen-of-the-meadow*				•
Foeniculum vulgare *Fennel*	•		•	•
Foeniculum vulgare 'Purpureum' *Bronze fennel*	•		•	•
Fragaria vesca *Wild strawberry*	•	•		•
Galium odoratum *Sweet woodruff*	•	•		•
Ginkgo biloba *Ginkgo*				•
Glycyrrhiza glabra *Licorice*				•
Humulus lupulus *Common hop*	•			•
Hypericum perforatum *St. John's Wort*	•		•	
Hyssopus officinalis *Blue hyssop*	•		•	•
Hyssopus officinalis 'Roseus' *Pink hyssop*	•		•	•
Inula helenium *Elecampane*	•	•	•	•
Isatis tinctoria *Woad*	•		•	•
Juniperus communis *Juniper*	•		•	•
Laurus nobilis *Bay*	•		•	•

Plant	SAND	CLAY	CHALK	LOAM
Laurus nobilis 'Aurea' *Golden bay*	•		•	•
Laurus noblis f. angustifolia *Willow leaf bay*	•		•	•
Lavandula x intermedia Old English Group *Old English lavender*	•		•	•
Lavandula angustifolia 'Hidcote' *Hidcote lavender*	•		•	•
Lavandula dentata var. candicans *Lavender Candicans*	•		•	•
Lavandula stoechas 'Kew Red' *Lavender 'Kew Red'*	•		•	•
Lavandula stoechas *French lavender*	•		•	•
Lavandula stoechas 'Helmsdale' *Lavender Helmsdale*	•		•	•
Lavandula x allardii *Lavender Allardii*	•		•	•
Lavandula x christiana *Lavender Christiana*	•		•	•
Lavandula 'Sawyers' *Lavender Sawyers*	•		•	•
Levisticum officinale *Lovage*	•			•
Linum perenne *Flax*	•		•	•
Luma chequen *Luma*	•			•
Lycopus europaeus *Gypsywort*		•		•
Lysimachia vulgaris *Yellow loosestrife*		•		•
Lythrum salicaria *Purple loosestrife*		•		•
Malva moschata *Musk mallow*	•			•
Malva sylvestris *Common mallow*	•			•
Mandragora officinarum *Mandrake*	•			•
Marrubium vulgare *White horehound*	•		•	•
Melissa officinalis *Lemon balm*	•	•	•	•
Melissa officinalis 'All Gold' *Golden lemon balm*	•	•	•	•
Melissa officinalis 'Aurea' *Variegated lemon balm*	•	•	•	•
Mentha pulegium 'Upright' *Pennyroyal upright*	•			•
Mentha x piperita *Peppermint*	•	•	•	•
Mentha x piperita f. citratus *Eau-de-cologne mint*	•	•	•	•
Mentha x piperita 'Logee' *Logee mint*	•	•	•	•
Mentha spicata *Spearmint*	•	•	•	•
Mentha spicata var. crispum *Curly mint*	•	•	•	•
Mentha x villosa var. alopecuroides 'Bowles' *Bowles mint*	•	•	•	•
Meum athamanticum *Meu*	•			•
Monarda fistulosa *Wild bergamot*	•			•
Murraya koenigii *Curry tree*	•			•
Myrrhis odorata *Myrrh*		•		•
Myrtus communis *Myrtle*	•			•
Myrtus communis 'Merion' *Myrtle Merion*	•			•
Myrtus communis 'Microphylla Variegata' *Variegated small-leaved myrtle*	•			•
Nepeta cataria *Catnip*	•	•	•	•
Nepeta x faassenii *Catmint*	•		•	•
Nigella sativa *Black cumin*	•			•
Ocimum basilicum *Sweet basil*	•			•
Ocimum basilicum 'Cinnamon' *Cinnamon basil*	•			•
Ocimum basilicum 'Dark Opal' *Dark opal basil*	•			•
Ocimum basilicum 'Horapha Nanum' *Thai basil*	•			•
Ocimum basilicum 'Siam Queen' *Siam Queen basil*	•			•
Ocimum minimum 'Greek' *Greek basil*	•			•
Ocimum tenuiflorum *Holy basil*	•			•
Oenothera biennis *Evening primrose*	•	•	•	•
Olea europaea *Olive*	•		•	•
Origanum dictamnus *Cretan oregano*	•			•
Origanum majorana *Sweet marjoram*	•		•	•
Origanum vulgare *Oregano, Wild marjoram*	•		•	•
Origanum vulgare 'Acorn Bank' *Oregano Acorn Bank*	•		•	•
Origanum x onites *French marjoram*	•		•	•
Pelargonium 'Apple scented' *Apple-scented pelargonium*				•
Pelargonium 'Atomic Snowflake' *Atomic snowflake pelargonium*				•
Pelargonium 'Attar of roses' *Attar of Roses pelargonium*				•
Pelargonium 'Chocolate Peppermint' *Pelargonium Chocolate Peppermint*				•
Pelargonium 'Lady Plymouth' *Lady Plymouth pelargonium*				•
Pelargonium 'Peach Cream' *Peach Cream pelargonium*				•

Plant	SAND	CLAY	CHALK	LOAM
Perilla frutescens var. crispa *Green shiso*	•			•
Perilla frutescens var. purpurascens *Purple shiso*	•			•
Persicaria odorata *Vietnamese coriander*	•			•
Petroselinum crispum *Parsley*	•	•	•	•
Petroselinum crispum 'French' *French parsley*	•	•	•	•
Phytolacca americana *Pokeroot*	•			•
Portulaca oleracea *Purslane*	•			•
Primula vulgaris *Primrose*			•	•
Prostanthera cuneata *Australian mint bush*	•			•
Rosmarinus officinalis *Rosemary*	•		•	•
Rosmarinus officinalis 'Aureus' *Golden rosemary*	•		•	•
Rosmarinus officinalis 'Roseus' *Pink rosemary*	•		•	•
Rosmarinus officinalis Prostratus Group *Prostrate rosemary*	•		•	•
Rumex scutatus *French sorrel*	•	•		•
Ruta graveolens *Rue*	•			•
Salvia clevelandii *Jim sage*	•			•
Salvia elegans 'Scarlet Pineapple' *Pineapple sage*	•			•
Salvia lavandulifolia *Narrow-leaved sage*	•			•
Salvia microphylla var. microphylla *Blackcurrant-scented sage*	•			•
Salvia officinalis *Sage*	•		•	•
Salvia officinalis Purpurascens Group *Purple sage*	•		•	•
Salvia viridis *Painted sage*	•		•	•
Sambucus nigra *Elder*	•	•	•	•
Sanguisorba minor *Salad burnet*	•	•	•	•
Santolina chamaecyparissus *Lavender cotton*	•			•
Saponaria officinalis *Soapwort*			•	•
Satureja douglasii *Yerba buena*	•			•
Satureja hortensis *Summer savory*	•			•
Satureja montana *Winter savory*	•		•	•
Scutellaria lateriflora *Virginia skullcap*	•			•
Sempervivum tectorum *Houseleek*	•			•
Solidago virgaurea *Goldenrod*	•		•	•
Stachys officinalis *Betony*	•		•	•
Symphytum officinale *Comfrey*	•	•	•	•
Symphytum x uplandicum *Russian comfrey*	•	•	•	•
Tagetes lucida *Winter tarragon*	•			•
Tagetes patula *Wild Mexican marigold*	•			•
Tanacetum balsamita *Alecost*	•			•
Tanacetum cinerariifolium *Pyrethrum*	•		•	•
Tanacetum parthenium *Feverfew*	•	•	•	•
Tanacetum vulgare *Tansy*	•	•	•	•
Teucrium chamaedrys L. *True valerian*	•		•	•
Teucrium scorodonia *Wood sage*	•	•	•	•
Teucrium scorodonia 'Crispum' *Curly wood sage*	•	•	•	•
Teucrium x lucidrys *Hedge germander*	•		•	•
Thymus 'Fragrantissimus' *Orange-scented thyme*	•		•	•
Thymus 'Peter Davis' *Peter Davis thyme*	•		•	•
Thymus caespititus *Azores thyme*	•		•	•
Thymus coccineus *Creeping red thyme*	•	•	•	•
Thymus pulegioides *Broad-leaved thyme*	•		•	•
Thymus pulegioides 'Bertram Anderson' *Bertram Anderson thyme*	•		•	•
Thymus serpyllum *Creeping thyme*	•		•	•
Thymus serpyllum 'Minimus' *Minimus thyme*	•		•	•
Thymus vulgaris 'Compactus' *Compact thyme*	•		•	•
Thymus vulgaris 'Snow White' *Compact white-flowering thyme*	•		•	•
Thymus x citriodorus 'Silver Queen' *Silver Queen thyme*	•		•	•
Tropaeolum majus 'Empress of India' *Nasturtium Empress of India*	•	•	•	•
Tropaeolum speciosum *Flame nasturtium*	•			•
Ugni molinae *Chilean guava*	•			•
Valeriana officinalis *Valerian*		•		•
Verbena officinalis *Vervain*	•		•	•
Viola odorata *Sweet violet*	•	•	•	•
Viola tricolor *Heart's ease*	•	•	•	•

Preparing new beds for planting

Before you start planting a new herb garden, take time to prepare the ground by eradicating weeds, especially perennial ones like bindweed, which can be persistent and deep rooted. (A weed basically is an invasive plant in the wrong place.) If you have heavy soil, dig it in early winter after rain, when the top soil is easier to work but before it becomes waterlogged. Winter frosts will also help to erode and break up clods of soil. If your soil is light, leave it undug until early spring so that nutrients do not leach out of the soil in wet winter weather. Once you have cleared the site, cover the soil with some form of sheeting or mulch (see below) to inhibit weed seed that lays dormant until exposed to the light. This way you will avoid having to weed the site before planting. Also, when newly planted with young herbs, do not irrigate the area with a spray hose or sprinkler because jets of water can spread weed seed. Use leaky pipes or seep irrigation instead, which also reduces water consumption.

Plastic sheeting to cover new beds

1 Cover newly prepared soil
Once your soil is clear of weeds, cover it with mulch or plastic sheeting. By excluding the light from the soil, you are effectively preventing weed growth. Here, I am using black plastic sheeting (400 gauge), which is excellent for keeping the ground clear before planting. Lay the sheet over the newly prepared soil for a month to exclude light, lock in moisture, and warm up the soil before planting. A permeable membrane like coir matting (see opposite), which allows the soil to breathe and water to permeate, is best as a long-term cover for herb beds.

2 Anchor plastic sheeting
Bury the edges of the plastic sheeting in soil or under stones or planks to stop it from lifting in strong winds. Planks are good because they give you access to the site and spread your body weight without compacting the soil structure – which is, after all, what you are trying to improve. Other suitable soil covers include cardboard. Place torn-up strips of cardboard between rows of annual herbs like coriander and dill to inhibit weeds. Cardboard is biodegradable, so when it is no longer useful in the herb bed, break it up and add it to the compost heap (see page 37).

Preparing existing beds

The best time for preparing an existing bed is in the spring, when the soil has started to warm up and seedlings are starting to grow. Clear the ground of weeds, add any soil improvers or fertilizers (see page 36–39), then apply a mulch to inhibit further weed growth. Keep your herb garden as weed-free as possible so that herbs are easy to pick and the nutrients are not depleted. Suppress weeds with a permeable plastic membrane or bark chippings, leaf mold, gravel, coir, or cocoa shells. I personally do not like cocoa shells because they have a strong smell and are environmentally unsound, having been transported across the world. Plus there is little information on whether the cocoa bush is sprayed with pesticides. I have similar ecological concerns about coir, the coarse fiber from coconut shells, which I find does not break down well. When applying mulch around established plants, always leave some bare soil close to the plant crown and roots to allow air to circulate and prevent rot.

Mulch and coir matting on mature beds

1 Spreading leaf mold mulch
The mulch in an established garden should be both nutritious and moist, helping to improve the soil condition as well as stifling weeds. My favorite mulches are leaf mold and bark (see page 37) because herb plants prefer these low-nutrient versions. In addition to being of benefit to the soil, a layer of mulch will improve the appearance of the flower bed.

2 Using permeable mulch covers
Permeable mulches made from fibrous matting materials are also available from garden centers. Fibrous coir matting (shown above) is useful for supressing weeds around established low-growing herbs where it is often awkward to weed. The coir mat will also help to protect the plant's root system in winter from cold and damp. Avoid old carpet or sacking because they look unattractive and may encourage pests like mice or other rodents that feed on herbs.

Designing an herb garden

Herbs are very versatile plants, and the pleasure in designing an herb garden is that there is a species of herb to suit every soil type and location. Whether you are planning to give over the whole of your garden to herbs, or you just want to plant herbs in individual pots, take time deciding how you want to use your chosen species. Are you growing herbs purely for their color and fragrance? Or do you want to be able to harvest herbs all year round to flavor cooking, or be able to pick herb leaves for use in summer salads? Maybe you just want to grow a selection of medicinally beneficial herbs to make tisanes?

Top left A rockery in the garden designed to face south or south-west, creates a Mediterranean-style habitat suitable for herbs like thyme, oregano, sage, and prostrate rosemary.

Top right A raised herb bed is a good solution if your soil type is unsuitable for the herbs you wish to grow. It is also a practical solution if you suffer from back problems and find it difficult to bend down.

Bottom left A path edge is planted with low-growing herbs like sage, which cascade over the edge, softening the architectural lines. When you walk along the path and brush past the sage, it fills the air with a heady aroma.

Bottom right I like to grow herbs in mixed herbaceous beds, because many have soft gray and silver foliage that looks attractive mixed in with other shrub and tree leaf colors. Blue-flowering herbs like borage are always attractive to insects, so pollination in the flowerbed is increased.

Planning the design

Before you start planting, consider your soil type and which way your garden faces (see page 19 for more information). Plan the best position for each herb plant in the garden design by researching each one's growth habit. Information on specific herbs can be found in my Top 100 herbs (see pages 114–267). Consider height; for example, angelica reaches 8ft (2.5m) so it is best placed at the back of the herb bed, while some herbs like mint spread very quickly, so you may wish to grow them in containers instead of the herb bed to keep their growth in check. Another factor is the growing cycle; for example, salad herbs like wild rocket are short-lived and are only productive for a few months, while others such as box are evergreen and will remain in leaf throughout the year. Also consider which herbs grow well together and make good companion plants. Think of your garden ecosystem, and which herbs attract birds, bees, and butterflies. By their very nature, all herbs are born survivors and self-seed freely. To keep the herb garden looking its best, you will need to maintain it, clipping evergreen foliage to shape and cutting off flowerheads before they run to seed.

If you already have an existing herb garden that you have inherited from a previous owner, do not be afraid to replace old plants, like lavender and rosemary that have become woody and are now no longer productive. Equally, if you do not particularly like certain herbs, remove them to create more space for herbs you are eager to grow.

Sources of inspiration

To help you plan a successful herb garden design, try to visit established herb gardens for inspiration. The Herb Society in Britain (see Resources) has information on herb gardens that are open to the public. Flower shows also offer a wealth of ideas for planting schemes and often have ideas on how to use herb plants to provide structure, or as path edges and hedges. Armed with this information, you will be equipped to make an enthusiastic start.

Traditional herb garden design

Herbs have been cultivated for thousands of years as medicine and as a food, but they were also planted near temples and used as part of religious rituals. By 1066, European monasteries were the custodians of medicinal herbs. The gardens were laid out in simple rectangles, and a dedicated physic garden was a feature. After the dissolution of the monasteries in Britain, herbs became the province of the manor house garden; and by Tudor times (1558) herb gardens had become very formal. In 1621, the first Botanic garden opened at Oxford University, and in 1673 the Chelsea Physic Garden followed suit. By the eighteenth century, herbs became an informal part of the flowerbed and vegetable plot. Today, herbs are grown in beds and as part of formal herb gardens, the design of which reflects their history.

Herb garden styles

Physic The design of this herb garden is influenced by the monastic gardens. The beds are rectangular and divided by grassy paths, giving access to each area of the garden. Herb beds were carefully ordered and divided up so that each bed was planted with herbs from one family, or with herb plants that healed specific areas of the body such as the head, heart, or circulatory system.

Formal knot In the early sixteenth century, knot gardens became fashionable. The feature of this style of planting is that regular geometric and symmetrical patterns are picked out in evergreen herbs like lavender cotton (*Santolina chamaecyparissus*), thyme (*Thymus vulgaris*), hyssop (*Hyssopus officinalis*), or hedge germander (*Teucrium* x *lucidrys*). An "open knot" garden was filled with flowers: a "closed knot" was a more complex pattern with no flowers, but with a sand or brick dust infill to enhance the pattern. Box (*Buxus sempervirens*), was introduced as a hedging plant in the seventeenth century.

Culinary Over 200 years ago, herbs were a staple food of everyday life. The term herb had many different meanings: vegetables were known as "pot herbs," because they added bulk to the cooking pot; "salad" (salet) herbs and "sweet" herbs were used for flavoring, and "simples" were medicinal herbs. The culinary herb garden evolved from being primarily a vegetable and herb garden combined, to a garden that now contains mainly evergreen and annual herbs. The design of a culinary herb garden is such that plants are easily accessible for picking, so stepping stones or paths running between narrow beds are an important feature.

Left The herb garden is visually linked to the vegetable garden by a archway of climbing hops (*Humulus lupulus*).

Opposite, top row left This formal knot garden has fragrant rosemary (*Rosmarinus officinalis*) and clipped evergreen box hedges (*Buxus sempervirens*) in-filled with purple sage (*Salvia officinalis* Purpurascens Group).

Opposite, top row right Here the natural mound shape and silver foliage of lavender cotton (*Santolina chamaecyparissus*) are used to great effect.

Opposite, middle row left Specimen plants are displayed against a dark hedge. Gravel keeps the weeds at bay and sets off the plant structure.

Opposite, middle row right This is the typical layout of a physic garden showing grass paths between rectangular beds.

Opposite, bottom row left This is my favorite style of herb garden — formal box hedges contain an informal planting of herbaceous herbs.

Opposite, bottom row right Hops and nasturtiums like the warmth and shelter a wall site has to offer and grow quickly to cover the surface.

Formal versus informal garden design

Every gardener has a different idea of the style of herb garden they would like to create. Formal herb garden designs generally follow traditional lines and feature clipped evergreen hedges infilled with perennials and annuals. They are often placed near the house as a showpiece. The choice of herbs is restrained to fit into the grid system of beds and paths and consists of the same plant repeated several times to create a sense of symmetry. To maintain the appearance of formal elegance, the herb plants need regular clipping and shaping as by their very nature herbs are vigorous plants. A formal design gives you clear paths and a strong sense of direction, while informal gardens are often more relaxed with meandering paths that slow down your progress and encourage you to stop and take in the colors and fragrances. As with formal designs, paths running through the informal herb garden are important for picking and maintaining the plants, which grow in large groups and self-seed rather than being restricted to one specific area or bed.

Square formal design

This simple design is based on the principles of an "open knot" garden. It offers a successful low-maintenance design for a small town garden or a "room" in a larger garden. The path ensures easy access to all four beds, making it an ideal design for harvesting and maintaining herbs. In the first year the garden will establish itself. In the second year, trim the top of the box hedge to keep the plants at a uniform height. The bay trees will put on growth, so pinch out growing tips to maintain their shape. Lightly cut back sage, thyme, and oregano after flowering. Make sure that these plants do not smother the base of the bay trees. After winter, check that herbs growing in the beds have room to spread, and if necessary, remove some plants to create more space. Fill any empty spaces in the beds where plants have died back. In late summer, cut back all herbs after flowering to prevent them from self-seeding and to stop the stems from becoming woody. By the third year, the box hedge will have started to knit together and the bay trees will have grown up.

Informal rectangular design

This relaxed-style garden is bordered by a soft silvery hedge of lavender cotton and has a slow, winding path running through it, planted up with a selection of thymes. These features contribute to the country garden style of this fragrant herb garden planted with mint and lemon verbena. In the first year the sages, thymes, and oreganos will need trimming once they have flowered to maintain their loose shapes, as will the lavender cotton hedge. In winter, tender plants like lemon verbena will need protecting with horticultural fleece. In the second year, check that the sorrel, wood sage, and oreganos have not spread out too much. If they have, lift and divide them (see page 57). Cut back the lemon verbena and southernwood and remove the growing tips from bay, myrtle, and luma. By the third year the garden will have filled out and the hedge will be established. If you wish your informal garden to keep its shape, cut it back in spring. The thyme plants on the path may also need replacing.

Choosing a shape

Before you decide upon a shape, consider the space you have available and whether you want to plant up your whole garden with herbs. Or would you like the herbs to occupy "a garden room" within a larger garden, or just fill a flowerbed or corner site? Round or oval-shaped herb gardens are a lovely solution because you can happily wander around or through this garden shape. The curved edge also allows access from all sides which makes picking and maintaining culinary and medicinal herbs in a small site very easy. A triangular herb bed is a good solution if you wish to plant up herbs in the corner of a larger garden. Using this geometric shape you can create a very sheltered herb garden by growing a rosemary hedge along two or three sides. This will protect Mediterranean herbs like oregano and thyme from exposure to cold winds and driving rain throughout the growing season, and they will thrive. Clip the hedge to give the triangular herb garden a more formal appearance.

Oval garden

Oval and round gardens are good for making the most of a small space. This oval design has been conceived with an S-shaped path edged with golden box, which runs like a golden ribbon through the design. The path creates the illusion that the garden is more spacious than it really is, and makes picking the culinary and medicinal herbs a pleasure. As the herb plants mature, the overall design will produce a tapestry effect as the different herbs start to grow and blend together. To achieve this harmonious effect, keep invasive plants like French sorrel in check so that they do not dominate the rest of this small garden. Trim back any tall plants for the same reason. Cut back lavender, sage, and thymes after flowering to maintain their shape, and cut off the flowers of feverfew to prevent them from self-seeding. Protect the wild rosemary with horticultural fleece if the weather is cold, and mulch in the spaces between plants in the fall. By the third year the box hedge should be well established and the thyme plants cascading over the edge of the oval.

Triangular corner garden

Here the border of rosemary plants has only recently been planted and needs time to grow up into a hedge. In the center of this simple design, creeping thymes have been planted to create an aromatic carpet of herbs. In summer when the thymes and rosemary are in flower they will attract butterflies to this aromatic corner garden. The garden has been mulched with gravel to inhibit weeds and to enable thyme to gain a foothold. In the first year, only trim the top growth of the young rosemary hedge. It is best to wait until it is well-established before starting to cut it to shape. In summer, trim the thymes after flowering to encourage them to put on new protective growth for the winter. In spring, check to see if any gravel has been washed away, and spread more gravel if necessary. By the third year, the rosemary hedge can be properly trimmed and shaped to the required height. Make sure that there is a gap in the hedge for access to the thyme plants.

Herbs and planting design

Herb ideas

Height and structure

Angelica archangelica (angelica); *Angelica gigas* (Korean angelica); *Buxus sempervirens* (box); *Calomeria amaranthoides* (incense plant); *Chenopodium giganteum* (tree spinach); *Cynara cardunculus* (cardoon); *Eupatorium purpureum* (Joe Pye weed); *Humulus lupulus* (common hops); *Juniperus communis* (juniper); *Laurus nobilis* (bay); *Myrtus communis* (myrtle); *Olea europea* (olive); *Sambucus niger* (elder); *Ugni molinae* (Chilean guava).

Leaf texture

Anethum graveolens (dill); *Artemisia abrotanum* (southernwood); *Foeniculum vulgare* (fennel); *Meum athamanticum* (meu); *Perilla frutescens* var. *purpurascens* (purple shiso).

Ground cover

Centella asiatica (gotu kola); *Chamaemelum nobile* 'Treneague' (lawn chamomile); *Satureja douglasii* (yerba buena); *Sempervivum tectorum* (houseleek); *Thymus species* (thyme).

Decorative herbs

Achillea millefolium (yarrow); *Agastache foeniculum* (Anise hyssop); *Alchemilla mollis* (lady's mantle); *Allium schoenoprasum* (chives); cichorium intybus (chicory); *Echinacea* species (echinacea); *Hyssopus officinalis* (blue hyssop); *Lythrum salicaria* (purple loosestrife); *Malva sylvestris* (common mallow); *Monarda fistulosa* (wild bergamot); *Oenothera biennis* (evening primrose); *Primula vulgaris* (primrose).

Describing how she first sets out a planting design, the influential plantswoman Beth Chatto says she treats the garden like any other room in the home – large plants are the "furniture," creeping plants the "carpet," and decorative plants the "ornaments." This simple yet effective approach is, in my experience, the key to successful planting and design in the herb garden. When clipped and trained into shape, herbs such as box provide the furniture for the garden and create the necessary height and structure for the design, while paths of creeping thyme or lawn chamomile make a wonderfully fragrant carpet. For ornament and decoration, groups of annual and perennial herbs will bring the garden alive with their changing colors and textures, coming into flower and dying back as the year progresses.

Creating a planting plan

The key to a successful planting is to work with nature. Look carefully at your previous planting and take note of which plants grew well without needing constant attention. The secret is to understand your garden environment (see pages 18–19) and learn how to work within your specific site. Once you know where to position herbs in the garden, the creative process of planting design becomes much simpler. When selecting herbs for your planting scheme, consider each plant's characteristics, such as height and structure, leaf texture and flower color, and which herbs will provide all-year-round interest. A thoughtful planting plan with a range of plant heights and shapes will, in my experience, look most effective (see pages 28–29), as will a scheme that has been designed to evolve over time as the plants mature.

Also look to the work of garden designers for inspiration. If you want to inject your herb planting design with color, consider Sandra and Nori Pope's planting combinations with their striking color contrasts. If you favour the wild, naturalistic approach look to Piet Oudolf, or to Beth Chatto for wonderful gravel-garden plantings. When you have decided on the effect you wish to achieve, and have considered the shape and scale of the site, you are ready to put your planting plan into action.

Above This magical walled herb garden manages to combine a wonderful freedom of planting while maintaining a sense of underlying structure. One device the owner has used to create this informality is to allow frothy masses of lady's mantle (*Alchemilla mollis*) to overrun the gravel areas between clipped box (*Buxus sempervirens*) "lollipops."

Opposite This area of the garden has been skilfully designed to make the mix of perennial herb species look natural. In reality, the owner has planned the seasonal planting design so that a purple and yellow color mix dominates in early summer.

Good combinations

White herbs
Allium ursinum (wild garlic);
Carum carvi (caraway);
Chamaemelum nobile
(Roman chamomile); *Meum*
athamanticum (meu);
Myrrhis odorata (myrrh);
Valeriana officinalis
(valerian).

Silver-gray herbs
Artemisia absinthium
(wormwood); *Cynara*
cardunculus (cardoon);
Marrubium vulgare (white
horehound); *Nepeta* x
faassenii (catmint); *Olea*
europaea (olive).

Blue herbs
Borago officinalis (borage);
Centaurea cyanus
(bachelor's buttons);
Cichorium intybus (chicory);
Hyssopus officinalis
(hyssop); *Lavandula* x
christiana (lavender
Christiana); *Linum perenne*
(flax); *Nigella sativa* (black
cumin); *Salvia clevelandii*
(Jim sage).

Mauve/purple herbs
Allium schoenoprasum
(chives); *Lavandula stoechas*
'Willow Vale' (Lavender
Willow Vale); *Mentha spicata*
var. *crispa* (curly mint):
Monarda fistulosa (wild
bergamot); *Origanum*
vulgare (wild marjoram);
Symphytum x *uplandicum*
(Russian comfrey); *Thymus*
pulegioides (broad-leaved
thyme); *Thymus serpyllum*
(creeping thyme).

Pink/red herbs
Angelica gigas (Korean
angelica); *Cedronella*
canariensis (Balm of gilead);
Centella asiatica (gotu kola);
Pelargonium 'Attar of Roses'
(rose-scented pelargonium);
Sanguisorba minor (salad
burnet); *Teucrium*
chamaedrys (true valerian);
Thymus coccineus (creeping
red thyme); *Tropaeolum*
majus 'Empress of India'
(nasturtium Empress
of India).

Herbs in existing beds

Herbs can be successfully planted into existing flowerbeds. Their subtly colored foliage and flower colors combine well with trees and shrubs. Equally, they look stunning in decorative vegetable gardens planted in formal patterns. In flowerbeds herbs mix well with wildflowers, especially in gravel gardens where they can self-seed and enjoy well-drained Mediterranean-type growing conditions. If the reason you like an herb is purely because of its color or leaf shape, rather than its culinary or medicinal value, feel free to grow it for its appearance with other plants that you enjoy. Another reason for growing herbs with flowers in the garden is that they are popular with insects and butterflies. Plants such as Korean angelica and cardoon are particularly attractive to beneficial insects.

Herbs mixed with other plants

Herbs and vegetables In an organic garden, herbs make good companion plants for flowers and vegetables. For example, blue borage flowers (*Borago officinalis*) grown alongside climbing beans will attract bees that will pollinate the beans, producing large harvests. Chives (*Allium schoenoprasum*) planted next to rose bushes deter blackspot and help fix nitrogen in the soil. Catnip (*Nepeta cattaria*) grown between rows of carrots deters carrot-root fly and flea beetle from brassicas.

Herbs and roses Historically, when monks were planting medicinal herb and vegetable gardens, they would plant a rose bush at the edge of the herb bed to symbolize themselves at work. I have seen this use of roses and herbs in a number of historic gardens, notably the famous potager at Barnsley House, in Gloucestershire, Britain, where white standard roses are underplanted with lavender to stunning effect.

Herbs and flower color In a formal garden, flowerbeds filled with black tulips and sweet woodruff (*Galium odoratum*) and edged with clipped evergreen box hedges look striking. I also enjoy the skillful use of tall silver-gray cardoons (*Cynara cardunculus*) as architectural plants in gray and pink color-themed beds. In the flowerbed next to my house, I have mixed ceanothus (*Ceanothus thyrsiflouris*), jasmine (*Jasminum officinale*), and tree peony (*Paeonia delavayi*), and underplanted this with lungwort (*Pulmonaria officinalis*) and lady's mantle (*Alchemilla xanthochlora* syn. *vulgaris*). This combination of herbs and flowers works well, giving color interest through the seasons.

Left Spires of foxgloves (*Digitalis purpurea*) fill the flowerbed in this walled herb garden, and lady's mantle (*Alchemilla mollis*) creates a soft path edge.

Opposite top row left A long bed containing drifts of borage (*Borago officinalis*) with nasturtiums (*Tropaeolum majus*).

Opposite top row right A vegetable garden containing chard (*Beta vulgaris* 'Ruby Chard') and purslane (*Portulaca oleracea*).

Opposite bottom row left Here, tree spinach (*Chenopodium giganteum*) makes a useful windbreak to protect lettuce in a vegetable garden.

Opposite bottom row right A lovely mixed bed containing white borage (*Borago officinalis* 'Alba') in the foreground and acer behind.

Choosing containers

Drainage Make sure your container has adequate drainage holes. Add broken terracotta shards or large stones to the bottom of the pot for extra drainage and to prevent the root ball from sitting in water and rotting.

Size Choose the container to suit the plant. A tall plant will need a wide-based container to prevent it from becoming too top-heavy and blowing over in strong winds. Also, many plants such as bay and olive trees like to have their roots confined, so do not plant them in too large a container.

Materials Terracotta pots look wonderful but can harbor disease from previous use. Scrub them well before planting, and if they need sterilizing, dry them in an oven at 245°F (120°C) for 30 minutes. To age new terracotta pots, cover the outside of the pot with live yogurt to encourage moss to grow. Glazed pots are not as porous as plain terracotta and retain water better; but they may be prone to crack in frost. Plastic offers the lightest and least expensive of container materials. However, sunlight can make plastic brittle. Woven willow containers look lovely, but will only last a couple of seasons as they rot in wet weather. Line woven willow containers with moss before planting up with herbs to hold the substrate in place and retain moisture. Make sure metal containers have adequate drainage holes, and place them out of the midday sun, because the hot metal will heat up the soil and may damage the root ball of the plant.

Herbs in containers

By growing herbs in containers, you can choose the soil and position to suit the plant. Containers of culinary herbs by the back door or on a windowsill are easy to access and are an effective way to grow herbs if space is limited. Most herbs adapt well to growing in containers. Details of the best conditions for growing individual herb species in pots are provided in my Top 100 herbs (see pages 214–267). Tender herbs like lemon grass or invasive herbs like mint are best grown in containers. Tender herbs in pots can be sunk into the flowerbed for the growing season and then lifted in winter for protection against frost, without damaging their roots. The rampant spread of invasive herbs like mint and horseradish can be kept in check when they are grown in pots because their roots are contained.

Maintaining herbs in containers

Choose a quality substrate so the plant will thrive in this restricted environment. I find that the most reliable all-round substrate is a loam mix. To make your own loam-based potting substrate mix 7 parts loam, 3 parts fine bark, and 2 parts coarse sand. Alternatively, buy an organic multipurpose potting substrate from a garden center.

Seaweed and liquid comfrey are ideal fertilizers for feeding container plants (see page 39), or you can make your own fertilizer mix using: 8 oz (225g) seaweed meal; 4 oz (110g) bonemeal; 3 oz (85g) hoof and horn and 2 oz (55g) ground limestone. This fertilizer mix will make enough for 35 quarts of potting substrate. Use it once a week during the growing season.

It is difficult to judge how often a container plant needs watering, and too much or too little can cause stress or long-term damage. Watering is dependent on the size and type of the plant and the container material. Do not allow container plants to dry out; once the substrate is dry, it is very difficult to get it to take up water again. Water the substrate rather than the plant to avoid damaging delicate foliage.

Above Creeping pennyroyal (left) grown on a windowsill is a good herb for repelling ants and for treating insect bites. Common thyme (center) is Mediterranean in origin and likes well-drained soil. If your garden soil is heavy clay, container growing in a loam-based potting substrate may offer a solution. Cultivate parsley (right) in terracotta pots for use in cooking.

Opposite Old stone pots look lovely planted up, but do not be tempted to overplant the containers or you will need to divide and replant them every year. The disadvantage of stone pots is that they are heavy, so changing their position is not a simple operation.

Feeding the soil

Bulky organic waste products can be added to the soil in winter or spring, or both, to improve the soil structure (see page 20) and increase its supply of plant food. Organic material is spread over the soil as a mulch or dug into the top 6–8in (15–20cm). Spring feeding gives a boost to the soil at the start of the growing season, while winter feeding offers a slow, steady release before the following year's planting. Recycled organic waste forms the basis of all the organic soil improvers. If you have a small yard, it may be difficult to generate enough material to make your own compost. Make sure that any compost you buy is approved by an organic body such as the Soil Association or Henry Doubleday Research Association (HDRA).

Making compost from organic waste

Stage 1, left The key to healthy compost is a good mix of materials. Just kitchen waste or grass cuttings creates wet slurry. I start off with woody prunings, which are slow to compost and allow air to circulate.

Stage 2, right Next add a layer of organic kitchen waste, about 3–4in (8–10cm) deep. Follow this with a layer of straw or cardboard. Repeat the layers. If your compost is too dry, add more grass or kitchen waste. If it is too wet, add more straw or woody prunings. The compost is ready when it is dark brown and crumbly. This will take about 16 weeks in summer.

Making leaf mold

Stage 1, left In the fall, gather up fallen leaves from deciduous trees and shrubs in your yard. Do not take leaf material from woodland, which will upset the natural ecosystem.

Stage 2, right Place a heap of leaves either in an open bin or lay some sheeting over the mound to stop the leaves from blowing away. Leave them to rot down to a mulch. One-year-old leaf mold is good as a mulch; two-year-old leaf mold is excellent as a soil improver that can be dug into the soil, in spring or fall.

Composts and mulches

Manure This is available from farms that are organic or non-intensive, and from garden centers. Make sure the manure is well rotted before use; this stabilizes the nutrients, preventing them from being washed away by rain. To check the quality, smell the farmyard manure. It should smell sweet, not strong and acrid.

Leaf mold This is a useful soil improver and mulch. It has a low-nutrient content so it suits most herbs. Dug into clay soil, it improves the structure and the airflow; and added to sandy soil, it helps retain moisture. As a mulch, leaf mold is effective for suppressing weeds.

Composted bark This mulch is useful for weed control since it is low in nutrients. Make sure it is well rotted: fresh green bark has a high content of ammonium nitrate and can burn young seedlings and tree trunks.

Composted waste This organic compost is made from a mixture of garden waste, woody stems, and household waste such as fruit and vegetable peelings. Once composted, it has a medium fertility, ideal for feeding all plants. It is best applied in spring, either as a mulch or dug into the soil.

Natural compost accelerators

Chamomile, yarrow, and comfrey plants can be added to the compost heap to speed up the decomposition process. The heat they release accelerates decay and kills weed seed. Comfrey leaves rot down quickest and are high in minerals.

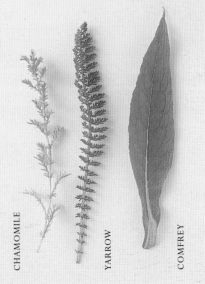

CHAMOMILE YARROW COMFREY

Chamomile plants being placed on the compost heap

Seasonal use of compost

The soil is the engine of the garden, and to maintain healthy plants it needs to be fed with organic compost: ideally, twice a year. In spring, dig in compost with a spade for an "instant" feed, if you have lifted herbs from the soil and wish to replace them with new ones. Compost again in the fall when the herbs have flowered and died back. In the fall, a layer of compost on top of the soil will feed the soil with nutrients and improve the soil structure over the winter months. I discourage the use of chemical fertilizers which can upset the microorganisms in the soil which, in turn, will upset the natural ecosystem of the garden. If you do not make your own organic compost (see pages 36–37) or do not have access to organic farmyard manure, there are now organic fertilizers available from garden centers. "Hoof and horn" is a source of slow-release nitrogen, while seaweed meal adds nitrogen, phosphorous, and potassium.

Preparing the ground for planting  **Fall** **Spring**

1 Weeding
Before you start adding compost to the soil, it is important to remove as many weeds as possible. Otherwise, the rich compost will feed the weeds and encourage their rapid growth. Use a fork to lift the weeds and then carefully pick them out by hand.

2 Turning over the topsoil
Next, dig over the ground with a spade to help aerate the soil. Always stand on a wooden board when turning over the soil to spread your body weight evenly so you do not compress the soil and damage its structure. Turning the soil also makes it easier to dig at a later date, when you are planting the garden.

3 Laying on compost
Spread the compost over the soil with a fork in a thick layer. I recommend feeding the soil with compost in the fall to activate the microorganisms in the soil. The action of the microorganisms in the compost warms up the soil, while rainwater helps to release nutrients into the soil.

4 Digging in compost
The following spring, dig in any compost that remains on the soil surface which has not been absorbed or washed away. Established herb plants and newly planted annuals will benefit from composted soil. If you have not laid compost on your soil the previous fall, you can still dig in compost in spring to provide an instant feed for newly-planted herbs.

Organic liquid feed

Comfrey is perhaps the best natural fertiliser as it is rich in potassium, calcium, iron, and manganese. The comfrey plant provides an abundant crop of leaves, which are available to harvest from spring through to late summer and can be simply and quickly made into a liquid feed. This liquid feed is ideal for foliar feeding salad herbs, such as wild rocket and chicory, for root feeding container plants like box, and for restoring mature garden plants to health like southernwood or licorice. For root feeding, dilute the liquid feed concentrate to 1 fl oz (25ml) per quart of rainwater. For foliar feed, dilute to ½ fl oz (12ml) per quart of rainwater. Comfrey leaves can also be placed on the compost heap to speed up decomposition (see page 37).

Making liquid comfrey leaf feed

1 Pick comfrey leaves in the early morning when they are at their freshest. Wear gloves; some people are allergic to the hairs on the comfrey leaves, which can cause a rash. Choose a bucket that will not rust and contaminate the liquid, and which has a tight-fitting lid to contain the strong odor of the comfrey leaves as they start to break down. To make approximately 1 quart (1 liter) of liquid feed concentrate, use a bucket that holds 8 quarts (8 liters). Pack the container with the leaves, weigh them down with something heavy like a concrete block, and pour 1 pint (500ml) of rainwater over the leaves. Cover with the lid and place in a warm position but not direct sun. Leave for 3–4 weeks.

2 After 3 weeks remove the bucket lid to check the progress of the comfrey liquid feed. The leaves should have started to rot down, producing a murky brown liquid. If you cannot see any brown liquid, or the leaves are still taking up more than half the bucket space, replace the lid and leave to mature for a further week.

3 Strain the liquid through a piece of cheesecloth or a pair of old panty hose into a clean bucket or bowl. Discard any leaf material that collects on the strainer. This concentrated comfrey liquid feed will keep for up to 6 months stored in a screw-top bottle, out of direct sunlight. Dilute as described above to make a root or foliar feed.

Herb propagation

For me, propagation is the most exciting job on the farm. I never cease to be amazed that from a cutting you can produce a new plant. Equally, there is nothing more satisfying on a cold winter morning than to enter the warm glasshouse and see the seedlings emerging in row upon row of trays. When I started the farm, I used to propagate every herb in a makeshift building attached to the house, with my children crawling around my feet. From the start, I taught myself how to grow plants without growth-promoting hormones like rooting powder. It is not necessary for herb cuttings and is particularly harmful to women, upsetting their delicate hormonal balance. The first few weeks are critical and will determine both the health of the plant and resistance to disease in later life.

When to propagate?

Propagation is not a complicated science. For successful seeds and cuttings, simply watch and imitate the natural cycle. The fruity mellow scent of fall in the air is the signal to sow all autumn seeds like angelica and foxgloves. Leave them outside in their containers to expose them to winter weather, especially fluctuating temperatures, which will encourage them to germinate. The change in the air temperature is also the signal to cut back hardy perennials to encourage them to put on new growth, which not only gives protection in winter, but also makes strong new shoots in spring, from which successful softwood cuttings can be taken. In spring, look for the first signs of weeds growing. As soon as weeds appear, you know the soil is warming up and that day length is increasing, so it is time to sow annual herbs in open ground and to take softwood cuttings from established plants.

Propagation tips

Growing herbs from seed and cuttings under protection is very different from planting them in open ground. In an artificial environment, you can control the soil, water, and temperature, and mimic the plant's preferred germinating conditions.

Light

Plants need light to grow, but seedlings and cuttings do not like being exposed directly to the hot sun which scorches young leaves. Cover seed trays with lightweight horticultural fleece to shade them.

Temperature

Cuttings need warmth to encourage roots to form and grow. Every seed has an optimum temperature for germination. Although most seeds germinate within a fairly wide temperature range, some have limits, so it is worth checking (see page 49).

Water

Cuttings need to replace moisture lost to put on top growth and to encourage roots. Seeds need water to penetrate the outer seed coat to begin the germination process.

Air

In winter or early spring, open your home or greenhouse windows on warm days. Good ventilation encourages growth and prevents disease. Oxygen is needed for plant respiration and carbon dioxide for photosynthesis.

Greenhouse propagation

Balancing the natural ecosystem in an artificial environment, such as a greenhouse or conservatory, requires constant surveillance because soft, lush seedlings that have no natural protection are easy pickings for pests. Also, the more seedlings you grow in one site, the more food there will be for pests, and they will thrive in the warmth of this sheltered environment. To save having to check under every plant leaf and examine every tray for pests, you can hang yellow sticky traps throughout the glasshouse as an organic method of pest control. Any pest present will stick to the traps, making it easier to diagnose the problem, be it an infestation of whitefly, scarid fly, or greenfly. If you find signs of pest damage, you will need to introduce some form of biological control to restore the balance; i.e, a natural predator that will prey on the pest. For whitefly the best predator is the parasitic wasp, *Encarsia formosa*. Both sticky traps and predators are available from garden centers.

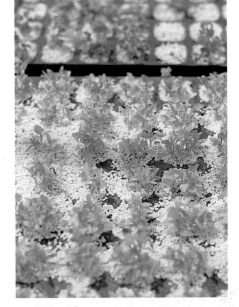

Coriander seedlings in a greenhouse

Propagation methods

There are five key techniques used to propagate herbs, and the one you choose depends on the time of year and the plant's growing cycle. The chart (opposite) indicates the most successsful techniques for propagating my Top 100 herbs (see pages 114–267).

In the case of myrrh (*Myrrhis odorata*), one of three techniques can be used: from seed (winter); from root cuttings (spring); or by division (fall or spring). The best technique, in my opinion, is indicated by a black dot, the others by gray dots.

From seed

Any herb that produces flowers will produce seed. Seed is the only propagation method for annual herbs. After flowering, annual herbs set seed in late summer and then die. Biennials – herbs that survive for two years – are also only propagated from seed. In the first year, they produce leaf, and in the second flowers, then seed. For perennial herbs, seed is not the best method of propagation; it takes longer to achieve an established plant from seed than from a cutting, plus seedlings are more prone to disease than cuttings.

Pricking out seedlings, see page 50

From soft- or hardwood cuttings

The technique of taking softwood and hardwood cuttings is identical, but softwood cuttings are taken in spring and hardwood in fall. Softwood cuttings are a successful way to propagate herbs, especially those whose seed is sterile (these include hybrids, variegated plants, and double-flowered herbs) or slow to develop from seed, like thyme. It also works well for herbs like lemon verbena that come from warmer climates and do not set seed because either the day length is too short, or the temperature is too cold, or it is too damp.

Softwood cuttings, see page 52

By layering

With this method you propagate the plant where it grows, encouraging it to form roots while it is attached to the parent plant. Layering is one of the oldest forms of propagation, no doubt based on observation of plants propagating themselves. Quite often, branches on a shrub, weighed down to the ground by their leaves, will take root. Herbs that are successfully propagated by layering include sage and rosemary which both have low-growing branches. Layer in spring or fall when the soil is warm.

Layering, see page 54

From root cuttings

Herbs that spread by creeping roots, such as sweet woodruff and herbs with long taproots like horseradish are propagated from root cuttings. The best time is spring when the plant's energy is concentrated in the roots before growth begins or, in the fall, as top growth slows. Depending on the type of root, one of three methods is used: for taproots, a slice of root is taken; for creeping roots, a thin piece of root with two growing nodes; and for roots that have both, like mandrake, a piece of root is sliced off with a growing node.

Sliced root cutting, see page 56

By root division

Root division involves digging up the root ball and breaking it up to produce smaller plants. It is suitable for hardy herbaceous herbs that, in time, can die off at their central core. By dividing the plant you are keeping it vigorous and healthy. The other benefits of root division include: creating more plants quickly; freeing up space in the garden, and encouraging new growth. Herbs that are best propagated by division include lady's mantle. Like root cuttings, the best time of year to divide the roots is spring or fall.

Root division, see page 57

Which Propagation method

● = best method   • = other methods

Methods columns: Seed | Softwood cuttings | Layering | Root cuttings | Division

Plant	Seed	Softwood cuttings	Layering	Root cuttings	Division
Achillea ageratum *English mace*		•			•
Achillea millefolium *Yarrow*	•				•
Agastache foeniculum *Anise hyssop*	•	•			
Alchemilla xanthochlora *Lady's mantle*	•				•
Allium cepa Proliferum Group *Tree onion*	•				
Allium fistulosum *Welsh onion*	•				
Allium sativum *Garlic*	•				
Allium schoenoprasum *Chives*	•				•
Allium tuberosum *Garlic chives*	•				•
Allium ursinum *Wild garlic*	•				
Aloe vera *Aloe*		•			
Aloysia triphylla *Lemon verbena*		•			
Angelica archangelica *Angelica*	•				
Angelica gigas *Korean angelica*	•				
Anethum graveolens *Dill*	•				
Anthriscus cerefolium *Chervil*	•				
Armoracia rusticana *Horseradish*			•	•	
Arnica chamissonis *Arnica*	•			•	•
Artemisia annua *Sweet Annie*	•				
Artemisia abrotanum *Southernwood*			•	•	
Artemisia absinthium *Wormwood*	•				•
Artemisia dracunculus *French tarragon*		•		•	•
Artemisia vulgaris *Mugwort*	•				•
Borago officinalis *Borage*	•				
Borago pygmaea *Prostrate borage*	•				•
Buxus sempervirens *Box*		•			
Buxus sempervirens 'Latifolia Maculata' *Golden box*		•			
Calendula officinalis *Pot marigold*	•				
Calomeria amaranthoides *Incense plant*	•				
Carum carvi *Caraway*	•				
Cedronella canariensis *Balm of Gilead*		•			
Centaurea cyanus *Bachelor's buttons*	•				
Centella asiatica *Gotu kola*					•
Chamaemelum nobile *Roman chamomile*	•	•			
Chamaemelum nobile 'Treneague' *Lawn chamomile*					•
Chamaemelum nobile 'Flore Pleno' *Double-flowered chamomile*	•				•
Chenopodium bonus-henricus *Goosefoot*	•				
Chenopodium giganteum *Tree spinach*	•				
Cichorium intybus *Chicory*	•				
Coriandrum sativum *Coriander (cilantro)*	•				
Crithmum maritimum *Sea fennel*	•				•
Cymbopogon citratus *Lemon grass*	•				•
Cynara cardunculus *Cardoon*	•				•
Digitalis purpurea *Foxglove*	•				
Diplotaxis muralis *Wild rocket*	•				
Echinacea purpurea *Purple coneflower*	•				•
Echinacea angustifolia *Narrow-leaved echinacea*	•				
Echinacea pallida *Echinacea*	•				•
Elettaria cardamomum *Cardamom*		•			•
Eriocephalus africanus *Wild rosemary*		•	•		
Eupatorium purpureum *Joe Pye weed*	•				•
Filipendula ulmaria *Queen-of-the-meadow*	•				•
Foeniculum vulgare *Fennel*	•				•
Foeniculum vulgare 'Purpureum' *Bronze fennel*	•				•
Fragaria vesca *Wild strawberry*	•	•			
Galium odoratum *Sweet woodruff*	•		•		•
Ginkgo biloba *Ginkgo*	•	•			
Glycyrrhiza glabra *Licorice*	•		•		
Humulus lupulus *Common hop*		•		•	•
Hypericum perforatum *St. John's Wort*	•				•
Hyssopus officinalis *Blue hyssop*	•	•			
Hyssopus officinalis 'Roseus' *Pink hyssop*	•	•			
Inula helenium *Elecampane*	•				•
Isatis tinctoria *Woad*	•				
Juniperus communis *Juniper*		•			
Laurus nobilis *Bay*	•	•			

Plant	Seed	Softwood cuttings	Layering	Root cuttings	Division
Laurus nobilis 'Aurea' *Golden bay*		•			
Laurus nobilis f. angustifolia *Willow leaf bay*		•			
Lavandula x intermedia Old English Group *Old English lavender*		•	•		
Lavandula angustifolia 'Hidcote' *Hidcote lavender*		•			
Lavandula dentata var. candicans *Lavender Candicans*		•			
Lavandula stoechas 'Kew Red' *Lavender 'Kew Red'*		•			
Lavandula stoechas 'Helmsdale' *Helmsdale lavender*		•			
Lavandula stoechas *French lavender*	•	•			
Lavandula x allardii *Lavender Allardii*		•			
Lavandula x christiana *Lavender Christiana*		•			
Lavandula 'Sawyers' *Lavender Sawyers*	•	•			
Levisticum officinale *Lovage*	•				•
Linum perenne *Flax*	•				
Luma chequen *Luma*		•			
Lycopus europaeus *Gypsywort*	•				•
Lysimachia vulgaris *Yellow loosestrife*	•				•
Lythrum salicaria *Purple loosestrife*	•				•
Malva moschata *Musk mallow*	•				
Malva sylvestris *Common mallow*	•				
Mandragora officinarum *Mandrake*	•			•	•
Marrubium vulgare *White horehound*	•				•
Melissa officinalis *Lemon balm*	•	•			•
Melissa officinalis 'All Gold' *Golden lemon balm*		•			•
Melissa officinalis 'Aurea' *Variegated lemon balm*		•			•
Mentha pulegium 'Upright' *Pennyroyal upright*		•			•
Mentha x piperita *Peppermint*		•		•	•
Mentha x piperita f. citratus *Eau-de-cologne mint*		•		•	•
Mentha x piperita 'Logee' *Logee mint*		•		•	•
Mentha spicata *Spearmint*		•		•	•
Mentha spicata var. crispum *Curly mint*		•		•	•
Mentha x villosa var. alopecuroides 'Bowles' *Bowles mint*		•		•	•
Meum athamanticum *Meu*	•				•
Monarda fistulosa *Wild bergamot*	•	•			•
Murraya koenigii *Curry tree*	•	•			
Myrrhis odorata *Myrrh*	•			•	•
Myrtus communis *Myrtle*		•			
Myrtus communis 'Merion' *Myrtle merion*		•			
Myrtus communis 'Microphylla Variegata' *Variegated small-leaved myrtle*		•			
Nepeta cataria *Catnip*	•	•			•
Nepeta x faassenii *Catmint*	•	•			•
Nigella sativa *Black cumin*	•				
Ocimum basilicum *Sweet basil*	•				
Ocimum basilicum 'Cinnamon' *Cinnamon basil*	•				
Ocimum basilicum 'Dark Opal' *Dark opal basil*	•				
Ocimum basilicum 'Horapha Nanum' *Thai basil*	•				
Ocimum basilicum 'Siam Queen' *Siam Queen basil*	•				
Ocimum minimum 'Greek' *Greek basil*	•				
Ocimum tenuiflorum *Holy basil*	•				
Oenothera biennis *Evening primrose*	•				
Olea europaea *Olive*		•			
Origanum dictamnus *Cretan oregano*		•			•
Origanum majorana *Sweet marjoram*	•	•			
Origanum vulgare *Oregano, Wild marjoram*	•				•
Origanum vulgare 'Acorn Bank' *Acorn bank marjoram*		•			•
Origanum x onites *French marjoram*	•	•			•
Pelargonium 'Apple scented' *Apple-scented pelargonium*		•			
Pelargonium 'Atomic Snowflake' *Atomic snowflake pelargonium*		•			
Pelargonium 'Attar of roses' *Attar of Roses pelargonium*		•			
Pelargonium 'Chocolate Peppermint' *Chocolate peppermint pelargonium*		•			
Pelargonium 'Lady Plymouth' *Lady Plymouth pelargonium*		•			
Pelargonium 'Peach Cream' *Peach cream pelargonium*		•			
Perilla frutescens var. crispa *Green shiso*	•	•			

Plant	Seed	Softwood cuttings	Layering	Root cuttings	Division
Perilla frutescens var. purpurascens *Purple shiso*	•	•			
Persicaria odorata *Vietnamese coriander*		•	•		•
Petroselinum crispum *Parsley*	•				
Petroselinum crispum 'French' *French parsley*	•				
Phytolacca americana *Pokeroot*	•			•	•
Portulaca oleracea *Purslane*	•				
Primula vulgaris *Primrose*	•				•
Prostanthera cuneata *Australian mint bush*		•			
Rosmarinus officinalis *Rosemary*	•	•	•		
Rosmarinus officinalis 'Aureus' *Golden rosemary*		•	•		
Rosmarinus officinalis 'Roseus' *Pink rosemary*		•	•		
Rosmarinus officinalis Prostratus Group *Prostrate rosemary*		•	•		
Rumex scutatus *French sorrel*	•				•
Ruta graveolens *Rue*	•	•			
Salvia clevelandii *Jim sage*	•	•			
Salvia elegans 'Scarlet Pineapple' *Pineapple sage*		•			
Salvia lavandulifolia *Narrow-leaved sage*		•	•		
Salvia microphylla var. microphylla *Blackcurrant-scented sage*	•	•			
Salvia officinalis *Sage*	•	•	•		
Salvia officinalis Purpurascens Group *Purple sage*		•			
Salvia viridis *Painted sage*	•				
Sambucus nigra *Elder*	•	•	•		
Sanguisorba minor *Salad burnet*	•				•
Santolina chamaecyparissus *Lavender cotton*	•	•			
Saponaria officinalis *Soapwort*	•	•	•		
Satureja douglasii *Yerba buena*		•	•		
Satureja hortensis *Summer savory*	•				
Satureja montana *Winter savory*	•	•			
Scutellaria lateriflora *Virginia skullcap*	•	•		•	•
Sempervivum tectorum *Houseleek*	•				•
Solidago virgaurea *Goldenrod*	•				•
Stachys officinalis *Betony*	•				•
Symphytum officinale *Comfrey*				•	•
Symphytum x uplandicum *Russian comfrey*				•	•
Tagetes lucida *Winter tarragon*	•	•			•
Tagetes patula *Wild Mexican marigold*	•				
Tanacetum balsamita *Alecost*		•			•
Tanacetum cinerariifolium *Pyrethrum*	•				•
Tanacetum parthenium *Feverfew*	•	•			•
Tanacetum vulgare *Tansy*	•			•	•
Teucrium chamaedrys L. *True valerian*	•	•			
Teucrium scorodonia *Wood sage*	•	•			•
Teucrium scorodonia 'Crispum' *Curly wood sage*		•			•
Teucrium x lucidrys *Hedge germander*		•	•		
Thymus 'Fragrantissimus' *Orange-scented thyme*	•	•	•		
Thymus 'Peter Davis' *Peter Davis thyme*		•	•		
Thymus caespititus *Azores thyme*		•	•		
Thymus coccineus *Creeping red thyme*		•			
Thymus pulegioides *Broad-leaved thyme*		•			
Thymus pulegioides 'Bertram Anderson' *Bertram Anderson thyme*		•			
Thymus serpyllum *Creeping thyme*	•	•			
Thymus serpyllum 'Minimus' *Minimus thyme*		•			
Thymus vulgaris 'Compactus' *Compact thyme*		•	•		
Thymus vulgaris 'Snow White' *Compact white-flowering thyme*		•	•		
Thymus x citriodorus 'Silver Queen' *Silver Queen thyme*		•	•		
Tropaeolum majus 'Empress of India' *Empress of India nasturtium*	•				
Tropaeolum speciosum *Flame nasturtium*	•		•		
Ugni molinae *Chilean guava*		•			
Valeriana officinalis *Valerian*	•				•
Verbena officinalis *Vervain*	•				•
Viola odorata *Sweet violet*	•				•
Viola tricolor *Heart's ease*	•				•

Choosing seed and seed containers

Take care when buying herb seed. Many producers offer enhanced germination, and to achieve this they have used fertilizers and pesticides. For example, "pelleted" seeds have an added outer case of nutrients, and "primed" seeds have been modified to germinate quicker. Once your own herb garden is established, it offers the best source of seed because you know its origins. First make sure harvested seeds have no signs of pests or diseases. Keep a record of when they were collected because some only remain viable for a year.

Pot

Sowing directly into pots is ideal for seeds that are slow to germinate like gingko (see page 166), which may take up to five years before it is ready to plant out. A pot is also suitable if you only intend to grow one type of herb since it occupies far less space than a seed tray. If you have a 3in (8cm) pot, you can plant several seeds and then thin out the seedlings leaving only the strongest to grow on. Also pots offer more space for large seeds – so seedlings will not need potting on as quickly. The disadvantage of growing herbs from seed in pots is that you can only grow one species from seed at a time, whereas you can grow many different types in multicell modular trays.

Plug or modular tray

These are multicell trays with 6–200 cells made from plastic, styrofoam, or pressed peat. Plastic modules are perhaps the easiest to use because rooted seedlings can be slipped out of the container. These trays are useful for plants that dislike having their roots disturbed. Plastic modules can also be washed out and reused, which makes them more acceptable to the organic gardener, and many different species of herb can be propagated from seed at one time in each of the separate cells. The disadvantage is that the substrate in each module dries out much more quickly than in a seed tray or pot, so they need checking and watering regularly in hot weather.

Seed tray

These trays should be 2–3in (5–7cm) deep and sturdy enough to hold their shape when filled with wet substrate, or when you pick them up. The disadvantage of using seed trays is that you have to "prick out" (see page 50) each seedling, and when doing so, it is very difficult not to damage their fine roots. Root damage slows down the growth of the seedling until the roots repair themselves. The advantage of seed trays is that they do not dry out as quickly as modules, and they are useful for propagating seedlings whose germination is erratic – if you only produce one or two seedlings, you have not wasted rows and rows of cells in a modular tray.

Ground

Sowing seed in a prepared open site in the garden is ideal for those herb seeds like dill and coriander that dislike being disturbed and need to establish a taproot before they produce a crop. The disadvantage of sowing into open ground is that you have to wait until the soil is warm enough before you can begin sowing your herbs, so you cannot start your crop early in the year.

Choosing seed-growing substrate

To give plants the best start in life, choose a quality seed-growing substrate. Do not use soil taken from the garden – it is not sterile, and seeds will have to compete with weed seed, while last year's commercial substrate may harbor pests or disease. Each year, I make my own mix from the following ingredients: 1 part fine bark + 1 part perlite (or 1 part vermiculite) + 2 parts coir. As seeds have their own food supply, I do not add fertilizer. I find extra fertilizer can inhibit seed germination and growth.

Fine bark

Tree bark is available in many different grades from garden centers. For seed sowing you will need a fine or propagating-grade bark. If you are using your own composted bark from the yard, make sure it has had time to rot down – this usually takes 6–8 months. Fresh green bark is harmful to seedlings because it contains ammonium nitrate that can either burn the seedlings or stunt their growth.

Perlite

Perlite is not a trade name, but a generic term for naturally occurring siliceous rock that has been heated to produce light, sterile granules. It is available in fine, medium, or coarse grades. Root cuttings can be grown in 100 percent perlite because the structure of the perlite encourages strong root growth. Perlite is also mixed in with other seed-growing substrates to improve drainage and protect young root systems. It has a neutral pH, which means it will not upset the acid or alkaline balance of the chosen substrate. Perlite granules can also be sprinkled on top of the seed-growing substrate in modules, trays, and pots to help reflect light, keep seeds warm, and speed up germination.

Vermiculite

This is the mineralogical name give to hydrated laminar magnesium-aluminum-iron-silicate that resembles the volcanic rock, mica. When heated, vermiculite expands, and it is this substance that is used in horticultural practice. It has properties similar to perlite (see above), but retains more water and less air. It is available in fine to coarse grades. Vermiculite can be added to seed-growing substrates to improve drainage or aeration. It can also be used as a covering for seeds, helping to keep moisture in. In my opinion, it is not as good as perlite as a general seed covering.

Coir

Coir is the outside layer of husk that surrounds the shell of a coconut. It consists mainly of fibers which have been used traditionally to manufacture rope, carpets, and brooms. Coir is recognized as a growing medium. The inherent qualities of coir improve aeration and water retention in the substrate and it is ideal for encouraging roots to form quickly. The disadvantage of coir is that it can be difficult to tell if the seedlings need watering because the surface dries out quickly, while farther down the substrate is still wet.

Germinating seed

For successful germination, try to mimick the natural conditions the seed will experience in the wild. These will vary according to whether it grows in the cold of the mountains (with extreme temperature fluctuations) or the humid climate of the tropics. Copying these will improve your chances, especially with seeds that are difficult or erratic germinators. In spring, germination is triggered by a temperature increase, but some seeds require extra triggers like extreme cold. The germinating conditions for my Top 100 herbs are listed on page 49.

Scarification

Some seeds have hard outer coats that are impervious to water. In the wild, this coating can be broken either by the seed falling from the tree, by a sudden change in temperature, or by being ingested by an animal and passing through the digestive tract. In a controlled situation, you can break down a seed coating by placing the seeds into freshly boiled water. Leave the seeds to soak until the water cools down to room temperature. Other methods of scarification include: rubbing the seed coating with fine-grit sandpaper (as shown here), or using a knife to nick the outer seed coating, but taking care not to damage the "eye" (the little depression where the seed is attached to the ovary). Scarified seeds do not store well and should be planted immediately after treatment.

Herbs that require scarifying include: *Ginkgo biloba* (ginkgo); *Laurus nobilis* (bay); *Olea europaea* (olive).

Stratification

Stratification breaks down the seed's protective coating by subjecting it to sudden changes in temperature from cold to warm or vice versa. This mimicks winter followed by spring, or summer followed by winter.

Natural stratification: Where winter temperatures drop below 32°F (0°C) for a period of 3 weeks, natural stratification is possible. Sow the seeds into a container and leave outside to experience all weathers. The temperature change will help break down the protective outer coat.

Artificial stratification: Where winter temperatures remain warm, you may need to use an artificial stratification technique. Mix the seed with some moist vermiculite, sand, or coir (contact with a cold damp substrate will make the seed colder). Place the seed mixture in a plastic bag, label it clearly, and place it in the refrigerator. Keep it at a constant temperature of 32–41°F (0–5°C) for 3–4 weeks. Turn the bag from time to time to allow air to circulate.

Herbs seeds that need stratifying include: *Angelica archangelica* (angelica); *Digitalis purpurea* (foxglove); *Meum athamanticum* (meum); *Myrrhis odorata* (myrrh); *Solidago virgaurea* (goldenrod); *Viola odorata* (sweet violet).

Sowing seed in pots, trays, or modules

Before you start sowing, gather up the equipment you will need, including clean pots, trays, or modules, plant labels and a waterproof pen, the seed substrate mix (see page 45), the seeds for sowing, and a paper clip to reseal the seed pack when you have finished. Make sure your hands are clean and that you work on a clean surface so as not to infect the seed or contaminate the substrate. Seal and store any packs containing leftover seed in a dry, cool environment so they will remain viable.

Sowing fine seed on the surface

Very fine seeds are usually sown on the surface of the substrate and left uncovered. This allows the maximum light, air, and water to come into contact with the seed. A useful technique when sowing very fine seed is to mix it with flour or fine sand so the seed becomes more visible. Then place this mixture into the crease of a folded piece of cardboard. Gently tap the cardboard to sow the seeds thinly on the surface.

Fine seed

Calomeria amaranthoides, (incense plant); *Viola odorata*, (sweet violet); *Viola tricolor* (heart's ease).

Seeds to cover with perlite

Perlite is a useful cover for small seed because its drainage properties help prevent seeds from sitting in water, while its pale color reflects light and warms up the seed, speeding up the germination process.

To sow small seeds, tip a small amount of seed into the palm of your hand. Let the seeds settle in the crease of your palm, then carefully control the flow of the seed onto the surface of the substrate. Cover the seed with a thin layer of perlite to approximately the same depth as the seed.

Small seed

Agastache foeniculum (anise hyssop); *Allium fistulosum* (Welsh onion); *Foeniculum vulgare* (fennel); *Hyssopus officinalis* (hyssop); *Lavandula angustifolia* (lavender); *Ocimum basilicum* (basil).

Please check the species list on page 49 for more details.

Seeds to cover in substrate

Some medium-sized seeds benefit from being sown in a dark, covered environment. These are often the seeds of herb plants that self-seed naturally in open ground, and their leaves would have fallen in autumn, covering and protecting the seed throughout the winter and blocking out the light.

To sow medium-sized seeds that are easy to handle, space the seeds evenly on the surface of the substrate. Then gently press the seed into the surface before covering with substrate.

Medium-sized seed

Eupatorium purpureum (Joe Pye weed); *Filipendula ulmaria* (queen-of-the-meadow); *Phytolacca americana* (pokeweed); *Primula vulgaris* (primrose); *Saponaria officinalis* (soapwort).

Please check the species list on page 49 for more details.

Seed growing techniques

The most important factors for germinating and growing seedlings well are water, light, and temperature. Before germination, keep watering to the minimum or the seed will rot, but equally do not allow the substrate to dry out. Germination is usually 10–14 days, but times vary from species to species. Once a seedling appears, water it in the morning so it is not sitting in the cold and wet at night, when temperatures fluctuate. Water the substrate not the seedling, to avoid fungal disease.

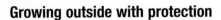

INDOORS

Growing inside with extra warmth

Propagator: This will let you control temperature, air flow, and light to suit the seed's needs and give it the best conditions for germination. There are many different propagators available, and some have a heating element that provides the seedlings with extra warmth and a constant temperature. Make sure the propagator lid has a vent so you can regulate humidity and prevent the seedlings from "damping off."

Windowsill: Place seed trays or pots on windowsills to encourage germination. Avoid south-facing windows, which may become too hot and scorch the seedlings. To stop seedlings from bending toward the light, turn the tray once a day.

Conservatory or greenhouse: A conservatory offers similar growing conditions to a greenhouse, but is usually hotter. Take care not to allow the seed trays to dry out. To provide good ventilation, open the window during the day. A greenhouse is ideal for germination, offering all-round light. If it is unheated, protect seedlings in cold weather. .

Seed modules on windowsill

OUTDOORS

Growing outside with protection

Outdoor covers offer valuable protection from cold weather and are more flexible than a greenhouse structure because they can be moved from site to site. Cloches and cold frames are good for those who want to start growing herbs from seed early in the season, to prolong the cropping season for salad herbs, to help establish young plants and protect them from pest attack, and to shelter hardy herbs like thyme for winter picking. Change the location of the cloche or cold frame from time to time, and weed the soil and remove slugs, which like to congregate in and around the structure.

Cold frame: Use a cold frame structure to propagate seeds that need cold to germinate (see page 46), and to protect tender perennial herbs.

Cloche: These are now available in all shapes and sizes. You can create a mini-cloche from a sawn-off plastic bottle, or buy a glass cloche to protect single plants. Or, you can use an A-shaped cloche in the same way as a cold frame.

A-frame cloche

OUTDOORS

Covered with horticultural fleece

Horticultural fleece is available in different weights depending on how much protection you wish to provide. In exposed sites, use a 1 oz (30g) fleece; in sheltered sites or in a cold frame, 1/2oz (17gm) fleece. On a cold spring morning on my farm, you will see the young and tender herb plants covered with fleece to protect them during nights when frost is forecast. Later in the morning, we lift off the fleece and hang it out to dry. Always remove the fleece during the day to prevent the plant from becoming too soft, and to check for weeds and slugs. Fleece is not only good for protecting plants from frost damage, but it is an organic way to deter pest attack. I use fleece to cover parsley seedlings as a protective barrier against carrot-root fly attack and to protect wild rocket crops from flea beetle. Fleece can also act as a windbreak to protect young stock.

Which herbs may be grown from Seed

● = best method   • = other methods

Herb	STRATIFY	SCARIFY	INSIDE WITH EXTRA WARMTH	OUTSIDE WITH PROTECTION	IN COIR/BARK/PERLITE	IN SEED-SOWING MIX (see p.45)	SOWING INTO OPEN GROUND	COVERED WITH SOIL/SUBSTRATE	COVERED WITH PERLITE	COVERED WITH FLEECE	SOWING ON THE SURFACE
Achillea millefolium *Yarrow*			●		●	•		●			
Agastache foeniculum *Anise hyssop*			●		●			●			
Allium fistulosum *Welsh onion*			•		•		●	•			
Allium schoenoprasum *Chives*			•		•		●	•			
Allium tuberosum *Garlic chives*			•		•		●	•			
Allium ursinum *Wild garlic*			•		●			●			
Angelica archangelica *Angelica*	●					•	•	●			
Angelica gigas *Korean angelica*			●		●			●			
Anethum graveolens *Dill*			•		•		●	•			
Anthriscus cerefolium *Chervil*			•		•		●	•			
Arnica chamissonis *Arnica*				●	●			●			
Artemisia annua *Sweet Annie*			●		●			●			
Artemisia absinthium *Wormwood*			●		●			●			
Artemisia vulgaris *Mugwort*			●		●			●			
Borago officinalis *Borage*			•		•		●	●			
Borago pygmaea *Prostrate borage*			●		●			●			
Calendula officinalis *Pot marigold*			●		●	•		●			
Calomeria amaranthoides *Incense plant*				●	●						●
Carum carvi *Caraway*				•	●			•			
Centaurea cyanus *Bachelor's buttons*			●		●			●			
Chamaemelum nobile *Roman chamomile*			●		●			●			
Chenopodium bonus-henricus *Goosefoot*			•		•		•				
Chenopodium giganteum *Tree spinach*			•		•		•				
Cichorium intybus *Chicory*			•		•		●	•			
Coriandrum sativum *Coriander (cilantro)*			•		•		●	•			
Crithmum maritimum *Sea fennel*				●	●			●			
Cymbopogon citratus *Lemon grass*			●		●			●			
Cynara cardunculus *Cardoon*			●		●			●			
Digitalis purpurea *Foxglove*	●					•		●			
Diplotaxis muralis *Wild rocket*			●		●		•	●			
Echinacea purpurea *Purple coneflower*			●		●			●			
Echinacea angustifolia *Narrow-leaved echinacea*			●		●			●			
Echinacea pallida *Echinacea*			●		●			●			
Eupatorium purpureum *Joe Pye weed*				●	●	•		●			
Filipendula ulmaria *Queen-of-the-meadow*				●	●			●			
Foeniculum vulgare *Fennel*			●		●		•	●			
Foeniculum vulgare 'Purpureum' *Bronze fennel*			●		●		•	●			
Fragaria vesca *Wild strawberry*				●	●			●			
Galium odoratum *Sweet woodruff*				●	●			●			
Ginkgo biloba *Ginkgo*		●		●				●			
Glycyrrhiza glabra *Licorice*			●		●			●			
Hypericum perforatum *St. John's Wort*				●	●			●			
Hyssopus officinalis *Blue hyssop*			●		●			●			
Hyssopus officinalis 'Roseus' *Pink hyssop*			●		●			●			
Inula helenium *Elecampane*			●		●			●			
Isatis tinctoria *Woad*			•		•		●	•			
Laurus nobilis *Bay*		●	●		●			●			
Lavandula angustifolia 'Hidcote' *Hidcote lavender*			●		●			●			
Lavandula x intermedia *Old English lavender*			●		●			●			
Lavandula stoechas *French lavender*			●		●			●			
Levisticum officinale *Lovage*			●		●			●			
Linum perenne *Flax*			•		•		•	•			
Lycopus europaeus *Gypsywort*				•	•	•		•			
Lysimachia vulgaris *Yellow loosestrife*				•	•	•		•			
Lythrum salicaria *Purple loosestrife*				•	•	•		•			
Malva moschata *Musk mallow*				•	•		•	•			
Malva sylvestris *Common mallow*				•	•		•	•			
Mandragora officinarum *Mandrake*			●		●			●			
Marrubium vulgare *White horehound*			●		●			●			
Melissa officinalis *Lemon balm*			●		●	•		●			
Meum athamanticum *Meu*				●	●	•		●			
Monarda fistulosa *Wild bergamot*			●		●			●			
Myrrhis odorata *Myrrh*	●					•	•	●			
Myrtus communis *Myrtle*			●		●			●			
Nepeta cataria *Catnip*			●		●			●			
Nepeta x faassenii *Catmint*			●		●			●			
Nigella sativa *Black cumin*			●		●			●			
Ocimum basilicum *Sweet basil*			●		●			●			
Ocimum basilicum 'Dark Opal' *Dark opal basil*			●		●			●			
Ocimum minimum 'Greek' *Greek basil*			●		●			●			
Ocimum tenuiflorum *Holy basil*			●		●			●			
Oenothera biennis *Evening primrose*				●	●			●			
Origanum majorana *Sweet marjoram*			●		●			●			
Origanum vulgare *Oregano, Wild marjoram*			●		●			●			
Perilla frutescens var. crispa *Green shiso*			●		●			●			
Perilla frutescens var. purpurascens *Purple shiso*			●		●			●			
Petroselinum crispum *Parsley*			•		•		•	•	•		
Petroselinum crispum 'French' *French parsley*			•		•		•	•	•		
Phytolacca americana *Pokeroot*				●	●			●			
Portulaca oleracea *Purslane*			●		●			●			
Primula vulgaris *Primrose*				●	•			•	•		
Rosmarinus officinalis *Rosemary*			●		●			●			
Rumex scutatus *French sorrel*			•		•		•	•			
Ruta graveolens *Rue*			●		●			●			
Salvia clevelandii *Jim sage*			●		●			●			
Salvia elegans 'Scarlet Pineapple' *Pineapple sage*			●		●			●			
Salvia officinalis *Sage*			●		●			●			
Salvia officinalis Purpurascens Group *Purple sage*			●		●			●			
Salvia viridis *Painted sage*			•		•			•			
Sambucus niger *Elder*	●		●					●			
Sanguisorba minor *Salad burnet*				●	●			●			
Saponaria officinalis *Soapwort*				●	●	•		●			
Satureja hortensis *Summer savory*			●		●			●			
Satureja montana *Winter savory*			●		●			●			
Scutellaria lateriflora *Virginia skullcap*			●		●			●			
Sempervivum tectorum *Houseleek*			●		●			●			
Solidago virgaurea *Goldenrod*	●		●					●			
Stachys officinalis *Betony*				●	●			●			
Tagetes lucida *Winter tarragon*			●		●			●			
Tagetes patula *Wild Mexican marigold*			●		●			●			
Tanacetum cinerariifolium *Pyrethrum*			●		●			●			
Tanacetum parthenium *Feverfew*				●	●			●			
Tanacetum vulgare *Tansy*				●	●			●			
Teucrium chamaedrys L. *True valerian*				●	●			●			
Teucrium scorodonia *Wood sage*			●		●			●			
Thymus 'Fragrantissimus' *Orange-scented thyme*			●		●			●			
Thymus serpyllum *Creeping thyme*			●		●			●			
Tropaeolum majus 'Empress of India' *Nasturtium Empress of India*			●		●			●			
Tropaeolum speciosum *Flame nasturtium*			●		●			●			
Valeriana officinalis *Valerian*				●	●			●			
Verbena officinalis *Vervain*			●		●			●			
Viola odorata *Sweet violet*	●				●			●			•
Viola tricolor *Heart's ease*			●		●			●			•

Pricking out to potting on

Having nurtured seedlings through germination, the next stage in the plant's development is pricking out and potting on. The seedlings are ready when they have formed their second set of leaves and are well rooted. To check if the roots are well formed, lift up the container and see if the roots are growing out of the bottom. Alternatively, gently tap and ease the seedlings out of the pot or module. Do not leave the seedlings too long, because the roots become more intertwined each day, and they will suffer stress and damage when transplanted. Equally, if you leave seedlings in a module for too long, the root ball will become too tight for the seedling to grow, and plant growth will be weak. Pot on into a commercial organic potting substrate or make your own using 1 part coir, 1 part fine bark, 1 part sterilized loam, and 1 part vermiculite. I also make my own fertilizer to encourage the seedlings to put on root and top growth. To make enough fertilizer for 4 quarts of substrate, mix: 1oz (28g) seaweed

Pricking out seedlings

1 Seedlings in modules and pots
The seedlings in both the modules and pots have formed their second set of leaves and are ready for pricking out.

2 Fill a container with substrate To fill the container correctly, scoop the chosen substrate into the container so that it is overflowing. Do not pat or tap it down – you are trying to maintain as much air as possible within the substrate.

3 Removing seedling from modules Gently squeeze the base of the module with one hand and pull the seedling from the module with the other. If you are pricking out seedlings from a seed tray or pot, water the substrate first to make this process easier. Then, using a stick, carefully lever the seedlings out of the substrate. Hold the seedlings by the leaves, not the stems.

meal; 2 tsp (14g) bonemeal; 2 tsp (14g) hoof and horn and 1 tsp (7g) ground limestone. Or, purchase a good commercial organic fertilizer. Add the fertilizer to your substrate mix at the recommended rate. You will find that herbs raised in modules will grow twice as fast when potted on as those grown in seed trays or pricked out from pots. The root ball of seedlings grown in modules is hardly disturbed when it is transplanted, so the plant does not go into a state of shock and its growth remains unchecked.

When potting on, do not compress the substrate because this will remove the air from the soil and make it harder for the root system to develop. Once the plants are potted up, they need to be watered regularly. When ready to plant out in open ground, move to a protected site to "harden off" for at least one week, prior to planting. Hardening off is a gentle introduction to outdoor growing conditions and prevents herb plants from becoming stressed when they have been planted out early in the season.

Potting on into a container

4 Potting up Make a hole in the substrate with one finger, then gently position the module into it. Do not push the module down into the substrate because this will compact the roots and reduce the air flow to the roots, which will inhibit growth.

5 Position the module Once the module is in the substrate, tap the container hard on a firm surface. This action will be enough to position the module within the container.

6 Watering in Once the module is happily in position, water it in well using a fine rose on a watering can so as not to flatten the young leaves. When ready to plant out, place the young plant in a cold frame or under a cloche to harden off.

Propagation from cuttings

There is something miraculous about creating a new plant from a cutting. The secret of success is to use the fresh material at once to prevent it from drying out. Make a cutting substrate mixture to fill the modules using 1 part coir + 1 part fine bark + 1 part perlite. I also use a small amount of organic fertilizer to encourage root growth without stimulating too much top growth. To make up your own fertilizer (enough for a 4-quart volume of substrate), mix 2 teaspoons (14g) seaweed meal, 1 teaspoon (7g) bonemeal; ½ teaspoon (3g) hoof and horn and ½ teaspoon (3g) ground limestone. Use within 6 weeks. The technique for taking softwood (spring to early summer), semi-hardwood (summer to early fall), and hardwood cuttings (fall) is the same, but the name given to the cutting, for example, softwood, hardwood, or semi-hard, indicates the time of year it is taken. The herbs listed opposite can all be grown from cuttings.

Taking softwood cuttings

1 Selecting cuttings
Choose only healthy strong stems with fresh growth. Cut off the young stems with clean sharp scissors or pruners. Place them in a plastic bag and seal to prevent the cutting from drying out. To keep the cuttings moist, spray-mist the inside of the bag with water, before taking the cuttings. The best time of day to take cuttings is early in the morning before the sun has started to dry them out.

2 Preparing cuttings
Remove the lower leaves from the stem with care, so as not to tear the stem. (Torn stems attract disease.) Then, using a clean, sharp knife, cut the stem just below a leaf node. The length of the space between nodes can vary from species to species, but try to include the growing tip, plus some leaf plus some stem.

3 Planting cuttings
Gently push the stem end of each cutting into the substrate in a module until only the leaves are visible. Spray-mist the cutting with water to keep it moist.

4 Growing on cuttings
Cover the cuttings. I use a small propagator (shown here). Alternatively, cover the cuttings with a plastic bag, but remember to turn it inside out each day to prevent the bag from becoming too moist. In the morning and again early in the evening, spray-mist the cuttings with water. They should root within 14–21 days, depending on the time of year – cuttings taken late in the year take longer.

Which herbs may be grown from Cuttings

• = best method   • = other methods

	SOFTWOOD CUTTINGS: UNDER PROTECTION WITH WARMTH AND PROTECTED FROM SUN	SEMI-HARD CUTTINGS: COLD UNDER PROTECTION	HARDWOOD CUTTINGS: COLD
Achillea ageratum *English mace*	•		
Agastache foeniculum *Anise hyssop*	•		
Aloysia triphylla *Lemon verbena*	•	•	
Artemisia abrotanum *Southernwood*	•	•	
Artemisia dracunculus *French tarragon*	•		
Buxus sempervirens *Box*	•	•	•
Buxus sempervirens 'Latifolia Maculata' *Golden box*	•	•	•
Cedronella canariensis *Balm of Gilead*	•	•	
Chamaemelum nobile *Chamomile*	•		•
Chamaemelum nobile 'Flore Pleno' *Double-flowered chamomile*	•		•
Chamaemelum nobile 'Treneague' *Lawn chamomile*	•		•
Eriocephalus africanus *Wild rosemary*	•	•	
Ginkgo biloba *Ginkgo*			•
Glycyrrhiza glabra *Licorice*	•		
Humulus lupulus *Common hop*	•		
Hyssopus officinalis *Blue hyssop*	•		
Hyssopus officinalis 'Roseus' *Pink hyssop*	•		
Juniperus communis *Juniper*	•	•	•
Laurus nobilis *Bay*	•	•	•
Laurus nobilis 'Aurea' *Golden bay*	•	•	•
Laurus nobilis f. angustifolia *Willow leaf bay*	•	•	•
Lavandula x intermedia Old English Group *Old English lavender*	•	•	
Lavandula angustifolia 'Hidcote' *Hidcote lavender*	•	•	
Lavandula dentata var. candicans *Lavender Candicans*	•	•	
Lavandula stoechas 'Kew Red' *Lavender Kew Red*	•	•	
Lavandula stoechas 'Helmsdale' *Helmsdale lavender*	•	•	
Lavandula stoechas *French lavender*	•	•	
Lavandula x allardii *Lavender Allardii*	•	•	
Lavandula x christiana *Lavender Christiana*	•	•	
Lavandula 'Sawyers' *Lavender Sawyers*	•	•	
Luma chequen *Luma*	•	•	•
Melissa officinalis *Lemon balm*	•		
Melissa officinalis 'All Gold' *Golden lemon balm*	•		
Melissa officinalis 'Aurea' *Variegated lemon balm*	•		
Mentha pulegium 'Upright' *Upright pennyroyal*	•		
Mentha x piperita *Peppermint*	•		
Mentha x piperita f. citrus *Eau-de-cologne mint*	•		
Mentha x piperita 'Logee' *Logee mint*	•		
Mentha spicata *Spearmint*	•		
Mentha spicata var. crispum *Curly mint*	•		
Mentha x villosa var. alopecuroides 'Bowles' *Bowles mint*	•		
Monarda fistulosa *Wild bergamot*	•		
Murraya koenigii *Curry tree*	•	•	•
Myrtus communis *Myrtle*	•	•	•
Myrtus communis 'Merion' *Myrtle merion*	•	•	•
Myrtus communis subsp. tarentina 'Variegata' *Variegated myrtle tarentina*	•	•	•
Nepeta cataria *Catnip*	•		
Nepeta x faassenii *Catmint*	•		
Olea europaea *Olive*	•	•	•
Origanum dictamnus *Cretan oregano*	•		
Origanum majorana *Sweet marjoram*	•		
Origanum vulgare *Oregano, Wild marjoram*	•		
Origanum vulgare 'Acorn Bank' *Acorn Bank marjoram*	•		
Origanum x onites *French marjoram*	•		
Pelargonium 'Apple Scented' *Apple-scented pelargonium*	•		
Pelargonium 'Atomic Snowflake' *Atomic snowflake pelargonium*	•		
Pelargonium 'Attar of roses' *Attar of Roses pelargonium*	•		
Pelargonium 'Chocolate Peppermint' *Chocolate peppermint pelargonium*	•		
Pelargonium 'Lady Plymouth' *Lady Plymouth pelargonium*	•		
Pelargonium 'Peach Cream' *Peach cream pelargonium*	•		
Perilla frutescens var. crispa *Green shiso*	•		
Perilla frutescens var. purpurascens *Purple shiso*	•		
Persicaria odorata *Vietnamese coriander*	•		
Prostanthera cuneata *Australian mint bush*	•	•	
Rosmarinus officinalis *Rosemary*	•	•	
Rosmarinus officinalis 'Aureus' *Golden rosemary*	•	•	
Rosmarinus officinalis 'Roseus' *Pink rosemary*	•	•	
Rosmarinus officinalis Prostratus Group *Prostrate rosemary*	•	•	
Ruta graveolens *Rue*	•	•	
Salvia clevelandii *Jim sage*	•	•	
Salvia lavandulifolia *Narrow-leaved sage*	•	•	
Salvia microphylla var. microphylla *Blackcurrant-scented sage*	•	•	
Salvia officinalis *Sage*	•	•	
Salvia officinalis Purpurascens Group *Purple sage*	•	•	
Salvia elegans 'Scarlet Pineapple' *Pineapple sage*	•	•	
Sambucus nigra *Elder*	•	•	•
Santolina chamaecyparissus *Lavender cotton*	•	•	
Saponaria officinalis *Soapwort*	•		
Satureja douglasii *Yerba buena*	•		
Satureja montana *Winter savory*	•	•	
Scutellaria lateriflora *Virginia skullcap*	•		
Tagetes lucida *Winter tarragon*	•		
Tanacetum balsamita *Alecost*	•		
Tanacetum parthenium *Feverfew*	•		
Tanacetum vulgare *Tansy*	•		
Teucrium chamaedrys L. *True valerian*	•	•	
Teucrium scorodonia *Wood sage*	•		
Teucrium scorodonia 'Crispum' *Curly wood sage*	•		
Teucrium x lucidrys *Hedge germander*	•	•	
Thymus 'Fragrantissimus' *Orange-scented thyme*	•	•	
Thymus 'Peter Davis' *Peter Davis thyme*	•	•	
Thymus caespititus *Azores thyme*	•	•	
Thymus coccineus *Creeping red thyme*	•	•	
Thymus pulegioides *Broad-leaved thyme*	•	•	
Thymus pulegioides 'Bertram Anderson' *Bertram Anderson thyme*	•	•	
Thymus serpyllum *Creeping thyme*	•	•	
Thymus serpyllum 'Minimus' *Minimus thyme*	•	•	
Thymus vulgaris 'Compactus' *Compact thyme*	•	•	
Thymus vulgaris 'Snow White' *Compact white-flowering thyme*	•	•	
Thymus x citriodorus 'Silver Queen' *Silver Queen thyme*	•	•	
Tropaeolum speciosum *Flame nasturtium*	•	•	
Ugni molinae *Chilean guava*	•	•	•

Propagation by layering

This traditional method of propagation encourages the plant to form roots while it is still attached to the parent plant. The technique requires a healthy well-established plant with strong growth that hangs down to the ground. For this reason, it is a useful propagation method for shrubby herbaceous herbs like rosemary, sage, and thyme where a pendulous growth habit is natural, and lower branches often root anyway when they come into contact with the ground. All you are doing by layering the stem is encouraging the plant's natural tendency to put out roots and propagate itself. The best time for layering an herbaceous herb is in spring or fall when the soil is warm. On the site where you want the stem to take root, prepare the ground well, remove all weeds, and dig it over. If the soil is low in nutrients, add some organic fertilizer or leaf mold to improve its condition. Then, take hold of a long stem from the parent plant that you wish to layer, and remove its leaves and side shoots. Then, with a

How to propagate by stem layering

1 Scrape the stem For large shrubs like sage (shown here), choose a strong, healthy stem and remove all side shoots and leaves from a 12in (30cm) section. For smaller herbs with much shorter branches like thyme, scrape away only 4–6in (10–15cm).

2 Prepare the ground Dig over the soil well, removing all weeds and stones. For woody herbs like sage, bay, and elder, feed the ground with organic fertilizer to provide the cuttings with extra nutrients so they will take better. For thyme and Vietnamese coriander, good drainage is the most important factor for successful propagation by layering. To improve soil drainage, add fine grit or sharp sand to the prepared site.

3 Anchor to the ground Remove a slice along the side of the stem that is going to come into contact with the earth. Pin the herbs stem into the soil with a U-shaped piece of wire – this is more than adequate to hold it in place. For thicker herb stems, anchor the stem with metal and bury in a trench for successful propagation.

sharp knife, slice off the outer bark to expose the soft inner stem that is going to come into contact with the soil. Gently pull the stem down to the ground and anchor it to the soil with a piece of wire bent into a U-shaped hook. Having pinned the stem in place, cover it with soil to a depth of at least 3in (8cm). Water in well. Make sure at least one growing tip on the stem remains above soil level. Throughout the year, check the layered stem and the ground around it. Remove any weeds that

may have grown up after the soil was turned over during planting, and water the stem layer because it is probably sheltered from the rain by the parent plant. After at least one year, check to see if the layered stem has rooted, if not, leave it alone for a another year. If the stem has successfully taken root, cut the stem that joins it to the parent plant. A few weeks later, dig up the rooted layer and replant it into a new, well-prepared site where it will grow into a new plant.

4 Cover up the stem layer Spread a layer of soil over the stem, but leave the growing tip exposed. Herbs like thyme and Vietnamese coriander will put down roots within one growing season. (If you layer the stem in spring, you will be able to separate it from the parent plant by the fall). If this is the time span, do not replant the layered stem outdoors in autumn. Instead lift it and pot it up and place in a cold frame to protect it over the winter months. Plant out the following spring.

Which herbs may be propagated by # Layering

Artemisia abrotanum *Southernwood*

Eriocephalus africanus *Wild rosemary*

Lavandula x intermedia Old English Group *Old English lavender*

Origanum x onites *French majoram*

Persicaria odorata *Vietnamese coriander*

Rosmarinus officinalis *Rosemary*

Rosmarinus officinalis 'Aureus' *Golden rosemary*

Rosmarinus officinalis 'Roseus' *Pink rosemary*

Rosmarinus officinalis Prostratus Group *Prostrate rosemary*

Salvia lavandulifolia *Narrow-leaved sage*

Salvia officinalis *Sage*

Salvia officinalis Purpurascens Group Purple *Purple sage*

Sambucus nigra *Elder*

Santolina chamaecyparissus *Lavender cotton*

Satureja douglasii *Yerba buena*

Thymus 'Fragrantissimus' *Orange-scented thyme*

Thymus 'Peter Davis' *Peter Davis thyme*

Thymus pulegioides *Broad-leaved thyme*

Thymus pulegioides 'Bertram Anderson' *Bertram Anderson thyme*

Thymus vulgaris 'Compactus' *Compact thyme*

Thymus vulgaris 'Snow White' *Compact white-flowering thyme*

Thymus x citriodorus 'Silver Queen' *Silver Queen thyme*

Propagation from root cuttings

The technique you use to propagate an herb plant from a root cutting depends on the size and type of root the plant produces. All root cuttings are taken in the fall or early spring when the plant's energy is in the roots. Plants with thick taproots like comfrey and horseradish can be propagated by taking from the parent plant a slice of root that is then placed in a pot and covered in substrate – the root slice is too big to grow in a module. Herbs with long, thin creeping roots like French tarragon, sweet woodruff, and mint can be propagated by cutting off a section of root about 1in (2.5cm) long which has at least two root nodes; this is known as an internodal root cutting (see below). Nodal root cuttings are a mixture of the two techniques described above. It works well for plants that produce a solid mass of roots like mandrake, and involves slicing off a section of root while making sure you take a growing node.

Sliced root cutting

1 Taking a slice of root
Wash any excess soil from the root. With a sharp knife, cut the root up into into approximately 1in (2.5cm) thick slices.

2 Planting
Using cutting substrate mix (see page 52), fill your pot two-thirds full with substrate. Make a small hole in the substrate with your finger, drop the cutting into the hole, and cover with more substrate to just below the rim of the pot. Water well and label.

Internodal root cutting

1 Cutting a node
Having selected your thin roots, wash them well to remove excess soil so the growing nodes become visible. Use a sharp knife to divide the cuttings so that each length has two growing nodes. If you look carefully at these sweet woodruff cuttings, you will see that at each root node, small roots have begun to grow.

2 Planting the cutting
Using the cutting substrate (see page 52), half-fill a module tray. Then lay the root cuttings on the surface of the substrate. Cover the cuttings with more substrate to just below the rim. Do not compact the substrate into the modules, which could damage fine roots. Water well.

Propagation by division

Dividing established herbaceous herbs is a useful way to produce more stock and to keep plants healthy. Quite often, herbaceous herb plants like lemon balm become invasive, and as the plant ages, the central core can die away. Division prevents these problems from occurring. Divide plants in early fall when they start to die back or in early spring, before they put on too much top growth – any later in the season and you could inhibit flowering. When propagating by division, carefully dig up the whole plant plus its root ball and shake off any excess soil. Divide the root ball in two with your hands or use two garden forks placed back to back if extra leverage is required to separate the roots. If you wish to replant one section of root back in the same site, dig in some well-rotted compost to give the plant a boost. Replant the other section where required, or, if you don't have space, offer it to a friend with a garden.

How to propagate by division

1 Dig up roots Dig up the plants that are to be divided in spring or fall. Both wild garlic and French tarragon are best divided in the fall, but for different reasons: the garlic because it will give the plant time to settle in for winter and allow time for it to mature enough to provide a crop the following spring; the French tarragon, especially in a damp cold climate, will allow you to put some in a cold frame over winter as insurance. Specific guidance and information on individual plants is given in the Top 100 (see pages 114–267).

2 Divide roots Either shake the excess soil off the root prior to dividing or hold the root ball under running water to loosen the soil.

3 Replant Replant the divisions into a prepared site as soon as possible to prevent them from drying out. Always water the plant in well. Divisions can also be potted up either for insurance against bad winter weather, or to create a container plant. See page 58 for a list of herbs that can be propagated successfully by division.

Which herbs may be propagated from Root cuttings

• = best method   • = other methods

	INTERNODAL ROOT CUTTINGS	ROOT CUTTINGS INCLUDING GROWING NODE	SLICED ROOT CUTTINGS
Armoracia rusticana *Horseradish*			•
Arnica chamissonis *Arnica*		•	
Artemisia dracunculus *French tarragon*	•		
Galium odoratum *Sweet woodruff*	•		
Glycyrrhiza glabra *Liquorice*			•
Humulus lupulus *Common hop*		•	
Mandragora officinarum *Mandrake*		•	
Mentha x piperita *Peppermint*	•		
Mentha x piperita f. citratus *Eau-de-cologne mint*	•		
Mentha x piperita 'Logee' *Logee mint*	•		

	INTERNODAL ROOT CUTTINGS	ROOT CUTTINGS INCLUDING GROWING NODE	SLICED ROOT CUTTINGS
Mentha x villosa var. alopecuroides 'Bowles' *Bowles mint*	•		
Mentha spicata *Spearmint*	•		
Mentha spicata var. crispa *Curly mint*	•		
Myrrhis odorata *Myrrh*		•	
Phytolacca americana *Pokeroot*		•	
Saponaria officinalis *Soapwort*		•	
Scutellaria lateriflora *Virginia skullcap*		•	
Symphytum officinale *Comfrey*			•
Symphytum x uplandicum *Russian comfrey*			•
Tanacetum vulgare *Tansy*		•	

Which herbs may be propagated by Division

• = best method   • = other methods

Achillea ageratum *English mace*	•	Fragaria vesca *Wild strawberry*	•	Origanum vulgare *Oregano, Wild marjoram*	•
Achillea millefolium *Yarrow*	•	Gallium odoratun *Sweet woodruff*	•	Origanum vulgare 'Acorn Bank' *Acorn bank marjoram*	•
Alchemilla xanthochlora *Lady's mantle*	•	Humulus lupulus *Common hop*	•	Origanum x onites *French marjoram*	•
Allium cepa Proliferum Group *Tree onion*	•	Hypericum perforatum *St. John's Wort*	•	Persicaria odorata *Vietnamese coriander*	•
Allium fistulosum *Welsh onion*	•	Inula helenium *Elecampane*	•	Phytolacca americana *Pokeroot*	•
Allium schoenoprasum *Chives*	•	Levisticum officinale *Lovage*	•	Primula vulgaris *Primrose*	•
Allium tuberosum *Garlic chives*	•	Linum perenne *Flax*	•	Rumex scutatus *French sorrel*	•
Allium ursinum *Wild garlic*	•	Lycopus europaeus *Gipsywort*	•	Sanguisorba minor *Salad burnet*	•
Aloe vera *Aloe*	•	Lysimachia vulgaris *Yellow loosestrife*	•	Scutellaria lateriflora *Virginia skullcap*	•
Armoracia rusticana *Horseradish*	•	Lythrum salicaria *Purple loosestrife*	•	Sempervivum tectorum *Houseleek*	•
Arnica chamissonis *Arnica*	•	Malva moschata *Musk mallow*	•	Solidago virgaurea *Goldenrod*	•
Artemisia absinthium *Wormwood*	•	Malva sylvestris *Common mallow*	•	Stachys officinalis *Betony*	•
Artemisia dracunculus *French tarragon*	•	Mandragora officinarum *Mandrake*	•	Symphytum officinale *Comfrey*	•
Artemisia vulgaris *Mugwort*	•	Marrubium vulgare *White horehound*	•	Symphytum x uplandicum *Russian comfrey*	•
Borago pygmaea *Prostate borage*	•	Melissa officinalis *Lemon balm*	•	Tagetes lucida *Winter tarragon*	•
Centella asiatica *Gotu kola*	•	Melissa officinalis 'All Gold' *Golden lemon balm*	•	Tanacetum balsamita *Alecost*	•
Chamaemelum nobile 'Flore Pleno' *Double-flowered chamomile*		Melissa officinalis 'Aurea' *Variegated lemon balm*	•	Tanacetum cinerariifolium *Pyrethrum*	•
Chenopodium bonus-henricus *Goosefoot*	•	Mentha pulegium 'Upright' *Pennyroyal upright*	•	Tanacetum parthenium *Feverfew*	•
Crithmum maritimum *Sea fennel*	•	Mentha x piperita *Peppermint*	•	Tanacetum vulgare *Tansy*	•
Cymbopogon citratus *Lemon grass*	•	Mentha x piperita f. citratus *Eau-de-cologne mint*	•	Teucrium x lucidrys *Hedge germander*	•
Cynara cardunculus *Cardoon*	•	Mentha x piperita 'Logee' *Logee mint*	•	Teucrium scorodonia *Wood sage*	•
Diplotaxis muralis *Wild rocket*	•	Mentha spicata *Spearmint*	•	Teucrium scorodonia 'Crispum' *Curly wood sage*	•
Echinacea purpurea *Purple coneflower*	•	Mentha spicata var crispum *Curly mint*	•	Thymus 'Coccineus' *Creeping red thyme*	•
Echinacea angustifolia *Narrow-leaved echinacea*	•	Mentha x villosa var. alopecuroides 'Bowles' *Bowles mint*	•	Thymus pulegioides *Broad-leaved thyme*	•
Echinacea pallida *Echinacea*	•	Meum athamanticum *Meu*	•	Thymus serpyllum *Creeping thyme*	•
Elettaria cardamomum *Cardamom*	•	Monarda fistulosa *Wild bergamot*	•	Thymus serpyllum 'Minimus' *Minimus thyme*	•
Eupatorium purpureum *Joe Pye weed*	•	Myrrhis odorata *Myrrh*	•	Valeriana officinalis *Valerian*	•
Filipendula ulmaria *Queen-of-the-meadow*	•	Nepeta cataria *Catnip*	•	Verbena officinalis *Vervain*	•
Foeniculum vulgare *Fennel*	•	Nepeta x faassenii *Catmint*	•	Viola odorata *Sweet violet*	•
Foeniculum vulgare 'Purpureum' *Bronze fennel*	•	Origanum dictamnus *Cretan oregano*	•	Viola tricolor *Heart's ease*	•
		Origanum majorana *Sweet marjoram*	•		

Propagation problems

The main reason seeds and cuttings fail is because of fungal diseases contracted from either too much water, a contaminated supply, or the wrong substrate. Too much water causes seedlings to "damp off" – the term to describe a fungal disease that thrives in cool, wet, poorly ventilated substrates. Hygiene can also cause problems since fungal infections remain in dirty trays and unsterilized substrates. Choosing a substrate with the right nutrient content to suit the seedling or cutting will also help prevent problems.

Overcrowded seedlings

It is very easy with fine seed to sow the seeds too thickly, which causes the seedlings to crowd each other out, which in turn inhibits their development into strong healthy specimens. For sowing techniques, see page 47. Also, if one seedling gets a disease because it is touching others, it can spread very quickly. If you have mistakenly sown too thickly, thin them as soon as the seedlings emerge so you only have two or three seedlings per 1in (2cm) module.

Watchpoints

Mix fine seed with flour or sharp sand for a thin sowing. Avoid sowing seedlings too close together to prevent the leaves of individual seedlings from touching one another, which may spread infection.

Primrose seedlings

Overwatered cuttings

Growing young plants from cuttings brings out the worst in the enthusiastic gardener. If their "offspring" look poorly, the gardener tries to help the ailing cuttings by watering them. Too much water puts young plants under stress since they do not have an established root system to cope. Overwatering also attracts pests, especially sciarid fly, which thrives on wet substrate. The fly lays its eggs in the substrate, the larvae hatch within a week and feed on the plant's roots; killing off the cuttings.

Watchpoints

The tray or pot feels heavy with water. When you lift a cutting, water seeps out. The cuttings start to die. Clouds of black sciarid fly appear when you knock the tray – a sure sign of very wet substrate.

Sage cuttings

Cuttings taken at the wrong time

As a general rule, it is best to take cuttings when the herb is not in flower so the leaves and stems are in peak condition. When the plant is in flower, all of its energy is taken up by flower production. For herbaceous herbs, it is best to take cuttings before flowering because by the fall the herbs have started to die back. Evergreen herb cuttings are best taken in summer or early fall. Any earlier and the sap will not have risen, so the cuttings are much slower to root.

Watchpoints

The cuttings are taking a long time to put down roots.

The cutting is weak and dies.

The cutting roots, but does not put on new growth.

Myrtle cuttings

Disease in cuttings

Cuttings taken from plants that have been attacked by pests are best avoided because the cutting is weak from the outset and will attract disease. Use a clean, sharp knife to take cuttings to avoid diseases like blackleg, which can occur if plant cells in the stem are crushed. Blackleg spreads rapidly, and the only organic solution is to throw away the cuttings and start again. Always wash out propagation trays well, especially if previous stock was diseased or attacked by pests.

Watchpoints

Look out for the stem of the cutting turning black, or the growing tip of the cutting bending over. If you notice mold growing on the leaves, it could be the first sign of mildew.

Pelargonium cuttings

Seasonal maintenance

I find it useful to keep a record each year of when we take cuttings, when we sow seeds, and what pests have caused problems during the year, to refer to in subsequent years. Although no two seasons are the same the maintenance routine changes very little, because in an organic herb garden there are always jobs that need doing as you have only natural rather than chemical methods for keeping pest and weeds under control. The secret of a well-managed herb garden is to keep the ecosystem in balance, to stay vigilant, and not to be fooled by nature. If spring comes early, for example, be prepared to guard against frost at night; have a roll of horticutural fleece ready to cover up tender plants or any plants that have started to put on new spring growth. When you prepare the ground for sowing annual herbs, take time to mulch around mature plants to suppress weed growth and to save time spent weeding. Container plants also require attention – they may need repotting, pruning, or moving outdoors. As summer approaches, growing tips need to be pinched out to keep plants bushy, and flowering herbs need regular deadheading to keep them in flower, while tender herbs are ready to plant out. By midsummer every herb is gearing up for harvest. Now is the time to choose which herbs you are going to let run to seed and those you wish to keep in cultivation through winter. This is also the time to cut back hardy herbs to encourage them to produce extra growth for winter protection and late pickings. As winter approaches, tender plants need protection from frost. Clear away annual herbs. Dig over and mulch the soil to feed and protect it. In winter, plants under protection are prone to disease so provide good ventilation. Take time in winter to select healthy seeds and plan next year's herb garden.

Top row left When frost is forecast, wrap up tender plants that are too large to be brought indoors with horticultural fleece.

Top row right In spring, check plants for pest damage like vine weevil. If damage is extensive, introduce a predator to restore the balance.

Bottom row left Late fall is the season to cut back herbs like thyme so they will burst into new growth the following spring.

Bottom row right Late summer is the time for trimming box. The hedge or container-grown plant will then keep its shape through winter and spring before the summer growing season.

Far right Weeding is a chore from spring until late fall. Remember container-grown herbs need weeding as regularly as garden herbs.

The maintenance calendar

Early season in the young garden If the soil has been dug and planted with annuals, you will have a good crop of weed seed as well as the young plants. It is essential to be diligent and keep weeds under control, or they will take all the nutrients from the soil intended for young plants.

Early season in the mature garden It is important to cut plants back to produce new growth. This not only protects the plant, but also creates lots of fresh leaf growth that can be used in cooking, the home, or for medicinal purposes.

Late season in the young garden Mulch well between perennial herbs. This not only inhibits weeds, but also protects the roots of young plants through winter.

Late season in the mature garden Remember to start feeding the birds so they stay in the garden for the season. Cut back hardy herbaceous top growth to prevent it from rotting if the weather is excessively wet.

Early season in the young garden

Spring in a young garden is exciting because you can start to see the results of your propagation and planning work. Having prepared the ground (see page 22), it is very difficult to remain patient and not to rush out and start sowing on the first day of good weather. But you need to wait for the soil to warm through. There is a saying that "if you can sit on the soil without feeling the cold it is time to plant." Alternatively, wait for weeds to start appearing, a sure sign that the soil is warming up

Planting annuals and salad herbs

If you live in an area prone to hard frosts or damp soil, sow seeds under protection rather than direct into open soil. Young seedlings grown under protection will need hardening off before they are planted outside. Start by taking them outside during the day for one week; then if there is no frost forecast, start leaving them outside at night. Plant salad herbs in rows to make them easy to harvest. As a general rule, plant seedlings 2in (5cm) apart. After planting, water the seedlings in well, and for the first week, cover them at night with horticultural fleece to encourage them to root.

Annual herbs to plant from seed

Anethum graveolens (dill); *Anthriscus cerefolium* (chervil); *Borago officinalis* (borage); *Calendula officinalis* (pot marigold); *Carum carvi* (caraway); *Chenopodium giganteum* (tree spinach); *Cichorium intybus* (chicory); *Coriandrum sativum* (coriander/cilantro); *Diplotaxis muralis* (wild rocket); *Ocimum basilicum* (sweet basil); *Ocimum basilicum* 'Dark Opal' (dark opal basil) *Ocimum tenuiflorum* (holy basil); *Origanum majorana* (sweet marjoram) *Perilla frutescens* var. *crispa* (green shiso) *Perilla frutescens* var. *purpurascens* (purple shiso); *Petroselinum crispum* (parsley); *Portulaca oleracea* (purslane); *Satureja hortensis* (summer savory); *Tropaeolum majus* 'Empress of India' (nasturtium 'Empress of India').

Please check the species list on page 43 for more details.

Shelter for young plants

When young plants are becoming established, they need protection from high winds and birds – I have watched a tiny wren eat her way through a row of French parsley (*Petroselinum crispum* 'French'). Make a shelter out of twigs to act as a windbreak and a protective cage. In addition to protecting the young plants, it will also allow water and sunlight to reach the seedlings. However, allow space between the sticks to pick out slugs. If you are also having trouble with birds eating larger plants, string up lines of twine that hum in the wind to scare them off. These are available through organic gardening mail-order catalogs.

Herbs that need protection from birds

Anethum graveolens (dill); *Anthriscus cerefolium* (chervil); *Carum carvi* (caraway); *Chenopodium giganteum* (tree spinach); *Cichorium intybus* (chicory); *Coriandrum sativum* (coriander/cilantro); *Foeniculum vulgare* (fennel); *Origanum majorana* (sweet marjoram); *Petroselinum crispum* (parsley); *Satureja hortensis* (summer savory).

and that it is time to plant. When planting, stand on a plank to spread your weight evenly so as not to compress newly dug soil. Use the side of the hoe to carve a straight shallow drill in the soil where you wish to plant. When sowing dark-colored seed, line the drill with sharp sand prior to sowing to make the seed visible and so easier to sow thinly. After sowing, check for signs of pests and disease. Young herbs are tender morsels for slugs, snails, aphids, and other pests that frequent the garden in spring.

Staking young plants

If you want to encourage a herb plant like bay to grow into a standard tree shape or make a rosemary hedge, the young plants will need to be staked and trained. This is also the case if you intend to grow herbs on an exposed site, where they will need staking to keep them upright in strong winds. Stake young plants with sticks or bamboo. If possible, support the plant without fastening it to the stake; otherwise, the stem may bend toward the pole; simply place the stake parallel to the plant stem. On exposed sites, a good solution is to make a ring of sticks around the herb to protect it from wind and keep it vertical.

Herbs to support

Laurus nobilis (bay); *Luma chequen* (luma); *Myrtus communis* (myrtle); *Rosmarinus officinalis* (rosemary).

Weed control

In a young herb garden where the plants are not yet established, it is essential to keep weeds under control to prevent them from taking all the nutrients from the soil. Weed by hand around seedlings rather than using a hoe so as not to damage new plants. Weeds are prolific in young gardens because the soil has been turned over and the weed seed has been exposed to the light, which kick starts it into growth. The key is to weed regularly; small weeds with tiny root systems are far easier to lift out than those that have become established. Applying a mulch of compost, leaf mold, or bark over bare soil is also an effective way to keep weed growth under control. See page 37 for a list of mulches and their properties.

Weeding techniques

Hoeing For best results, keep the hoe sharp, and hoe dry soil on a sunny day, cutting off the weeds where the stem joins the root. (Weed seedlings wilt in sunshine and do not take root again.) Make sure you pick up all the weeds when you have finished.

Flame gun, Thermal weed killer A thrilling way to exterminate perennial weeds is by torching them. This also sterilizes the soil.

Slashing and cutting A good short-term solution. Repeat cutting is effective because it weakens and slows down the growth of stubborn weeds.

Early season in the mature garden

In an established herb garden, as the soil starts to warm up early in the year, all your favorite hardy perennials like chives will reappear. This is the time to start weeding. Once weeded, apply a layer of mulch (see page 25) to "top up" the nutrient content of the soil after winter, so providing feed for established plants. Also, mulch beds that you intend to leave free of plants – mulch supresses weeds. In areas where you want to sow annual herbs, dig in well-rotted compost or mature leaf mold (see page

Trimming to shape

In spring, when all chance of hard frosts has passed, trim box plants and rosemary, especially if you are growing either plant as a hedge feature. When growing bay tree standards, spend time in spring cutting off the growing tips. This will encourage bay to put out side shoots and fill out. If you have been picking thyme through the winter for cooking, it is a good idea to give it a light trim to reshape it, and to encourage it to produce new growth.

Herbs that need trimming

Buxus sempervirens (box); *Eriocephalus africanus* (wild rosemary); *Laurus nobilis* (bay); *Luma chequen* (luma); *Myrtus communis* (myrtle); *Rosmarinus officinalis* (rosemary); *Thymus vulgaris* (thyme).

Removing pests

During winter, pests like slugs hibernate under low-growing evergreen herbs or the died-back growth of herbaceous herb plants. To keep pests under control organically, remove them by hand as and when they appear in spring. If you are growing herbs in containers, look out for signs of vine weevil, a small black beetle with a long snout that has orange splodges on its back. (Unhealthy-looking leaf growth may be the only visible "above ground" sign that vine weevil is present.) In summer, this beetle lays eggs in the container substrate and the larvae feed on the plant roots from winter until spring.

Early season pests include

Caterpillars – check plants where you have seen butterflies. Pick off eggs and caterpillars by hand. Encourage blue tits and wasps; both good predators.

Cutworm – is the larvae of a nocturnal moth. It feeds at night on seedlings, roots, and corms. Remove larvae by hand, or turn the soil and expose the cutworm for birds to feed on.

Slugs – remove by hand or from spring to late summer; introduce a biological control like the parasitic nematode *Heterorhabditis megidis*.

Vine weevil – attack species of primula and houseleek (*Sempervivum* species). Remove by hand or use the same biological control as for slugs.

37). In cold and wet geographical regions, spring rather than fall is the best time to cut back sun-loving, silver-foliage plants like artemisia – fall pruning will let water penetrate the plant and kill it off. Spring is also the time of year to reorganize the location of plants in an established garden. Dig up plants that have become invasive, and free space around tall herbaceous herbs like cardoons. Create more space around biennial herbs such as angelica in the year that they are going to flower.

Pruning

In spring, some herb plants may need pruning to remove dead branches and to cut out dead growth. Spring is the best time of year to prune because you can see more clearly what needs doing when there is little leaf canopy. It is also a good time for pruning and reshaping herb plants with Mediterranean origins like myrtle and olive, which favor dry conditions. Avoid pruning Mediterranean herbs in the fall because the wound caused by pruning may not heal over before cold and wet winter weather sets in, and the plant may become infected.

Herbs to prune in spring

Aloysia triphylla (lemon verbena); *Artemisia abrotanum* (southernwood); *Lavandula angustifolia* (lavender); *Olea europaea* (olive); *Rosmarinus officinalis* (rosemary); *Santolina chamaecyparissus* (lavender cotton); *Teucrium* x *lucidrys* (hedge germander).

Feeding

Some herbs are best fed in spring rather than fall to set them up for the year. This is particularly suitable for salad herbs and fruit-producing herbs since you will be harvesting them regularly and feeding will produce plenty of lush leaf growth. Take care, though, to get the balance right; overfeeding will lead to weak growth, which makes plants susceptible to damage from pests. Spring feeding is also a good idea for tender herbs that have been lifted in the fall and planted out again in spring – these extra nutrients will help to kick-start spring growth.

Plants that benefit from spring feeding

Allium fistulosum (Welsh onion); *Aloysia triphylla* (lemon verbena); *Buxus sempervirens* (box); *Levisticum officinale* (lovage); *Olea europaea* (olive); *Pelargonium* species (scented pelargoniums).

Late season in the young garden

By late summer, a young herb garden will have started to meld together to create a harmonious whole. There will be some herbs that have exceeded expectations and thrived in your chosen planting position, while for other's growth may have been disappointing. For plants that have romped away, cut them back dramatically, but if you are concerned that your pruning is too drastic, plant some of these vigorous herbs in pots and winter them in a cold frame as insurance against loss. For the poor

Mulching

Apply extra mulch to a young garden in the fall to help keep weed seeds at bay but also to keep the roots of young plants free from frost damage in their first season. Mulches, especially bark mulch (see page 37), allow water to permeate the soil more easily and reduce the likelihood of the young plants sitting in water, which rots the roots. To prevent the plant stem from rotting, do not lay mulch right up close to the herb. Leave a collar all the way around, of approximately 2in (5cm) to 4in (10cm). There are many different forms of mulch (see page 37), and one may be better suited to your soil type and plant species than another.

Young herbs that benefit from late season mulching

Aloysia triphylla (lemon verbena); *Cedronella canariensis* (balm of Gilead); *Ginkgo biloba* (ginkgo); *Humulus lupulus* (common hop); *Juniperus communis* (juniper); *Laurus nobilis* (bay).

Removing seed heads

Deadheading or removing seed heads can prolong flowering of herbs such as pot marigold and nasturtium, right up until the first frosts. It is also important to remove the flowers of feverfew and borage before they set seed; otherwise, they will self-seed and you could have swathes of white and blue flowers the following season. This can look wonderful if they grow in the correct position, but can be very frustrating when trying to establish a mixed herb garden. Another reason for removing the seed heads, especially from annual herbs, is to save them for drying and sowing the following season.

Herbs that become invasive if allowed to self seed

Anethum graveolens (dill); *Angelica archangelica* (angelica); *Borago officinalis* (borage); *Digitalis purpurea* (foxglove); *Lysimachia vulgaris* (yellow loosestrife); *Lythrum salicaria* (purple loosestrife); *Oenothera biennis* (evening primrose); *Portulaca oleracea* (purslane); *Tanacetum parthenium* (feverfew).

performers, lift and check their roots for signs of growth during the season. Pot them and put them in a cold frame for the winter, and move them to a new site the next year. Late season is also the time to protect young herbs, especially trees like olives and ginkgos, that are about to experience their first winter in the soil. Small trees should be covered with a cloche that is open at both ends for good air circulation. Larger trees may be wrapped in horticultural fleece when frosts are forecast.

Cutting back

Some young plants need more drastic cutting back than others at the end of the season. It is essential to cut the flowers of all lavender species as soon as they have finished flowering to help maintain shape and to prevent damage by winter weather. It also stops plant stems from becoming woody. This method also applies to thyme and sage. Herbaceous herbs require more vigorous cutting back of flowers and new growth to help them bush out and to prevent the flowering stems from falling back in on themselves and rotting out the plant center. (This happens when hillside plants are grown on flat sites; in their natural habitat the plant stems would fall away). Finally, there is the cutting back of all top growth to encourage new young leaves later in the year, which can be lightly harvested for cooking.

Young herbs to cut back in late season

Flowers and flowering stems: *Lavandula* species (lavenders); *Salvia* species (sages); *Thymus* species (thymes).

Flowers and new growth: *Scutellaria lateriflora* (skullcap virginia); *Symphytum officinale* (comfrey); *Tanacetum balsamita* (alecost); *Tanacetum cinerariifolium* (pyrethrum).

All top growth: *Melissa officinalis* (lemon balm); *Origanum vulgare* (oregano).

Lifting tender plants

As the winter months approach, it is important to check the weather forecasts and lift all tender herbs before frost occurs that will kill the plants. As soon as the night-time temperature dips below 39°F (4°C), lift the tender herbs, cut them back, pot up, and water them in. Then place them in a frostfree environment (without central heating) for the winter. They will need little water, just check that the substrate is not shrinking away from the sides of the pot. Replant in the garden the following spring once all threat of frost has passed.

Tender herbs to lift

Aloe vera (aloe); *Calomeria amaranthoides* (incense plant); *Centella asiatica* (gotu kola); *Cymbopogon citratus* (lemon grass); *Elettaria cardamomum* (cardamom); *Lavandula dentata var. candicans* (lavender Candicans); *Lavandula stoechas* 'Kew Red' (lavender 'Kew Red'); *Lavandula x christiana* (lavender Christiana); *Pelargonium* species (scented pelargoniums); *Persicaria odorata* (Vietnamese coriander); *Salvia clevelandii* (Jim sage); *Satureja douglasii* (yerba buena); *Tagetes lucida* (winter tarragon); *Tropaeolum speciosum* (flame nasturtium).

Late season in the mature garden

Hopefully you will have had a bountiful harvest from your herb garden, and your shelves will be groaning with produce to use in the kitchen during the winter months. Now is the time to put your garden to bed for the winter, so that it will perform as well, if not better, the following year. Dig up the older herbs that are past their best and no longer producing leaves full of flavor or looking fantastic. This is better done now than left to the spring because you can place the old plant on the compost heap, dig

Removing debris from plant crowns

In fall, I recommend cutting back and clearing the debris from around herbaceous herbs rather than letting the leaves and stems die back naturally. In cold damp climates, clearance will prevent the crown from rotting away over winter, and you will have a much healthier plant the following spring.

Herbs that benefit from crown clearance
Scutellaria lateriflora (virginia skullcap); *Tanacetum balsamita* (alecost); *Teucrium scorodonia* (woodsage).

Cutting hard back

In early fall, if you cut back all the season's growth of herbs like oregano, you will see a compact rosette of new growth appearing, encouraged by the warmth remaining in the soil. This growth will provide light pickings of fresh leaves for cooking throughout the winter months. Cutting mint hard back as the leaves start to turn also prevents the spread of disease like rust, to which mints are prone. By cutting hyssop hard back, you will encourage new growth, and help maintain the shape of the plant. Vietnamese coriander is a tender herb and is such a prolific grower that it also benefits from cutting back to prevent it from running out of energy and the leaves from becoming too coarse.

Herbs that benefit from cutting hard back
Hyssopus officinalis (hyssop); *Melissa officinalis* (lemon balm); *Mentha* species (mints); *Nepeta cataria* (catnip); *Origanum vulgare* (oregano); *Origanum x onites* (French marjoram); *Persicaria odorata* (Vietnamese coriander); *Teucrium scorodonia* 'Crispum' (curly woodsage).

over the bare soil, and add some well-rotted manure. By spring the ground will be ready to plant a young herb in the same place, which will grow well in its first season. At this time of year, choose a few herbs to shelter from the cold weather so you can continue to have fresh herbs for cooking through the winter; thyme, sage, and rosemary are good candidates. Either cover the plants in the soil with a cloche or pot up some of the plants and bring them into the greenhouse, conservatory or kitchen.

Encouraging birds and wildlife

I have been extolling the virtues of keeping your herb garden neat and tidy in order to minimize disease and maintain productivity. But to maintain a balanced ecosystem, it is necessary to create space for a pile of logs or leave parts of the garden undisturbed, so that both pest and predator have somewhere to hibernate during the winter and do not move out of the garden, so maintaining the ecobalance. In winter, you can also look after the bird population by erecting bird boxes and feeding them with nuts and seeds when their food supply is low.

Bird boxes made with untreated wood should have small entry holes and be placed so cats and squirrels cannot reach in.

Stack of wood, or logs will provide shelter for hedgehogs and beetles.

Mulches A mound of mulch left undisturbed during the winter is ideal shelter for frogs, toads, shrews, and spiders.

Mulching the crown

After mature hardy herbaceous herbs like myrrh (shown here) have been cut back in the fall, they will benefit from having the area of soil around the crown mulched with compost, but avoid well-rotted manure because it is too rich in nutrients. This layer of mulch will encourage the mature plant to produce lush new growth the following spring and come back healthy and vigorous.

Herbs that benefit from mulching
Levisticum officinale (lovage); *Myrrhis odorata* (myrrh); *Phytolacca americana* (pokeroot); *Scutellaria lateriflora* (virginia skullcap).

Harvesting techniques

An abundant harvest is the reward for having spent time nurturing your herbs. To enjoy the best flavor and medicinal benefit the plants have to offer, it is important to pick the leaves, flowers, seeds or berries, and roots or bulbs carefully and in the best possible conditions. For annual herbs, harvesting times vary according to the plant part you wish to obtain. For biennial herbs, good leaf harvests are achieved in the first year, while roots should be left alone until the second year to mature. For evergreen herbs, the first season is spent patiently feeding and shaping the plant to make sure that it puts on healthy growth. Although evergreen leaf trimmings can prove adequate for adding flavor to cooking or making a tisane, larger harvests are only an option in the second and third year. But it is well worth the wait because the leaf flavor of evergreen herbs like bay then remains consistent over the year, so they can be harvested at any time.

Herbaceous herbs, like French tarragon, can only be picked fresh in their own specific growing season. If they are being harvested for culinary use, however, the harvesting period is actually even narrower because the best leaf texture and flavor is generated before flowering (during flowering, the energy of the plant is diverted into producing flowers and the leaves become tougher in texture and have less flavor). After flowering, though, you can produce a second flush of tender young leaves if you cut back perennial herbs and give them a good feed. If you are harvesting herbs for their medicinal properties, you will want the best quality herb oil the plant leaf or root has to offer – this is best from mature roots while succulent young roots are better for cooking. More detailed harvesting information is provided on the following pages and in my Top 100 (see pages 114–267).

Top left Collecting the tasty fennel seeds (*Foeniculum vulgare*) from the flower head for drying in late summer.

Top right Echinacea flower (*Echinacea purpurea*) is harvested when the plant has died back to the ground. In fall, the root from mature plants can also be dug up for medicinal use.

Bottom left Pokeroot (*Phytolacca americana*) berries turn deep purple and are soft when the seed inside is ripe and ready for harvest, from late summer until late fall. It is advisable to wear gloves because the berry is toxic and its juice bright magenta, which dyes the skin.

Bottom right Myrrh seeds (*Myrrhis odorata*) are brown and shiny when ripe and should be harvested in late summer.

Harvesting times

Leaf from herbaceous and annual herbs. Pick fresh as soon as the leaf is large enough and continue throughout the growing season. Harvest evergreen leaves all year round.

Flower from early summer and in some cases until the first frosts in the fall. The flower is best picked when the bud is just about to open out fully.

Seed in late summer after the plant has flowered.

Berry in early fall after flowering and the berry is ripe. Usually this is signaled by a change in berry color.

Root in the fall. For culinary use, harvest the root just before the plant's top growth dies back, but for medicinal use wait until the plant has died back, but before it has used up its root store to grow again.

Bulb in late summer. Wait until the plant top growth has died back in the fall so the bulb has a rich store of nutrients.

Harvesting leaves

Fresh herb leaves can be picked throughout the growing season for use in cooking. For the best leaf flavor, harvest all types of herb just before flowering – but for soft-leaved herbs like parsley, lovage, and chervil, harvest before flowering, but after the plants have been well fed – the leaves respond to feeding by becoming lusher and sweeter. Pick all herb leaves in dry weather, before the heat of the midday sun or the leaf oils that give flavor will evaporate. All herb leaves can be dried or frozen for later use, but drying is preferable since it intensifies the herb flavor while freezing diminishes it. Herb leaves can also be easily preserved in mild olive oil or light vinegar (see page 88).

(see page 88)

Gathering leaves

Pick in the morning after the dew has evaporated, but before the heat of the day.

Choose lush, healthy leaves, not ones with holes or pest damage.

Harvest fresh leaves in small quantities to avoid waste, and keep different herb flavors separate so as not to taint them.

Evergreen leaves can be harvested all year and are best used fresh – there is no need to preserve them.

Collecting

Drying

Storing

1 Harvesting For perennial herbs like thyme and oregano, the leaf flavor is strong, so you will only need a few leaves. Also it is best not to pick more than a third of the available leaves at any time because perennial herb leaves grow back quite slowly. When picking annual herbs, especially salad leaves, you can take more leaves because they are grown to be cropped regularly and the leaf flavor is milder. Pick them quickly since their soft leaves are more likely to wilt. For all herb leaves, choose the healthiest looking as they are the ones with the most beneficial properties. Try not to bruise them as you pick them, which will damage their structure and impair flavor.

2 Drying The object of successful drying is to eliminate the water content of the leaf and at the same time retain the leaf oil that imparts flavor. Dry herb leaves separately from each other because small leaves will dry faster than large, and strong-scented herbs may taint more subtle aromatic ones. Spread the leaves on cheesecloth stretched over and stapled to a simple wooden frame (this is easy to make yourself). Place the rack of leaves in a dark room that is warm, dry, and well ventilated. Turn the herb leaves over several times during the first week since they will be moist and need air to reach every surface in order to dry.

3 Storing When the leaves are dry and crisp enough to crumble, they are ready to be stored. Herb leaves will quickly lose their flavor and color if not stored properly. Ideally, put the leaves into a dark glass jar with a screw top. Label the pot with the herb name, date, and year. Check the container for the first few days, and if moisture forms on the lid, the herbs are not totally dry. Return them to the drying rack. The shelf life for dried herbs is approximately one year. They are usually three to four times more potent in flavor than fresh herbs, so smaller amounts are needed in recipes.

Harvesting flowers

Herb flowers usually have only one flowering season per year, so it is important to get the timing right and harvest them at their best. Whichever herb flowers you harvest, always pick the flowers in loose bud just as they break open to maintain the best color, fragrance, and taste. There are a number of ways of preserving herb flowers, but the best method for preserving flowers for use in winter is to dry them. There are many herb flowers that dry well, from lavender to bachelor's buttons, and flowers like chamomile are popular in tisanes (see page 106). Hops are good in herbal pillows (see page 111).

Gathering flowers

Pick in the morning as soon as the dew has dried.

Gently shake the flower heads to remove any insects.

Pick the flower either in bud or just when it is starting to open.

Pick in small bunches so air can circulate and to prevent the flower buds from rotting.

Once cut, keep out of direct sunlight, or the flowers may wilt and deteriorate.

Collecting

Drying

Storing

1 Harvesting Herb flowers are best harvested just after the flower buds appear but before they open fully. At this stage in their development, they offer their most intense oil concentration and flavor. It is also best to pick flowers that are not completely open because they continue to open during the drying process. Younger flowerheads are also more beneficial; once overblown, their qualities are reduced.

2 Drying Once cut, keep the flowers out of sunlight. This advice is important if you want to maintain good petal color, fragrance, and taste. You can either cut off individual flowers like chamomile (shown here) and dry them on a cheesecloth frame, or you can cut whole flowering stems and tie them in small bunches. Dry bunches with the flower heads hanging down in an area where warm dry air circulates. By hanging bunches upside-down the stems will remain straight. When fully dried, the flower should feel stiff and dry, not limp or damp in any way.

3 Storing Dried single flowers can be stored in dark airtight jars for use in tisanes. Herb flowers dried in hanging bunches should only be picked off their stems and stored in dark airtight jars if they are going to be used for medicinal or culinary uses. Once exposed to the air and light, their aromatic and medicinal properties slowly deteriorate. Alternatively, use dried herb bunches in the home to make dried flower arrangements, potpourri, or to fill herbal sachets or pillows (see pages 103 and 111).

Harvesting seeds

It is important to know when seeds are ripe for harvesting. For example, borage seeds turn black when ripe and fall to the ground. Fennel seeds turn light brown and should be harvested just as the seeds become loose and start breaking free of the seed head. The seeds of elecampane are ripe when the petals of the flower have died back. If you are unsure the seeds are ripe, gently tap the plant. If seed falls off, it is time. Always harvest dry seed on a still, sunny day, once any morning dew has dried. Take a paper bag or a seed tray lined with newspaper to the plant to avoid dropping and spreading seed in the garden in areas you do not want the plant to grow.

Gathering seeds

Collect seeds from a plant as they start to fall or float away from the seed head.

Always use paper, not plastic, bags to collect seeds to avoid a build up of condensation, which may rot the seed.

Use separate bags or trays to collect different seeds so as not to confuse them.

Take a plant label with you to place in the bag or tray to identify the seed.

Collecting	Drying	Storing

1 Harvesting seeds Angelica seed (shown here) is ripe for harvest when it falls into the hand with a gentle tap of the seed head. Use a paper bag to gather a small number of seeds, or line a cardboard box with newspaper, cut the head from the plant and put it into the box.

2 Drying seeds Clean the seed by removing it from the stems, stalks, or any other chaff. Small seeds, like those of incense plant, are hidden in the bract and require a lot of cleaning before the seed is revealed, while foxglove seeds are easy to extract from the dry seed pods simply by shaking them vigorously. Once extracted, spread the seed out thinly on a piece of gauze or paper towel. Place in a dry, airy room and leave the seed for a few days to dry out completely.

3 Storing Check the quality of seeds before storing, and discard any damaged or half-eaten ones. Store them in a dark glass jar, cardboard box, or paper envelope, clearly labeled. Write the month and year that the seeds were collected, so you can check that the seed is still viable when you come to sow it in following seasons. Once harvested and dried, seeds have different lifespans: nasturtium seed can last for up to 5 years; pot marigold seeds for longer, while angelica seed is only viable for 3 months – after that, it is hard to germinate.

Harvesting berries

When berries start to form on bushes in the garden and hedges, fall is well on the way. Seeds encased in berries like pokeroot are best collected fresh, when they are soft and ripe. Drier, pithier berries like myrtle or luma can be left on the bush to shrivel slightly, which makes it easier to extract the seed from the pulp. However, if you leave berries on the tree, they may be eaten by wildlife like mice. Another proven method is to place the fresh or dry berries in a bowl of water for several days. Then, use a pestle and mortar to mash them to a pulp and return to clean water. The pulp and dead seed rises to the surface, while viable, heavy seeds settle at the bottom.

Gathering berries

Pick fresh berries when ripe and soft to the touch.

Pick dry berries just as they start to shrivel.

Berry seeds from either fresh or dry berries are best sown as soon as they are extracted rather than dried and sown the following season.

Wear protective gloves when picking toxic berries like pokeroot.

Fresh berries

1 Separating seed from pulp There are several methods of removing the pulp from fresh berries. You can place the berries in a strainer under running water and rub off the pulp. Or, wrap the berries in a piece of cheesecloth, hold the cloth under running water and, squeeze the berries. Wring out the cloth, then open it out and the seeds will have separated from the pulp. For toxic berries like pokeroot (shown here) that have a dark juice, wear gloves when extracting the seed.

2 Extracting the seed Having exposed the seed, you will need to lift it away from the pulp and place it on a clean paper towel. For best results, sow the moist seed immediately in substrate, and winter in a cold frame. If you are not ready to sow the seed immediately, keep the seeds damp (but not wet) by storing them in a refrigerator, buried in a tray of vermiculite (see page 45) until the following spring.

Dry berries

Harvesting dry berries These myrtle berries were left on the bush over winter until spring before they were harvested. To extract the seed, open the berry with your fingertips rather than a knife so as not to damage it. Gently rub the open berry between your thumb and index finger and the seeds will fall out. For successful germination results, sow the seed immediately or you can keep the seed for one month if you store it damp in the refrigerator in a tray of vermiculite (see page 45).

Harvesting roots

When harvesting herb roots for either culinary or medicinal purposes, it is best to dig them out of the ground at the end of the growing season, when the plant's top growth is just starting to die back and the maximum amount of nutrition has been stored in the root system. At this time of year, the root will be at its most potent, since its energy will not be used up by plant growth. Also for commonsense reasons it is best not to wait for the top growth to die back completely, or you may not be able to identify or locate your plant in the garden. The key herbs in my Top 100 whose roots I use are echinacea and Joe Pye weed for medicinal purposes, and licorice and horseradish for cooking.

Gathering roots

Dig up roots in the fall before the plant's top growth has died back fully so you can identify it correctly.

Wash the roots in cold running water. Do not soak roots or the flavor will leach out. Also, roots soaked in water tend to absorb water and rot.

If harvesting several different herb roots at the same time, keep them separate so as not to impair their individual flavor. Label each root to avoid confusion.

Collecting	**Washing**	**Grating**

1 Harvesting The first light frost is the signal for plants to start building up their energy reserves in their root system to help them survive the long winter months. It is also the time to harvest roots. Dig early in the morning or last thing at night, because at these times the plant's energy remains in the root system; on warm days it rises up to the top growth. Take care not to bruise the roots when you are lifting them.

2 Washing Rinse the roots under cold running water to wash off soil and dirt before you preserve them. If necessary, use a soft vegetable brush to gently clean off stubborn dirt without damaging them. If roots are caked in mud, perform the first wash outdoors with the hose so you do not block the kitchen sink with soil.

3 Grating Horseradish is the best culinary root in my Top 100 herbs (see page 132). Once washed, peel off the tough outer layers and then grate the fibrous white root flesh. Be warned, fresh horseradish root is very strong and will make your eyes water. The gratings can be used fresh or preserved in light vinegar, or you can dry the root. To prepare the root for drying, peel the root and slice it into sections. Arrange the slices on a cheesecloth frame until dry (dried slices remain slightly spongy in texture). Store the dried root slices in a clearly labeled dark glass jar.

Harvesting bulbs

The only herb bulb that I make reference to in my Top 100 is garlic (see page 122). There is an old country saying that it should be sown on the shortest day of the year, and harvested on the longest day. A more reliable indicator for the harvest is when the first leaves start to yellow. Sometimes garlic puts out a false seed stalk topped by small bulbils. These bulbils are edible and taste just like miniature cloves of garlic, but they are ready for harvest earlier than the bulb. Some people suggest that true garlic bulbs will be larger if these seed stalks are removed. To remove them, wait until the seed heads form a coil, and then cut them off as close to the ground as possible.

Gathering bulbs

The garlic you buy in supermarkets is not a named species. However, when it is planted, it will produce a small crop.

For a more reliable crop, buy seed garlic bulbs from a reputable organic source that have been acclimatized to the growing conditions of your area.

Gathering **Drying** **Storing**

1 Harvesting The best time to harvest garlic bulbs is midsummer as the top growth starts to die back and the soil is dry so the bulbs come away clean. Lift the garlic bulbs carefully – damaged bulbs can only be stored for short periods of time before they become diseased. Do not delay the harvest, for the following reasons: it makes garlic bulbs harder to clean because the outer leaves start to decay in wet soil; the skins stain as the bulbs mature, and late-harvested garlic does not store as well and may rot.

2 Drying This stage in the process is critical. In warm, dry climates where there is no rain for a period of two weeks, garlic can be dried outside. In unreliable or damp climates, it is best to dry garlic bulbs under shelter. Make sure there is good air circulation and that the bulbs are out of direct sunlight. Depending on the conditions, drying will take between 14–25 days, after which roots can be trimmed back and the top growth cut off just above where the bulb forms. If you wish to plait the bulbs together, leave a few strands of dried leaves (shown here).

3 Storing A bulb is ready to store when the skin feels papery and rustles when handled. Either plait into ropes or hang individual bulbs in net sacks. Place in an area with good ventilation that has a temperature above freezing but no higher than 39°F (4°C); otherwise, the garlic cloves will sprout green shoots. If the air circulation is poor or the air humid, the bulbs may start to become moldy and rot.

The Kitchen

Why use herbs in cooking?

My enthusiasm for using herbs to flavor food follows a long family tradition: in the 1950s, my grandmother, Ruth Lowinsky, wrote several cook books. My mother not only inherited her mother's love of cooking, but was also an avid gardener, growing all her own vegetables and herbs, and I have followed suit by setting up my herb farm. In the beginning, I only grew a limited selection of culinary herbs because there was little public demand for anything other than parsley, sage, rosemary, thyme, chives, tarragon, and fennel.

Today, tastes have moved on, and I produce a far more exotic, strongly flavored selection of herbs that are becoming as common in the kitchen as the standard ones. I believe, the increase in the use of pungent herbs in modern cooking has a

lot to do with people's desire to counter the bland flavor of intensively farmed foods and mass-produced readymade meals. But, as the organic movement gathers momentum and locally grown and seasonal food becomes more popular, the future of good flavorsome food is looking much brighter. Herbs are part of this desire to use fresh and simple ingredients.

Historically, herbs were used both as flavoring and as preservatives. Before refrigerators were invented, large households had underground cellars and cold rooms where they stored meat, which was covered in salt and wrapped in fresh sage leaves to preserve it. After shooting, fresh game was also left to hang to tenderize the meat, with bunches of fresh thyme that added flavor and imparted antiseptic properties to the meat to help prevent stomach upsets when it was eventually eaten.

Cooking with fresh herbs

Herbs have always been served as a traditional accompaniment to meat dishes and used as a flavoring for sauces. When you cook with fresh herbs, they release a wonderful aroma, which not only smells fantastic but makes your mouth water, and this release of saliva actually helps prepare your stomach for food. Herbs like mint also aid digestion, particularly of fatty meats like lamb, which goes some way to explaining the tradition of preparing meat with herbs.

Using herbs in Hot and cold drinks

There are many different hot and cold drinks that can be made from herbs. Herb teas, known as tisanes, can be drunk instead of ordinary tea, and can provide a helpful supplement to the daily diet. One of my favorite teas is lemon verbena, which is refreshing served hot or cold either on a summer's day or at the end of the day for a good night's sleep. An herb drink is one of the best ways of extracting both the medicinal properties of the herb and its aroma and flavor. Tisanes usually have a very delicate flavor, and herbs dried in poor conditions may impair this. For the best taste, I recommend using fresh herbs. But remember, you need to use more fresh herbs than dried – fresh herbs are less concentrated since they still contain moisture in their plant parts. For advice on harvesting and drying herbs, see pages 70–77.

Tisanes

Lemon verbena

Method You need either 5 fresh leaves or a sprig, 2in (5cm) long, or 2 teaspoons of dried herb, or 1 teaspoon of seed per cup of boiled water. Place the herb on paper towel, lightly crush, and then add to the cup. Pour on the boiled water that has been cooled to just below boiling. Cover the infusion to prevent the herb leaf oils, which are medicinally beneficial, from evaporating in the steam. Leave to infuse for 5 minutes. Strain if necessary. Tisanes may be sweetened with honey to taste. The teapot (above) contains lemon verbena leaves – a late-night tisane that aids sleep – and the tea cup, a sprig of rosemary – a refreshing morning pick-me-up.

Herb alternatives

Chamomile flower *tisane is lovely last thing at night to aid sleep.*

Dill seed *tisane is useful for calming gas pains in the abdomen.*

Lemon balm leaf *tisane is a mild antidepressant and relieves headaches.*

Peppermint leaf *tisane drunk after a meal aids digestion.*

Hot mead punch

Serves 4
1 bottle mead
2 cups (500ml) dry cider
2 cups (500ml) apple juice
2 oranges
12 cloves
5in (12cm) cinnamon stick
4 myrtle berries
1/4 cup (60g) honey, or to taste

Myrtle berry

Method Put the mead, cider, and apple juice in a saucepan. Cut the orange in thick slices and stick cloves into each slice. Add the fresh orange, cinnamon stick, and myrtle berries to the saucepan. Stir in the honey. Heat the punch to just below simmering point and keep it at that temperature for 20 minutes. Strain. Serve hot in warmed mugs or thick glasses. Mead blends well with these sweet spices, making a medium-sweet, full-flavored drink.

Herb alternatives

The following herbs can be used as a substitute for myrtle berries and cinnamon sticks.

Angelica stem *adds a wonderful spicy flavor, which combines well with apple and honey. Use a couple of 2in (5cm) slices of second-year stems.*

Caraway seeds *add a warm anise flavor. Use 2 teaspoons.*

Juniper berries *are spicier than myrtle berries. Use 4 berries.*

Sage leaves *add a warm herb flavor. Use 4 leaves.*

Elderflower cordial

*Makes about
3 x 1 quart (1l) bottles*

1 quart (1l) water
4lb (1.8kg) unrefined cane sugar
6 lemons, juice and peeled rind
2tbs (30ml) of dry cider or
 white wine vinegar
20 heads of elderflowers

Herb alternatives

*Lovage seeds add a celery flavor. Once
the sugar has dissolved, add 2 tbs seeds.
Use cider, not white wine vinegar.*

*Queen-of-the-meadow leaves add a
warm herb flavor. Use 4 leaves.*

*Myrrh flowers have a light anise taste.
Use 16 flowerheads.*

Elderflower

Method Pour boiled water into a sterilized container. Add the sugar, stirring until dissolved. Cool. Add the lemon rind, lemon juice, white wine vinegar, and elderflowers. Cover with a cheesecloth and leave to infuse for 24 hours. Strain the cordial through cheesecloth and pour into glass bottles with metal-levered caps. Once made, leave the cordial for 2 weeks. Serve chilled, diluted with spring water to taste. Store in a cool, dark place. Use within 3 months.

Herb wine cup

Serves 4
6 sprigs sweet woodruff
1 bottle dry white wine
1 cup (250ml) freshly
 squeezed orange juice
4oz (120g) strawberries
1/3 cup (90ml) brandy
1 cup (200ml) ginger ale
 (chilled)
20 borage flowers

Herb alternatives

*Hyssop stems Add 6 sprigs of hyssop,
lightly crushed. Substitute the borage
flowers for hyssop flowers. Hyssop has a
warm herby taste that enhances the flavors
in the wine cup.*

Sweet woodruff

Method Cut fresh woodruff sprigs and leave for 1 hour to bring out their vanilla flavor. Put them in a bowl and pour in the wine and orange juice. Leave for 1 hour; then strain. Put the strawberries in a punch bowl. Pour in the infused liquid. Cover and chill for 30 minutes. Pour in the brandy and the chilled ginger ale last so as not to lose its sparkle. Serve in tall glasses. Decorate with borage flowers.

*Rose-scented geranium leaves. Use 12
leaves, lightly crushed, to add a hint of
rose flavor to the wine cup.*

*Spearmint sprigs Add 6 sprigs, lightly
crushed. Mint with ginger is refreshing.*

Borage ice cubes

10 fresh borage flowers

Borage

Method Pick the fresh flowers when they are fully open. To keep the ice cube clear, use boiled water that has been left to cool. Fill the ice tray with the water, then add a single flower to each section. If you find the flowers difficult to handle, use a pair of tweezers to place the flowers in the ice-cube tray. Leave to set in the freezer. These flower cubes look pretty in drinks and added to fruit salads, or simply as decoration in an ice bucket.

Herb alternatives

Chicory flowers, a lovely blue flower. Pick when fully open.

*Heart's ease flowers look lovely in
fruit salads.*

*Pineapple sage flowers, a stunning red
flower that looks magnificent in cocktails.*

*Primrose flowers, a
charming yellow flower.*

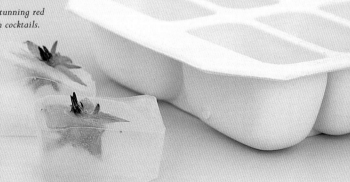

Using herbs in Salads

Fresh herbs can be added to all types of mixed leaf salads and offer perhaps the best way to experience the unique flavor and fragrance of the herb along with the benefits of its medicinal properties. Chive, caraway, and basil leaves, for example, aid digestion, while chervil is high in vitamin C, and parsley is rich in iron. To obtain the most intense flavor from fresh herbs in salad and their optimum medicinal qualities, it is best to use organically grown herbs. In growing herbs organically, the sun, rain, and soil have all worked to boost their natural oil content. Personally, I find that pot-grown supermarket herbs, grown on artificial nutrients under glass to encourage fast growth, can lack taste and fragrance. In salads, limit yourself to no more than five herb leaves, or the flavors may become confused.

Herb leaf salad

Use a generous handful of:
French sorrel
Chervil
Purslane
Salad burnet
Wild rocket

Salad burnet

Method This herb leaf salad presents a lovely mix of flavors. The French sorrel has a sharp, clean taste; salad burnet offers a hint of cucumber; chervil tastes of mild anise; wild rocket has a peppery edge, and purslane contributes a fresh pealike flavor. This selection of herbs works well served with fish, or as a starter to cleanse the palate. A wide range of leafy herbs can be used in a mixed salad and some other good alternatives are featured (right). Wash and dry the leaves before use if you do not know their place of origin. If home-grown, simply place the leaves in a salad bowl, since it is thought that water impairs their flavor.

Herb alternatives

Chive leaves and flowers have an onion flavor that combines beautifully with salad burnet, purslane, and chervil.

French parsley leaves have a strong parsley, works well mixed with salad arugula, sorrel, and purslane.

Summer savory leaves have a peppery flavor that mixes well with salad burnet, chervil, and purslane.

Mint french dressing

3 tbs (45ml) mild olive oil
1 tbs (15ml) white wine or balsamic vinegar
Pinch of sea salt, to taste
Freshly ground black pepper, to taste
1 tsp (5ml) wholegrain mustard
1 tsp (5ml) honey or soft brown sugar
Handful spearmint leaves, chopped

Spearmint

Method Place the oil and vinegar in a bowl and whisk together. Add all the remaining ingredients and blend. Taste to check the seasoning, then pour on the salad. Toss the leaves and serve. This simple mint dressing is suitable for green leaf and apple salads.

Herb alternatives

Chive and mint leaf *dressing for potato salad.*

Dill leaf *dressing for zucchini.*

Garlic and sweet marjoram leaf *dressing for tomato salad.*

Tarragon and sweet basil leaf *dressing for cold fish.*

Herb flower salad

Heart's ease flowers, green parts removed
Fennel flowers
Painted sage flowers and bracts
Wild rocket flowers

Wild rocket

Method Make the herb leaf salad (opposite) and decorate with edible herb flowers. Before adding the flowers to the leaf salad, remove all the flower parts from their stems. Add the flowers to the salad; toss and serve. You can use a very light mild dressing made from olive oil and white wine vinegar, but do not add more herbs to the dressing or it will overpower the flower flavors.

Herb alternatives

Chive flowers *add an onion flavor to salads.*

Nasturtium flowers *have a peppery taste.*

Pot marigold flowers *offer a mild, warm flavor.*

Wild bergamot flowers *add a strong herb flavor to salads.*

Herb ice bowl

Painted sage

Method Take two clear mixing bowls that fit inside one another. Half-fill the larger bowl with cool boiled water and float the smaller bowl inside about 1in (2cm) above the base of the larger bowl. Hold it in position by weighing it down with gravel and then tape it in place. Arrange the flowers or leaves by tucking them into the water between the two bowls. When you are happy with their position, top up the bowl with more water. Place the bowls in the freezer for 24 hours. Then, remove the tape and gravel, and leave the ice bowl to melt slightly to make it easier to slip it out of the glass bowls.

Herb alternatives

Borage flowers *have pretty blue or purple star-shaped flowers.*

English mace sprigs *have clusters of cream flowers and attractive stems.*

Painted sage stems *offer decorative pink and purple flowers and colorful bracts.*

Primrose flowers *add a soft pale yellow color, and their simple shapes look good in ice (see page 83).*

Nasturtium flowers *have vivid red flowers with a peppery flavor that are in bloom throughout the summer.*

Using herbs in Mayonnaise

When making a classic mayonnaise, there is something quite magical about watching the ingredients combine into a wonderful, shiny, glutinous substance. In my opinion, there is nothing to beat the flavor of homemade mayonnaise that has been blended with freshly harvested herbs or a single herb flavor to make a traditional green mayonnaise. When combining herb flavors in green mayonnaise, use herb mixes that complement one another and the food for which the mayonnaise is intended – parsley and garlic, fennel, and salad burnet, for example, make a delicious mayonnaise for fish. For a simpler herb mayonnaise, choose one herb that goes well with the meat, fish, or vegetable dish, such as French tarragon, which makes a wonderful herb mayonnaise to accompany cold chicken.

Herb mayonnaise

2 large egg yolks (at room temperature)
1 tsp (5ml) English mustard powder
Sea salt and freshly ground black pepper, to taste
1¼ cups (275ml) light olive oil or sunflower oil
1–2 tsp (5–10ml) white wine vinegar, to taste
½ tsp (2.5ml) lemon juice
1 bunch parsley, finely chopped
2 sprigs fresh basil, finely chopped

Parsley

Method Place the egg yolks, mustard, and salt in a bowl, and mix together. Add the oil, very slowly, one drop at a time, whisking until it starts to thicken. When half the oil has been added, add one teaspoon of white wine vinegar to thin the mixture. Now add the oil in a thin stream, whisking continuously. If the mixture is too thin, add a little more oil. When you are happy with the consistency, add the lemon juice, chopped herbs, salt and pepper to taste, and a little more white wine vinegar, if needed. Leave the mixture to infuse for an hour to bring out the herb flavors. Then use immediately – chopped basil leaves combined with vinegar may turn black on exposure to air.

Herb alternatives

Chervil leaves *create a delicate-flavored mayonnaise that is good with rice dishes.*

Garlic *mayonnaise is wonderful with fish, and great with French fries.*

French tarragon *mayonnaise is good with fish, chicken, and rice.*

Sorrel leaves *make another classic green mayonnaise that goes well with fish and cold chicken.*

Wild rocket leaves *add a peppery, beefy flavor, which combines well with new potatoes or egg dishes.*

Using herbs in Mustard

Mustards are increasingly popular and very easy to make. They are a condiment made from the whole or ground seed of three *Brassicaceae* family plants. Each plant produces a colored seed – white/yellow, brown, or black. The three seeds are substantially different in character and produce a huge number of differently-textured mustards, depending on the seed mix. These are then blended with ingredients like wine, vinegar, and herbs to create different flavors. Mustard is very versatile and works well with cheese, vegetables, poultry, red meat, and fish dishes. You can also add mustard to salad dressing (see page 85), or sauces. When adding mustard to food, remember that its flavor and character are destroyed by heat, so it should always be added at the last minute to hot dishes. Herb mustards are particularly good when combined with soured cream or cream cheese, as dips for vegetables or crisps. Dill mustard (described below) is a delicious accompaniment to smoked salmon.

Herb mustard

⅓ cup (80g) black mustard seed
⅛ cup (30g) white mustard seed
2 cups (500ml) water
½ cup (115g) English mustard powder
¾ cup (200ml) cider vinegar
1 tsp (5ml) salt
1 tsp (5ml) turmeric
¼ cup (50g) chopped dill

Dill

Method Place the mustard seed in a china or glass bowl, add the water, and soak for 24 hours. Then add the mustard powder, cider vinegar, salt, and turmeric. When thoroughly mixed, place the bowl over a saucepan of water, but do not allow the bottom of the bowl to touch the water. Using a low heat, gently cook the mustard seed for 4 hours, stirring occasionally. Check that the water in the saucepan does not evaporate, and do not let the mixture boil or the mustard will loose its flavor and become bitter. Once cooked, let it cool and add the chopped dill. Cover and keep in the refrigerator. Alternatively, you can cheat and simply mix together ¼ cup (50g) of good-quality coarse-grain mustard and ¼ cup (50g) of smooth Dijon mustard with ¼ cup (50g) chopped dill. If the mustard is too thick, add a small amount of white wine vinegar to thin it.

Herb alternatives

Horseradish root *is wonderful with red meat. Add 2 tablespoons of grated root to ¼ cup (50g) of coarse-grain and ¼ cup (50g) smooth mustard.*

Oregano leaves *taste good with goat's cheese and tomatoes. Add ⅛ cup (25g) of chopped leaves to the mustard mix given above.*

Rosemary sprigs *combine well with cold lamb. Add ⅛ cup (25g) of chopped leaves to the mustard mix given above.*

French tarragon leaf *mustard goes very well with fish and cold chicken, and is great for adding to sauces. Add ⅛ cup (25g) chopped leaves to to the mustard mix given above.*

Thyme sprig *mustard is good with cheese, meat, and fish. Add ⅛ cup (25g) of chopped leaves to the mustard mix given above.*

Winter savory leaves *are lovely used in a mustard dressing for a bean salad. Add ⅛ cup (25g) chopped leaves to the mustard mix given above.*

Using herbs in Oils and vinegars

Having grown up in a household where both my mother and my grandmother made their own herb oils and vinegars, it was only natural that I carried on the family tradition. Sweet basil leaf oil is perhaps one of the most popular herb oils I make each year. As soon as you uncork the bottle, the aroma brings the scent of summer into the kitchen, and dishes drizzled in basil oil seem to taste of sunshine. Herb oils are ideal for making classic mayonnaise (see page 86) and salad dressings (see page 85), or you can use them for marinades, sautés, and stir-frys. Vinegars infused with herbs are the cook's standby. Use them with herb oil for salad dressings, or add herb vinegars to sauces, or for making mustards (see page 87). A dash of tarragon vinegar added to light broth when poaching fish brings out the flavor.

Herb oil

2 cups (500ml) mild olive oil
2 good handsful of fresh basil leaves

Sweet basil

Method Tear up the basil leaves and place in a bowl. Pour over the olive oil, making sure that every leaf is submerged. Pour into an airtight container with a sealed lid and leave the oil in a warm place to infuse with the basil flavor. Stir once a week, and make sure the leaves stay below the surface of the oil or they will become moldy. After a month, strain the oil through unbleached coffee filter papers and discard the basil leaves. Place a few fresh leaves for both identification and decoration in a sterile glass container. Pour in the filtered basil oil, seal, and store in a cupboard out of sunlight. This method can be used with a range of herbs, except garlic, which does not preserve well in olive oil.

Herb alternatives

Fennel leaf oil has an aniseed flavor and goes well with broiled mackerel or barbecued pork.

Lemon balm leaf oil has a light lemon flavor. It is a good dressing oil for drizzling onto chargrilled eggplant slices.

Orange-scented thyme and French marjoram leaf oil has a mixture of herb and spice flavors. It is lovely poured over fish before broiling or barbecuing.

Parsley and sage leaves make a classic oil that combines well with salads, poultry, and fish.

Spearmint and rosemary leaf oil has a lovely fresh flavor, which is good with meat, barbecued lamb, and drizzled over tomatoes.

Sweet marjoram leaf oil is warm and aromatic. It is good for salad dressings or poured on sliced fresh tomatoes.

Herb vinegar

2 cups (500ml) white wine vinegar
2 handsful of fresh tarragon leaves

Method Fill a clean glass bottle full of fresh tarragon leaves. Make sure they are packed in tight against the container. Top up the bottle with white wine vinegar and seal. Do not use a metal top because vinegar is corrosive. Leave on a sunny windowsill for a month, shaking from time to time, so the tarragon leaves can infuse the vinegar with their flavor. Strain the liquid through unbleached coffee filter paper. Put a sprig of tarragon in the bottle for identification purposes.

French tarragon

For those who do not want to wait, here is a quicker method. Put the herbs and vinegar in a covered ceramic bowl over a pan of cold water. Bring the water to a boil to heat up the vinegar and infuse it with the tarragon leaf flavor. Then, remove the bowl from the pan. Leave it to cool for about 2 hours before using. You can infuse almost any herb with vinegar using either one of these simple methods. Tarragon vinegar is good for making salad dressing and sauces for white meat such as fish or chicken.

Herb alternatives

Dill leaves and seeds *make a vinegar that is wonderful for homemade gravalax. Use at least 1 teaspoon of crushed dill seeds.*

Hyssop and spearmint leaves *are good in sauces with vegetables or for making flavored mustard.*

Purple shiso leaves and caraway seeds *are lovely in dressings for rice or pasta salads. The purple shiso turns the vinegar a wonderful purple color, and the caraway seed adds a slight aniseed taste. Use 4 teaspoons of seed and 2 handfuls of leaves.*

Summer savory leaves *have a peppery flavor that permeates the vinegar, making it very useful in dressings and mayonnaise.*

Thyme and sage leaves *make strong-flavored vinegar, which is good for dressings.*

Wild bergamot leaves *are very pungent. Use this vinegar for making pickles, sauces, and mustards.*

Using herbs in Marinades

A marinade is a seasoned liquid in which meat, fish, and vegetables are soaked to absorb flavor and tenderize the food before cooking or serving chilled. The longer you marinate the food, the stronger the herb flavor and the more tender it will become. I recommend a minimum of four hours. This marinading time will also endow the food with the herbs' beneficial properties: oregano, sage, and thyme will inhibit the growth of bacteria and work as an antiseptic, while tarragon and crushed fennel seeds added to the marinades will aid digestion. Most marinades also contain an acid ingredient like lemon juice, vinegar, or wine, which acts as the tenderizer. Always marinate foods in the refrigerator, never at room temperature, in a covered glass or ceramic dish rather than metal, which may corrode in the acid liquid.

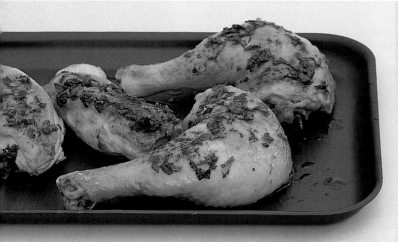

Herb fish marinade

1lb (500g) cod filet or other meaty white fish
For the marinade
1 cup (200ml) white wine vinegar
Juice of 1 lemon and juice of 1 lime
1 tbs sea salt
2 garlic cloves, sliced
2 handsful of finely chopped parsley, dill, lemon thyme, mint, and basil

Upright thyme

Method Mix all the marinade ingredients together. Slice the fish into ½in (2.5cm) pieces and place in a shallow glass dish. Pour in the marinade, cover the dish with a lid, and refrigerate for 4 hours, turning the fish every half an hour so it is completely saturated in marinade liquid. Drain the fish and pour on an herb dressing (see page 85). Toss the fish with the herbs of your choice, return covered to the refrigerator, and leave for one hour. Serve chilled with salad and crusty bread.

Herb alternatives

Chives, chervil, salad burnet, and fennel leaves *can be finely chopped and added to this marinade in any combination.*

Herb meat marinade

4 pieces of chicken, drumsticks and thighs
For the marinade
1 garlic clove, finely chopped
6 large leaves or 12 small leaves of sage, finely chopped
1 tbs (15ml) of lemon juice
½ cup (100ml) olive oil
1 tbs (15ml) soft brown sugar

Garlic

Method Using a sharp knife, cut slashes into the chicken pieces so the liquid marinade will seep into the meat. Place the chicken pieces in an glass or ceramic dish. Mix together the garlic, sage, lemon juice, and olive oil, and pour onto the chicken pieces. Cover the marinating chicken and place in the refrigerator for a minimum of 4 hours. Heat the oven to 350°F (180°C). Remove the dish from the refrigerator and drain off the liquid. Sprinkle the chicken pieces with brown sugar, and cook for 40 minutes, basting occasionally. Serve with crusty bread and a wild arugula and crisp lettuce salad.

Herb alternatives

Myrtle leaves *add a warm spicy flavor to meat marinades. Use 6 leaves.*

Juniper berries *are very good for strong meat marinades, adding a warm, rich, spicy flavor. Use 4 crushed berries.*

Using herbs in Butters

One of my first cooking memories is of helping my mother chop up herbs to make an herb butter to accompany broiled lamb cutlets. The old kitchen table was large and the chopping block thick, and their combined height meant that I had to stand on a kitchen stool to reach the tabletop and perform my task. The chopping of the herbs was fun, but I enjoyed mixing the herbs with the soft butter even more. Herb butters are incredibly useful. Not only can they be used in cooking for making sauces or broiling meat and fish, but they can also be used with sweet dishes. I use peppermint butter to make pancakes served with hot chocolate sauce, and I blend butter with marigold petals to give scones a distinctive flavor and a rich golden yellow color. I also use herb butter made with fresh elderflowers for baking cakes. Herb butters are simple and great fun to experiment with, and they offer an easy way to introduce a delicious herby flavor to all kinds of food.

Herb butter

2 tbs (30ml) thyme leaves, chopped
½ cup (125g) sweet butter

Mounding thyme

Method Remove the leaves of the thyme by rubbing your fingers up and down the stems. Once removed, chop up to release the leaf oils, then mix with the soft unsalted butter. It is important to use sweet butter so the herb flavor will come through. Use a fork to blend the herbs and butter. When thoroughly mixed, pack the butter in a roll of waxed paper and place in the refrigerator for up to 24 hours to set. The longer you leave it, the better the flavor.

Herb alternatives

Coriander leaf and garlic butter can be rubbed on trout before broiling. Use 1 tbs chopped coriander leaf and 2 cloves of garlic.

Dill leaf butter is ideal for salmon. Use one handful of dill leaf, chopped.

Parsley and lemon thyme leaf butter can be pushed under the skin of a chicken before roasting. Use 2 tbs of chopped herb leaves.

Rose-scented geranium leaf butter is excellent for making cakes. Use 3 leaves, chopped.

Sage leaf butter is great for using on broiled pork chops. Use 3 leaves, chopped.

Spearmint leaf and elderflower butter is very good for making a sweet sauce for ice-cream. Use 1 tbs of chopped spearmint leaf and 2 heads of elderflower.

Using herbs in Sweet sauces

It is generally presumed that herbs are used to flavor main dishes, but they taste equally good with cakes and desserts. Queen Elizabeth I loved lavender in sweet dishes and also drank lavender tea. In Europe, myrrh, or sweet cicely, was considered a natural sugar and was used as a sweetener for custards and puddings and to counteract sharp fruit flavors, such as gooseberry, rhubarb, and strawberry. In India, cardamom powder is still used to flavor rice pudding, and cardamom is combined with fennel seeds to make a sweet pancake syrup. It is not only the leaf, seed, or berry of herbs that is used in sweet sauces: licorice root, for example, is used to flavor milk for use in puddings. One of my favorite sweet herb sauces is spearmint syrup served with strawberries – the combination of flavors is sublime.

Herb custard

2½ cups (560ml) milk
5 bay leaves
6 egg yolks
⅓ cup (85g) white sugar

Herb alternatives

Cardamom seed custard is delicious served with hot dried fruit compote. Use 2 tsp of ground cardamom seeds.

Scented-pelargonium leaf custard is lemon flavored. Serve with fresh apricots. Use 4 pelargonium leaves, chopped.

Bay

Method Place the bay leaves and milk in a pan and bring to a boil to infuse the milk with the herb flavor. Whisk the egg yolk and sugar together until they change color from a deep gold to pale yellow. Pour in the hot milk and bay leaves. Stir over the heat in a double boiler for 10 minutes until it thickens. Take the pan off the heat, remove the leaves, and pour it into a cold pitcher. Serve with berries.

Herb fruit soup

1 quart (1l) water
½ cup (150g) white sugar
1 vanilla pod
½in (1cm) gingerroot, sliced
2 bay leaves
1 tsp (5ml) fennel seed
1 tsp (5ml) coriander seed
1 lime, juice and grated rind
Fresh fruit, sliced
2 sprigs fresh mint

Herb alternatives

Angelica stem syrup served with rhubarb. Use a 9in (25cm) piece of stem, instead of the ginger, bay, fennel, and coriander.

Elderberry syrup. Use 6 flowers with their stems removed.

Coriander seeds

Method Place the water and white sugar in a saucepan. Add the vanilla pod, ginger, bay leaves, fennel, and coriander seeds, and juice and grated rind of the lime. Bring to a boil and set aside to cool for about 2 hours. If you like a strong ginger flavor, leave it longer, but it should not overpower the fruit. Slice summer fruits into shallow bowls. Pour in the syrup and add sprigs of fresh mint leaves to garnish. Serve at room temperature rather than chilled. This dessert is perfect after a main course of fish as it cleans the palate and is very refreshing.

Using herbs in Non-sweet sauces

Fresh herbs are ideal in sauces, giving color, texture, and flavor. Simply by warming the sauce, the natural oils contained in the leaves of the herbs are released and infuse the sauce with their flavors. A good sauce can transform a simple pasta or rice dish, and liven up broiled fish or meat. To make a successful herb sauce, keep it simple, because if you use too many herbs, you will confuse the flavors. I recommend using herbs singularly or in pairs, for example, garlic and mint, or parsley and thyme.

Choose herbs that complement each other as well as the dish they are going to accompany. Two of my favorite sauces are based on hollandaise sauce. One is ideal for serving with fresh asparagus or fish, and requires a handful of freshly chopped French tarragon. Add this to the hollandaise sauce when it starts to thicken up. The second sauce is made with summer savory leaves. Add one tablespoon of chopped fresh leaves to the hollandaise sauce and serve it over fresh beans.

Chilled herb sauce

1 bunch fresh sorrel leaves
1¼ cups (250ml) soured cream
salt and freshly ground pepper

Herb alternatives

Anise hyssop sprigs make a good sauce for cold bean dishes or cold pasta. Use one small bunch of the herb.

English mace sprigs make a warm and mildly spicy sauce, excellent with cold chicken. Use one small bunch of the herb.

French parsley leaves are lovely with fish and chicken, or stirred into a cold pasta salad. Use one small bunch of the herb.

French sorrel

Method Remove the sorrel leaves from their stems. Tear the leaves into a bowl and stir in the soured cream. Place the bowl over a pan containing water and stir well over a very low heat for 2 minutes or until warmed through. Do not overheat the sauce, or the sorrel may become bitter. Season to taste with salt and pepper and serve. This sauce tastes good served with fresh salmon or chicken, or poured over potatoes.

Hot herb sauce

1lb (500g) English peas in pods
2 large sprigs mint
1 clove garlic, sliced
2 scallions, split lengthwise
1 tsp (5ml) sea salt
1 tsp (5ml) white sugar

Herb alternatives

Meum leaves Use one large handful of leaves instead of the mint. It combines well with the peas to make a sauce that is good with most vegetables, especially beets.

Summer savory leaves make a good substitute for mint. Use one large handful of leaves to make a sauce for white fish or chicken.

Spearmint

Method Place all ingredients in a saucepan and cover with boiling water. Boil for 2 minutes to soften the peas in their pods, but no longer or you will lose their fresh green color. Place all the ingredients in a liquidizer or a centrifugal juicer and whiz until liquid. Strain through cheesecloth. Wear rubber gloves so you can squeeze the cloth with your hands to extract the full flavor. Serve warm with white fish, such as flounder or sole. It is also very good as a hot herb sauce poured over salmon filets.

Using herbs in Cooked dishes

There is nothing more comforting than to enter a house and be greeted by the aroma of a casserole being cooked with fresh herbs, or vegetables being roasted with herbs and olive oil. This is how food should be cooked and enjoyed, for the pleasure of family and friends. Herbs are well-suited to this slow style of cooking since it allows time for the herbs to flavor the dish. Fennel and tarragon impart a delicious aniseed taste, and also work medicinally to help break down cholesterol in the bloodstream. Chives thin the blood and help improve metabolism. The addition of herbs to recipes like the herb and gruyere flan recipe outlined below, will also aid the digestion of cheese and eggs, which some people find difficult. By using herbs in cooking, you not only create a wonderful meal, but a healthy one as well.

Bouquet garni

1 bunch of parsley
3 sprigs of thyme
1 clove of garlic, peeled
2–3 bay leaves

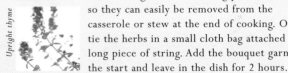

Upright thyme

Method Tie the herbs together with a long piece of string, so they can easily be removed from the casserole or stew at the end of cooking. Or tie the herbs in a small cloth bag attached to a long piece of string. Add the bouquet garni at the start and leave in the dish for 2 hours.

Herb alternatives

For fish *Fennel, lemon balm, French parsley, and sweet marjoram.*

For meat *Oregano, thyme, bay, and lovage; rosemary, sage, thyme, and parsley; thyme, sage, parsley, and bay.*

For poultry *Parsley, tarragon, chervil, and myrtle; bay, lemon thyme, lemon balm, and lemon grass (the grass tips); rosemary, summer savory, hyssop, and bay.*

For wild game *Myrtle, bay, orange-scented thyme, and parsley; luma, juniper berries, garlic, and parsley; winter savory, thyme, sage, and oregano.*

Roasted vegetables with herbs

Serves 4

2½lb (1.25kg) mixed root vegetables
2–8 garlic cloves
4 sprigs rosemary
4 sprigs classic thyme
salt and freshly ground pepper, to taste
3 tbs (15ml) olive oil

Rosemary

Method Use the tough leaves from evergreen herbs like rosemary because soft green leaves will disintegrate at high roasting temperatures. Chop up your chosen vegetables, such as onions, potatoes, carrots, and parsnips. Place them on a baking sheet and scatter the herbs over them. Sprinkle with salt and pepper to taste, and drizzle with olive oil. Roast the vegetables in a preheated oven at 350°F (180°C) for 30–40 minutes. Turn the vegetables every 15 minutes.

Herb alternatives

Bay leaves *add a warm flavor. Use 3–4 leaves.*

Luma sprigs *add a rich spicy flavor. Use 2 sprigs.*

Myrtle sprigs *add a warm spicy flavor. Use 4 sprigs.*

Winter savory leaves *add a spicy peppery flavor. Use 8 sprigs.*

Herb flan

12oz (350g) pastry, readymade or your own recipe
4lb (360g) Gruyère cheese
2 cups (500ml) soured cream
3 large eggs
salt and pepper, to taste
1 tsp (5ml) brown sugar
1 clove garlic, crushed
2 handful each of finely chopped tarragon, parsley, and fennel

Fennel

Method Heat the oven to 400°F (200°C). Finely grate half of Gruyere cheese and finely dice the other half. Roll out the pastry and line a metal loose-bottom pan 11in (28cm) in diameter. Leave in the refrigerator for 1 hour so the pastry does not shrink during cooking. Place the diced Gruyere on the pastry shell. To make the filling, beat all the other ingredients together in a bowl. Pour into the pastry shell. Cook in the oven for 40 minutes, occasionally checking and turning the pan so the top of the flan does not burn. Serve immediately or at room temperature with a sharp salad to counteract the rich taste. Use sorrel, wild rocket, and salad burnet with an herb dressing (see page 85).

Herb alternatives

Any of the following combinations can be substituted for the three herbs in the main recipe.

French parsley, chives, and sweet marjoram *use 2 handful of each herb.*

Mint, rosemary, and French parsley *use 2 handful of each herb.*

Summer savory, hyssop, and dill *use 2 handful of hyssop and dill, but less summer savory, which has a strong flavor.*

The Home

Why use herbs in the home?

Today, in our industrially developed world, using herbs in the home as natural alternatives to chemical cleaning products, for first aid, or simply to pamper yourself is beneficial for the family and the environment. If you grow herbs in the garden, herbal products are not only healthy, but inexpensive and fun to make.

Herbal uses

Historically herbs were central to the household, where they were used not only to flavor and preserve food, but to to sweeten and purify the air. Herbs were woven into roof thatch, scattered over floors, used to clean and polish furniture and ornaments, and to disinfect kitchen utensils and work surfaces. Although in the developed world the use and knowledge of herbs has decreased, in the third world, from the Amazon rain forest to the remote mountains of north Thailand, herbs are an important part of daily life.

Herbs as medicine

Traditionally, herbs have long been used as medicine for people and livestock. An herbal first aid kit is useful to have in the home for treating minor ailments, while herbs like aloe can be rubbed onto minor burns to relieve the pain, and a cup of herbal tea at the end of the day aids relaxation. Using herbs medicinally for more serious complaints is a complex issue, and self-treatment is not recommended. When I am ill, I consult a fully trained herbalist or a general practitioner. When taking herbs internally, it is important to remember that they contain potent medicinal properties and should be treated with the greatest respect. My animals also benefit from being treated for minor ailments with herbs, which make their coats glossy and their temperaments relaxed.

Herbs for relaxation

One of my favorite uses for herbs in the home is in the bath. Not only do herbs smell wonderful when they are infused in warm bath water, but they also help to relieve the aches and pains that accumulate after a day of physical work on the farm. I am also a great believer in herbal footbaths to soothe tired feet, and herbal pillows filled with hops or lavender to aid sleep.

Top row left

Water infused with fresh or dried lavender (*Lavandula angustifolia*) makes a fragrant, natural room spray for the home.

Top row center

Fresh tansy leaves (*Tanacetum vulgare*) rubbed into a dog's coat will deter fleas.

Top row right

Pot marigold cream (*Calendula officinalis*) is easy to make, and good for treating inflamed or minor wounds, skin rashes, and sunburn.

Middle row left

Sprigs of wormwood (*Artemisia absinthium*) tied in bunches and hung in a chicken coop prevent lice.

Middle row center

Aloe gel (*Aloe vera*) is a good natural remedy for soothing sunburn, minor burns, and insect bites.

Middle row right

A mixture of lemon verbena leaves (*Aloysia triphylla*), vinegar, water, and liquid soap make an effective natural window cleaner.

Bottom row left

Dried sprigs of southernwood (*Artemisia abrotanum*) are a good moth repellent. Place them between bedlinen and clothes that are kept in closets.

Bottom row center

Valerian leaves (*Valeriana officinalis*) made into a medicinal tisane will calm an anxious cat.

Bottom row right

Lemon balm leaves (*Melissa officinalis*) and beeswax make a wonderful natural furniture polish with a fresh lemon scent.

Using herbs for Furniture and fabric

There is nothing better for cleaning and restoring classic wooden furniture than good old-fashioned beeswax polish. Equally, soapwort shampoo is wonderful for cleaning curtains or delicate upholstery fabrics. The gentle cleansing power of the plant's saponins (see page 239) makes this natural shampoo ideal, and because of its cleansing properties, soapwort is still used as the main ingredient in manufactured cleaning products. Beeswax polish and soapwort shampoo are easy to make at home and offer a "green" alternative to commercial cleaning products, which contain a mixture of synthetics and chemicals. They are not only better for the furniture but also for your health, your hands, and the air quality in the home. In the following recipes, all the herbs smell wonderful and also work as a mild antiseptic.

Upholstery shampoo

1 tbs (15g) dried or fresh root of soapwort or 2 handsful of fresh stems
1 quart (750ml) water

If you wish to perfume the shampoo, add 6 drops of essential oil to the strained liquid. Lavender, thyme, rosemary, or rose-scented geranium oil are all suitable.

Soapwort

Method Wash the fresh soapwort root thoroughly in water. There is no need to peel it. If you are using dried soapwort root, prepare it by soaking it in water overnight. Put the soapwort in a saucepan with the water. Bring to a boil, cover, and simmer for 20 minutes. Let it stand until cool. Strain the liquid into a bottle and store in the refrigerator. To use, dampen a sponge with the solution and rub the fabric lightly. Let it dry before applying again, if necessary.

Natural furniture polish

1¼ cups (275ml) water
1 large handful of fresh lemon balm
1¼ cups (275ml) pure turpentine
2oz (60g) beeswax
½ cup (60g) soapflakes
2 x 1lb (500g) screw-top tins

Herb alternatives

Lavender stems *Use either a large handful of the dried herb or 6 drops of lavender essential oil.*

Sweet marjoram leaves *Use either a large handful of the dried herb or 6 drops of the essential oil.*

Lemon balm

Method Make an herb infusion by placing the lemon balm leaves and stalks into a bowl. Boil the water and pour over the leaves. Cover and let it stand for 15 minutes. Melt the beeswax and turpentine in a mixing bowl over a saucepan of simmering water. Take care when heating beeswax and turpentine since it has a low flash (ignition) point. Place the strained infusion and soapflakes in another saucepan and heat gently. Cool both mixtures a little and then stir the two together to make a thick cream. Pour into two tins and seal. Use a soft cloth to apply the polish to wood, metal, or painted surfaces. Buff to a shine with a clean soft cloth.

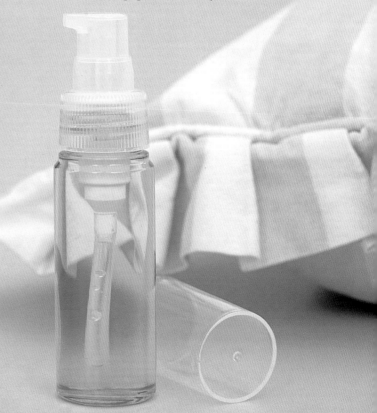

Using herbs for Surface cleaners

Using products made with herbs to clean surfaces will leave your home smelling delightfully fresh and fragrant, and they are just as effective as commercial cleaners. You can easily make these natural surface cleaners with just a few basic pantry ingredients, including fresh lemon, vinegar, baking soda, liquid soap, table salt, and fresh herbs. And there are several advantages: the ingredients are easy to obtain, they are inexpensive and have no damaging effects on the environment; they contain no additives, so are unlikely to cause allergic reactions; and they are not tested on animals. There is no need to rely on chemical sprays to keep surfaces and windows clean. Instead, an all-purpose surface cleaner (see below) can be made with 100 percent natural ingredients, and a handful of fresh sage leaves will add a natural disinfectant. And fresh lemon verbena leaves mixed with white wine vinegar, liquid soap, and water will help make your windows sparkle and smell fresh.

All-purpose surface cleaner

Handful of fresh sage
1¼ cups (300ml) water
2 tbs (30ml) baking soda
8 drops lemon juice

Herb alternatives

Thyme sprigs *Use 2 handsful of the herb.*

Rosemary sprigs *cut to fit into the saucepan. Use 1 handful.*

Common sage

Method Put the sage leaves and stems in a saucepan, add the water, cover, and bring to a boil. Once boiling, lower the heat and simmer for 20 minutes. Remove from the heat. When the liquid is cool, strain through fine mesh to remove any impurities. Pour the cooled liquid into a bottle, add 2 tablespoons of baking soda and 8 drops of lemon juice. Put a top on the bottle, and shake well. This liquid can be used to clean sinks, and bathroom and kitchen surfaces. Store this all-purpose cleaner in the refrigerator for up to 1 week.

Window cleaner

1 handful lemon verbena leaves, either fresh or dried
1 cup (230ml) water
2 tbs (30ml) white vinegar
3–4 drops liquid soap

Herb alternatives

Lemon balm leaves *fresh or dried. Use 1 handful.*

Wild bergamot leaves *fresh or dried. Use 1 handful.*

Lemon verbena

Method Put a handful of lemon verbena leaves in a saucepan, pour in the water, bring to a boil, and lower the heat to simmer. After 10 minutes, turn off the heat and let it cool. Strain through fine mesh into a bottle. Add 2 tablespoons of white vinegar and a few drops of liquid soap. Seal and shake well. Store in a labeled spray bottle and use within 3 weeks. If you apply this solution and then rub the windowpanes with old newspaper, it will increase the shine.

Using herbs for Home fragrance

Keeping your home fresh and sweet-smelling not only makes it a pleasant environment to live in but can also help deter insects. For centuries, herbs have been used in the home to improve the air quality and they are far more beneficial than synthetic room sprays, which are particularly harmful to those who suffer from asthma and allergies. In the Middle Ages, rosemary and majoram were strewn in doorways, and as they were crushed underfoot, they released their perfume and helped to prevent the spread of disease. Bunches of tansy leaves were hung in windows to repel flies and mint sprigs were added to flower arrangements to repel mosquitoes. Like my grandmother, I still tuck sprigs of southernwood between wool clothes to deter moths, and every time I smell this herb, I am reminded of her.

Herb garden potpourri

6 tbs peppermint or spearmint leaves
4 tbs rosemary leaves
4 tbs lemon balm leaves
2 tbs oregano flowers and leaves
1 tbs sage leaves
1 tbs bay leaves
1 tbs thyme flowers and leaves
2 tsp coarse salt
2 tsp orris root powder
1 tsp (5ml) rosemary essential oil
1 tsp (5ml) oregano essential oil

Herb alternatives

Incense plant flowers and bracts Use on its own or mixed with bay leaves.

Myrtle and juniper berries and cardamom pods This mix gives a spicy aroma.

Lemon balm

Method Start by drying the leaves in single layers on a piece of cheesecloth stretched over a frame, as shown below. Dry the herbs in small batches; do not mix herb types, as their drying times vary. Keep the frame in a warm, dry place out of direct sunlight. When each batch is dry and crisp, put the herbs in individual jars with tight-fitting lids. Before sealing the lids, sprinkle in 2 teaspoons coarse salt and 2 teaspoons of orris root powder. Put the sealed jars in a dark cupboard for 3 weeks. Mix all the dry ingredients in a bowl, sprinkle in the essential oils, and place in a room away from direct sunlight. Stir occasionally to allow the fragrance of the potpourri to perfume the room.

Herbal room spray

2 large handfuls of fresh lavender flowers or 1 large handful of dried lavender flowers or 10 drops of lavender essential oil
1¼ cups (275ml) water

Herb alternatives

Rose-scented geranium leaves Use either 2 large handsful of leaves or 10 drops of rose geranium essential oil.

Sage leaves Use 2 large handsful of leaves.

Lavender

Method Place the lavender flowers in a saucepan, add the water, cover, and bring to a boil. Then, lower the heat to simmering. Simmer for 15 minutes, then turn off the heat. Let the lavender cool in the water. Strain using a fine mesh to remove all impurities; this is important especially since the liquid will be sprayed. Pour the clear liquid into a spray bottle. Alternatively, use the essential oil for a quicker recipe. Add it to cold water (hot water will cause the oils to evaporate). Shake the container well to mix the oil and water together. The scent from the essential oil is slightly sharper than fresh lavender sprigs.

Meadowsweet fabric freshener

Dried herbs placed between clothes, towels, and sheets make them smell wonderful. Sweet woodruff is the traditional choice, smelling of newly mown hay. Or you could use dried Queen-of-the-meadow, which smells of almonds, or alecost, which has a camphorlike aroma.

Pennyroyal ant deterrent

This is incredibly useful. Simply pick some pennyroyal leaves, and where you have an infestation of ants, rub the surface with the leaves. Rub hard so that you release the juice of the plant.

Sweet basil leaf fly repellent

Place a sweet basil plant by a window or just outside the kitchen door. If flies are persistent, crush a leaf to release a more pungent aroma.

Herbal sachets for clothes drawers

1 handful of dried lavender flowers

Herb alternatives

Alecost leaves These have a warm, minty but camphorous scent when dried. Alecost is also a good moth repellent.

Lemon verbena leaves The dried lemon-scented leaves make clothes smell wonderful.

South African wild rosemary leaves have an aroma similar to a mixture of southernwood and rosemary.

Lemon verbena

Method Dry the lavender flowers on stretched fabric (see page 102). Then fill sachets with the flowers or leaves. Use enough flowers and leaves to fill the sachets loosely. Do not overfill. You can intensify the fragrance by adding a few drops of lavender essential oil. The scent of lavender perfumes clothes and repels moths.

Southernwood moth deterrent

Simply dry sprigs of southernwood on a stretched piece of cheesecloth (see page 102). When dry, lay whole branches between wool clothes to deter moths.

Using herbs in First aid

Herbal remedies can provide quick, effective relief for a whole range of household accidents, from wasp stings to minor burns or sprains. Many of these ailments can be treated by using the leaf picked straight from the plant. For example, aloe vera and pennyroyal are rubbed straight on the affected area. Other remedies take longer to prepare, but there is something very reassuring about using homemade products. Before using any plant medicinally, do make sure it has been correctly identified. If you are in any doubt about using a herbal remedy, seek professional medical advice and always seek help for more serious accidents.

Natural healing with herbs

I have aloe vera growing in a pot on my kitchen windowsill, because I am renowned as a clumsy cook. When I burn myself, I simply cut off a bit of leaf and rub the glutinous gel straight on the burn (see below), reapplying if the burn becomes uncomfortable. The burn then heals without blistering. Aloe gel is not only good for healing burns, but it can be used to control acne and eczema, and to relieve itching caused by insect bites and allergies. In cool climates, the succulent leaves of houseleek (see page 243) can be used in the same way as aloe vera, as can St. John's Wort oil (see page 169), while the mashed-up leaves of pennyroyal (see page 194) offer immediate relief from ant, mosquito, and fly bites.

Herbal first-aid kit

A good first-aid kit needs to cater for all basic minor ailments including stings, grazes, allergies, and sprains. Choose which natural herbal remedies to make and keep in your medicine cabinet, and make sure you do not store any for longer than the recommended time or they may lose their potency. Here are some suggestions:

Aloe *(Aloe vera) gel for cuts, burns, sunburn, or poison ivy. Use fresh from the plant or as a homemade gel (see page 107 for gel recipe).*

Arnica *(Arnica montana) ointment for painful bruises and muscle pain. Only use when the skin is unbroken (see page 106 for ointment recipe).*

Chamomile *(Chamaemelum nobile) dried flowers and leaves for an infusion to help sleep and relaxation, and cream to treat eczema and skin rashes (see pages 106–107 for cream and infusion recipe).*

Comfrey *(Symphytum officinale) ointment for bruises and cuts. It encourages the growth of scar tissue (see page 106 for ointment recipe).*

Lavender *(Lavandula angustifolia) oil for insect bites, stings, burns, and headaches. It has antiseptic and antibacterial properties (see page 107 for ointment recipe).*

Marigold *(Calendula officinalis) as a cream for inflamed or minor wounds, skin rashes, and sunburn (see page 106 for cream recipe).*

St. John's Wort *(Hypericum perforatum) oil for burns, grazes, and rashes. This oil is a good substitute for aloe vera when traveling (see page 107 for hot infused oil recipe). It can also be used to make a cream to treat cramp and neuralgia (see page 106 for cream recipe).*

Lemon balm *(Melissa officinalis) dried herb infusion for stomach upsets, and as a relaxant. It is a good herbal treatment to give to children (see pages 106–107 for infusion recipe).*

Marigold cream

5oz (150g) emulsifying
ointment
3oz (70g) glycerol
⅓ cup (80ml) water
1oz (30g) dried marigold
flowers (*Calendula officinalis*)
or 3oz (75g) fresh
whole flowers

*Apply marigold cream to
minor wounds, skin rashes,
or sunburn.*

Herb alternatives

*The following creams are made
from the flowering parts of the
herb in exactly the same way as
marigold cream.*

Chamomile (Chamaemelum
nobile) *cream for eczema and
other allergic skin conditions.*

St. John's Wort (Hypericum
perforatum) *cream for cramp
and neuralgia (the cream will
be pink in color).*

Method Melt the
emulsifying ointment
in a glass bowl over a
pan of boiling water.
Add the glycerol and
water, and keep stirring until all the
ingredients have melted. Add the
herb, stir well, and simmer for 3
hours. Make sure the water does not
boil dry. Strain the mixture through
a wine press or jelly bag set over a
pitcher. Once strained, stir the
molten cream constantly as it cools
to prevent it from separating. When
set, use a small spatula to fill a dark
glass jar with a screw-top lid. Label
and store in the refrigerator for up
to 2 months.

Comfrey ointment

1lb (500g) petroleum jelly or
soft paraffin wax
2oz (60g) dried or 5oz (150g)
fresh comfrey leaves
(*Symphytum officinale*)
finely chopped

*This ointment promotes the
healing of bruises and cuts,
helping scar tissue to form.*

Herb alternatives

Arnica (Arnica montana) *for
bruises, sprains, and chilblains.
Only use on unbroken skin. Use the
whole plant – flowers, leaves, and
stalks – to make the ointment.*

Heart's ease (Viola tricolor)
*for skin rashes. Use the flowers,
leaves, and stalks to make
the ointment.*

Method Melt the
petroleum jelly in a
glass bowl over a pan
of boiling water. Add
the leaves and simmer,
stirring continuously for about 1
hour. Pour the the mixture into a
jelly bag or strainer. Wearing rubber
gloves, squeeze the mixture through
the bag into the pitcher. Pour the
ointment into a jar before it sets.
Place the lid on the jar, without
securing it. When cool, tighten the
lid. Store in a refrigerator for
up to 3 months.

Medicinal infusions

1 tsp (5ml) of dried herb or 2 tsp (10ml) of fresh herb per teacup
Freshly boiled water

Method An herbal infusion is the simplest way to prepare the leaves and/or
flowers of herbs for use as a remedy for specific ailments, or as a relaxing or
revitalizing tea. Place the fresh or dried leaves or flowers of the herb in a cup and
pour in freshly boiled water. The water should be just below boiling, since water
at boiling point causes the valuable plant oils to evaporate in the steam. Cover and
infuse for 5–10 minutes, then strain. Sweeten with honey if desired. Some herbs like lemon balm
(*Melissa officinalis*) can be drunk every day, but other herbs like feverfew (*Tanacetum parthenium*)
are are too strong to be taken daily. Always check the recommended dosage and quantity. Do not
drink more than 2 cups of any one medicinal herb in 24 hours, except under guidance from a
qualified herbal practitioner.

Rosemary oil

½lb (250g) dried rosemary
sprigs (*Rosmarinus
officinalis*), or 1lb (500g)
fresh herbs, finely chopped
3 cups (750ml) olive,
sunflower, or other good-
quality vegetable oil

*This hot infused oil is good
for treating aches and pains.*

Method Stir the
chopped herbs and oil
together in a glass
bowl over a saucepan
of boiling water.
Cover and simmer gently for 2–3
hours. Remove from the heat and let
the mixture cool. Then strain the
infusion through a jelly bag into a
pitcher. Using a funnel, pour the
infused herb oil into dark glass
storage bottles. Seal and label. Place
the jars in a cool place out of direct
light. The oil will keep for
up to 1 year.

Herb alternative

Lavender sprigs *Use hot
infused oil to relieve insect bites,
stings, and burns, and to rub
into the temples to
treat headaches.*

Aloe gel

1 aloe vera leaf (*Aloe vera*),
taken from top of the plant
(do not use the leaves at
the base which are
very bitter)
4 drops of lavender
essential oil

*Use this gel to treat
sunburn, minor burns, and
insect bites.*

Method Peel the
tough outer skin off
the leaf using a potato
peeler or paring knife.
Extract the clear
gelatinous gel and place it in a
blender. For every ¼ cup (50ml) of
gel, add 4 drops of lavender essential
oil. Mix thoroughly. Pour the
mixture into a glass jar or plastic-
lined tin, seal, and label. Store in the
refrigerator for about 3–4 weeks.

Herb alternatives

Bergamot (Monarda fistulosa) *for
nausea and flatulence. Use 4 fresh leaves
or 1 teaspoon of dried herb per cup.*

Cardamom (Elettaria cardamomum)
*for indigestion after a meal. Use 4
crushed seeds per cup.*

****Catnip*** (Nepeta cataria) *for a chill,
rhinitis, or insomnia. Use 5 fresh leaves
or 1 teaspoon of dried herb per cup.*

Chamomile (Chamaemelum nobile)
for insomnia. Use 4 fresh flowers per cup.

Dill (Anethum graveolens) *for gripping
stomach pains and indigestion. Use 1
teaspoon of crushed seeds per cup.*

Elderflower (Sambucus nigra) *for colds
or as a refreshing cup of tea. Use 1*

*flowering top or 1 teaspoon of dried
flowers per cup.*

Fennel (Foeniculum vulgare) *for
indigestion and as a diuretic. Use 1
teaspoon of crushed seeds per cup.*

****Gotu kola*** (Centella asiatica) *is a
diuretic that cleanses toxins (see page 145
for more information). Use 1 teaspoon of
dried leaves per cup; infuse for 15
minutes, then strain.*

****Hops*** (Humulus lupulus) *for nerves
and insomnia. Use 1 teaspoon of dried
female flowers per cup.*

****Hyssop*** (Hyssopus officinalis) *for
coughs and rhinitis. Use 1 teaspoon of
dried or 2 teaspoon of fresh leaves
per cup.*

Lemon balm (Melissa officinalis) *for
tension, headaches, and upset stomachs.
Use 5 fresh leaves per cup.*

Lemon verbena (Aloysia triphylla) *for
insomnia and nasal congestion. Use 5
fresh leaves or 1 teaspoon of dried per
cup. Serve cold in summer.*

****Lovage*** (Levisticum officinale) *for
water retention. Use 1 teaspoon of
crushed seeds per cup.*

****Queen-of-the-meadow*** (Filipendula
ulmaria) *for indigestion, and as a
comfort during colds or flu. Use 1 head
of fresh flower, or 1 teaspoon of dried
flowers per cup.*

Peppermint (Mentha x piperita) *for
indigestion. Use 5 fresh leaves or 1*

*teaspoon of dried leaves per cup. Curly
mint (Mentha spicata) is equally good.*

Rosemary (Rosmarinus officinalis) *for
halitosis, and to improve concentration.
Use 2in (5cm) of a rosemary sprig or 1
tsp (5ml) of dried leaf per cup. Drink no
more than one cup a day.*

Sweet woodruff (Galium odoratum)
*for mild stomachache. Use either a 2in
(5cm) sprig of fresh leaf or 1 teaspoon of
dried leaves per cup.*

WARNING
*None of the plants marked * should be
taken during pregnancy.*

Using herbs for Beauty

Herbs have been used cosmetically for thousands of years. The ancient Egyptians perfumed their hair with marjoram oil and used many other herbs in beauty preparations, and for ceremonial occasions and religious rituals. Roman soldiers also used fragrant herb oils like lavender, to rub into their skin after bathing, which helped heal skin wounds after battle and acted as an insect repellent. Today, a whole commercial industry is based around beauty products, and it is big business. Many contain chemical preservatives, synthetic perfumes, and artificial colorings, but by making your own cosmetics, you can maintain control over the purity of the ingredients. There are also therapeutic reasons for using herbs in your daily beauty routine, plus their wonderful herb aroma will promote a sense of wellbeing.

Facial steam

3 tbs (45ml) dried herbs, comprising equal parts chamomile, chervil, lavender, lemon balm, spearmint, curly mint, and thyme
½ gallon (1.5l) freshly boiled water

Herb alternatives

For oily skin:
Pot marigold flowers, dried horsetail, sage leaves, and yarrow leaves.

For mature skin:
Dried elderflowers and tansy flowers, plus dried tansy and lemon verbena leaves.

WARNING Avoid facial steams if your skin is very dry or has visible red veins, or if you suffer from a heart condition or asthma.

Chervil

Method
Place the herbs in a bowl; pour in the slightly cooled, boiled water. Hold your face over the steam at a distance of 12in (30cm), or18in (45cm) for those with sensitive skin. Cover your head, shoulders, and the bowl with a towel, and inhale for 5–10 minutes. Rinse your face with tepid water, then splash with cold water. To close up pores, dab on an infusion (see pages 106–107) of elder-flower or peppermint with cotton balls.

Mouthwash

1 tsp (5ml) dried spearmint
1 tsp (5ml) dried rosemary
1 tsp (5ml) dried thyme
2½ cups (575ml) water

Herb alternatives

Use 1 teaspoon each of dried peppermint, sage, and rosemary leaves.

Creeping thyme

Method
Place all the dried herbs in a saucepan with the water. Cover, bring to a boil, and simmer for 20 minutes. Remove from the heat and cool. When cool, strain into a glass jar, seal, and store in the refrigerator for up to 4 days. Use a small quantity of this mouthwash twice a day. Rinse out your mouth with the mouthwash after you have brushed your teeth. Persistent bad breath is often a sign that the digestive system is not functioning properly. If this is the case, seek medical advice.

Nail strengthener

4 tbs (60g) fresh or 2 tbs (30g) dried
horsetail leaves
2 tbs (30g) crushed dill seed
1 quart (850ml) water

Dill seeds

Method To make the
nail-strengthening
solution, place the
horsetail and dill
leaves in a small
covered pan with the water. Bring to
a boil, lower the heat, and simmer
for a further 20 minutes. Leave to
cool, and then strain into a glass
bottle, seal, and label. Place in a
cupboard out of direct light. The
solution will keep for up to 4 weeks.
Soak your fingers in this solution for
10 minutes every other day over
several weeks, and the silicic acid,
which both dill and horsetail contain,
will strengthen your fingernails.

Shampoo

1 tsp (5ml) dried soapwort root or
10 fresh soapwort stems with
leaves each 6–8in (15–20cm)
long
1 quart (850ml) water

Herb alternatives

Oily hair *Add 1 tbs (15ml) dried or
10 leaves of fresh peppermint or
spearmint; 1 tbs (15ml) dried or 1 sprig
fresh rosemary; 1 tsp (5ml) dried sage or
3 leaves of fresh sage.*

Dry hair *Add 1 tbs (15ml) dried or 10
leaves of fresh mallow, chamomile, or
sweet marjoram leaves, or 1 tbs (15ml)
dried or 1 sprig of fresh rosemary.*

Soapwort

Method
Soapwort makes
a slight lather
when added to
water, but it
does not sting the eyes
like some synthetic
shampoos. You can use
soapwort on its own or
combine it with other
herbs that benefit your
hair type (see Herb
Alternatives). Crush the
soapwort root or
roughly chop up the
fresh stems. If you use
dried soapwort, soak
the root overnight in
water. Put the soapwort
and other herbs in a
saucepan with the
water, cover, bring to a
boil, and simmer for 20
minutes, stirring
occasionally. Remove
from the heat, cool, and
then strain the liquid
through a fine strainer
or cheesecloth. Store
the shampoo solution
out of direct light, for
up to 1 week.

Toning face pack

2 tbs (30ml) dried lady's
mantle leaves and flowers,
spearmint leaves, and
mallow leaves
1 tsp (5ml) crushed fennel
seed
1 tsp (5ml) crushed juniper
berries
2½ cups (575ml) water
2 tbs (30ml) ground oatmeal,
almonds, or Fuller's earth

Herb alternatives

For oily skin: *Chamomile,
yarrow, parsley, and peppermint
to equal either 2 handsful of
fresh leaves or 2 tbs (30ml) of
dried herbs.*

For dry skin: *2 handsful of
fresh houseleek, mallow, and
borage leaves, or 2 tbs (30ml)
of dried herbs and 1 tsp (5ml)
of crushed flax seed.*

Mallow

Method Combine
the herbs in a saucepan
with the water. Cover,
bring to a boil, and
simmer for 15 minutes.
Remove from the heat, strain, and
cool. Put the ground oatmeal in a
bowl. Add 2–3 tablespoons of the
herbal infusion and mix well to form a
paste. Spread fairly thickly over your
face, avoiding the area around the eyes
and mouth. Leave for 10 minutes.
Rinse with warm water. Use once or
twice a week to tone the skin.

Using herbs for Relaxation

A warm bath infused with herb oils or dried herb ingredients helps relaxation and has a soothing effect on the nervous system. By adding herbs to warm water, we are encouraging them to release their natural oils, which in turn help us relax our body and mind. As you stretch out in the bathtub, breathe in deeply and inhale the herbs and then slowly exhale several times to get the maximum benefit. As the Greek physician Theophrastus noted, fragrant herbs have an instant healing effect as the smell travels directly from the nerves in the nose to the part of the brain concerned with intuition, emotion, and creativity. He noted that when an aromatic herb poultice was applied to a leg, it could produce fragrant breath as its essences would permeate the skin and enter the circulatory system.

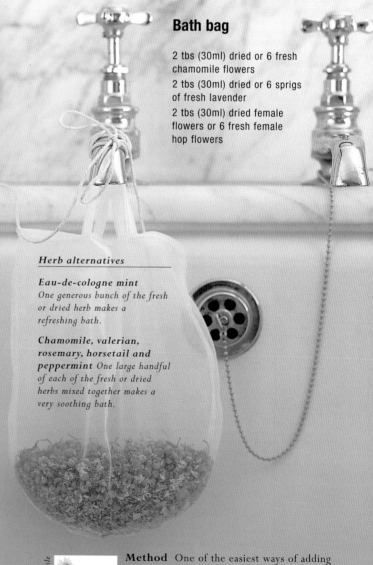

Bath bag

2 tbs (30ml) dried or 6 fresh chamomile flowers

2 tbs (30ml) dried or 6 sprigs of fresh lavender

2 tbs (30ml) dried female flowers or 6 fresh female hop flowers

Herb alternatives

Eau-de-cologne mint
One generous bunch of the fresh or dried herb makes a refreshing bath.

Chamomile, valerian, rosemary, horsetail and peppermint *One large handful of each of the fresh or dried herbs mixed together makes a very soothing bath.*

Bath tonic

I large handful of common thyme stems and leaves

2½ cups (575ml) water

Herb alternatives

Lemon balm leaves
relieve insomnia and soothe the nerves. Use 2 large handsful of fresh leaves. Simmer for 5 minutes.

Basil and sweet marjoram leaves
Use 2 large handsful (one of each herb) of fresh leaves, and simmer for 5 minutes. This bath relieves muscle cramps.

Sweet marjoram

Method I do not think that I could cope with the strenuous work on my farm without being able to soak in a relaxing herbal bath at the end of a hard day. It not only washes away the physical aches and pains, but also restores my equilibrium. This is one recipe I use frequently to alleviate backache. Place the thyme sprigs into the saucepan of water. Cover, bring to a boil, lower the heat, and simmer for 10 minutes. Remove the infusion from the heat and carefully strain the herbs – it is not romantic to have leaves floating in the bath water because when you get out they stick to the skin. Add the thyme infusion to a hot bath and soak.

Chamomile

Method One of the easiest ways of adding herbs to a bath is to hang a small cloth bag under the hot water faucet. Fill the bag with either a single dried herb or a mixture of herbs, and run the hot water through it, infusing the water and the air in the bathroom with herbs.

Hop pillow

2 handsful dried female hop flowers
1 handful dried chamomile flowers
1 handful dried lemon verbena leaves

Herb alternatives

Sweet marjoram leaves and lavender sprigs *Mix 1 handful of each dried herb to induce sleep and to lift the spirits.*

Chamomile flowers and rosemary sprigs *Mix 1 handful of each dried herb to prevent nightmares and to refresh the mind and body.*

Method Hop pillows are well known for their ability to aid sleep. If you do not like the beerlike aroma that hop flowers exude, mix them with other, more aromatic herbs, such as chamomile flowers and lemon verbena leaves. This will not detract from the hops' sleep-inducing properties. To make the herb pillow, sew a small cotton cover, and fill it with the dried herbs and stitch it up. It will last for up to 6 months.

Relaxing eye compress

5 leaves or 1 tsp (5ml) dried mint leaves
1 cup (200ml) water

Method Place the herbs in a ceramic bowl, pour in freshly boiled water, cover and let it infuse for 10 minutes. Strain through an unbleached coffee filter paper and

leave it to cool. To reduce dark circles under the eyes, dip 2 cotton pads in the liquid and place on the eyelids for 10–15 minutes.

WARNING Eyes are very delicate. Before use, test the solution on a tender patch of skin, such as underarm, for an allergic reaction.

Herb alternatives

Bachelor's buttons *to soothe the eyes and reduce puffiness in the eye area. Use 1 handful of fresh or dried flowers.*

Fennel leaves *reduce inflammation and brighten eyes. Use 1 teaspoon of crushed dried herb.*

Foot bath

Herb alternatives

Lovage leaves and seeds *are a good deodorizer for feet. Use 1 handful of fresh or dried leaves and 1 tsp (5ml) of crushed lovage seeds. Infuse for 10 minutes.*

Sweet marjoram leaves *are good for refreshing tired feet. Use 1 handful of fresh or dried leaves. Infuse for 10 minutes.*

1 handful of fresh lavender flowers or 2 tbs (30ml) dried flowers
2 bay leaves, fresh or dry
1 tbs (15ml) sea salt or Epsom salts

Method A foot bath is excellent for tired feet and aching leg muscles, particularly after vigorous exercise. Make an infusion with the herb of your choice, and leave to steep for 10 minutes. Fill a large bowl with hot water, add the herbal infusion and sea salt. Soak your feet for 10 minutes. Rinse in cold water and pat dry.

Using herbs in Petcare

Wild animals naturally turn to herbs if they are feeling unwell. Our domesticated animals have not lost this instinct and will treat themselves if, for example, they get a burr stuck in their throat by eating grass. We can use herbs to alleviate our pet's simple ailments. For instance, you can add parsley to a dog's diet to cure bad breath. Cats and dogs and other small creatures have much shorter digestive systems than humans, and they do not digest fresh herbs in the same way. For this reason, it is easier and safer to administer herbs as a herbal infusion, mixed with their food. Make the doses compatible with your pet's size – small amounts for small animals, larger amounts for large animals. But if your pet is not well, consult a qualified vet rather than attempting to treat it with herbs.

Flea powder

1 tsp (5ml) dried rosemary
1 tsp (5ml) fennel seeds, crushed
1 tsp (5ml) dried wormwood
1 tsp (5ml) dried rue

Method Mix together the dried herb ingredients. Comb sparingly into your pet's hair. Alternatively, you can pick a handful of tansy *(Tanacetum vulgare)* and rub your pet's coat with the crushed leaves. This will soothe the pet and deters fleas. Or, you can bathe your dog in a strong rosemary *(Rosmarinus officinalis)* infusion (see pages 106–107). This infusion can also be used to wash your dog's bedding and to soak its collar to deter fleas.

Pyrethrum

Lice deterrent

Wormwood

Method Free-range hens will control their own lice infestations by taking dust baths. You can help control lice in a coop by hanging large bunches of dried wormwood *(Artemisia absinthium)* inside the coop and placing dried leaves in the hens' bedding straw. Dried bunches of pyrethrum *(Tanacetum cinerariifolium)* will deter flies, and tansy *(Tanacetum vulgare)*, mice.

Calming tonic

Method Pets, like humans, can be frightened by thunderstorms, car travel, or loud noises. Here, a hamster is being given a few drops of chamomile tea *(Chamaemelum nobile)*. It calms the nerves and is an excellent cleanser and toner of the digestive tract, helping to expel worms and parasites and so improve the appetite. It also helps to control dry, flaking skin. For cats, add one tablespoon of chamomile tea to their feed, for dogs up to 3 tablespoons, depending on their size. Another calmative is valerian *(Valeriana officinalis)*, which works well for anxious cats. Cats are notoriously fussy about their food, but are partial to valerian, which reduces anxiety and soothes the nervous system. Add 3–4 drops of valerian tisane to food using a dropper.

Chamomile

Worming mixture

Garlic

½–1 raw garlic clove, grated or minced
(depending on pet's size)
1 tsp–2 tbs (5–30ml) of brewer's yeast
powder (depending on pet's size)

Method Garlic is very beneficial for dogs, acting as a wormer, a flea deterrent, and an all-round tonic for the immune and cardiovascular system. Some dogs are happy to eat garlic grated on to their food, but others will refuse it. To disguise the aroma of garlic, add brewers' yeast to the garlic to make a more palatable worming mixture. It is also good for the coat condition.

WARNING This mixture is not suitable for dogs under six months old.

Cat toy

Catnip

Method My two cats both adore the two species of catnip *(Nepeta cateria)* and *(Nepeta x faassenii)*. They can be found lying outdoors in ecstasy among the fresh plant in summer. To give them all-year-round pleasure, dry catnip leaves and use them to fill a small cat toy or make a small cotton sachet and sew it up.

Top 100 herbs

Reasons for choice

Over the past decade, as we have become more familiar with the negative effects of processed foods and prescription medicines, herbs as both healing foods and natural remedies have increased in significance as the key to good health. When I first started growing herbs organically more than twenty years ago, I was thought eccentric, but now these ideas have been integrated into the mainstream with more and more people becoming aware of the health benefits of foods that are grown free from pesticides and other harmful chemicals.

Choosing my Top 100 herbs for this book was difficult, as I have a passion for all these useful plants including those from farflung outposts of the world. There are so many dimensions to herbs: not only are they used in the kitchen or

medicinally, but they also work as companion plants in the organic garden, helping other plants to grow successfully – or they can form the basis of natural beauty products and household cleaners to help create a toxic-free home. One of the main criteria for the herbs that feature here was that they had to be grown on the farm. One species, curry tree (*Murraya koenigii*), is tropical, but I have placed it in my Top 100 because I have successfully managed to raise a cherished specimen in the warmth of my farm greenhouse. As a rule, I have tried to stick to everyday herb species that have a role in the kitchen or have an indispensable use as an herbal remedy, like sage, thyme, mint, and garlic. I describe how to grow each one using the tried and tested organic methods we practice on the farm. I have also included herbs, like shiso (*Perilla* species), that are common in the East but need their profile raised in the West. I especially like the purple variety (*Perilla frutescens var purpurascens*), which is not only wonderful in cooking, but looks stunning in the garden. I have also included medicinal herbs to reflect the increased interest in these plants, for example, *Echinacea* species for their immune-boosting properties, and lemon balm (*Melissa officinalis*), for healing and preventing cold sores. Finally, I have chosen herbs for their perfume, such as lemon verbena (*Aloysia triphylla*) with its refreshing lemon fragrance, and the scented *Pelargonium* 'Attar of Roses' with its sweet rose perfume. Once you start growing and using herbs, I defy anyone not to become hooked.

Top row left Sweet marjoram (*Origanum marjorana*). Medicinal and culinary herb quintessential for Mediterranean cooking.

Top row center Lettuce leaf basil (*Ocimum basilicum* 'Napolitano'). Wonderful for pesto sauce or for tearing over a tomato salad.

Top row right Pink rosemary *Rosmarinus officinalis* 'Roseus.' Great for barbecues, rinsing dark hair, or settling the stomach.

Middle row left Angelica (*Angelica archangelica*) is a magnificent structural plant for a large herb garden.

Middle row center Pineapple sage (*Salvia elegans* 'Scarlet Pineapple'). By simply rubbing the leaves of this plant, a sweet pineapple scent fills the air.

Middle row left Sweet woodruff (*Galium odoratum*). A lovely little traditional herb that is very useful in the home.

Bottom row left Fringed lavender (*Lavandula dentata*). A highly aromatic lavender, lovely when grown in containers.

Bottom row center Golden oregano (*Origanum vulgare* 'Aureum'). The leaves of this oregano add warmth and spice to tomato dishes, or taste good scattered over zucchini.

Bottom row right Rue (*Ruta graveolens*), the herb of grace and bitterness, is medicinally very important in ophthalmology.

Cultivation

Propagation In the fall, sow seeds in a container and winter in a cold frame. Germination is erratic. In spring, plant young plants 8–12in (20–30cm) apart. Since yarrow can be invasive, I do not advise sowing seeds directly into the ground. To control its spread, divide mature plants in spring or early fall.

Site Once established, yarrow will survive in most soils. It is drought tolerant.

Maintenance This plant is prone to self-seeding. Cut back after flowering to prevent it from setting seed.

Harvesting Cut the leaves and flowerheads for drying when it comes into flower, or to use fresh.

Uses Yarrow is known as a "plant doctor," and when it is planted near unhealthy plants, secretions from its roots actively help the ailing plant by triggering its disease resistance. Its leaves can be infused to make a copper fertilizer to prevent fungi and cure downy mildew, and a few leaves added to the compost heap will speed up decomposition. Before using leaves for medicinal or culinary purposes, wash them well, then pat dry with paper towel. Add young leaves to salads. Yarrow is well known for staunching the flow of blood. Simply crush the leaves to release its tannins; then apply it to the wound to stop the bleeding. An infusion made from the flowers is a good remedy for fever. The flowers can be also used in dried-flower arrangements.

Achillea Yarrow ASTERACEAE

The plant name "Achillea" is taken from Greek mythology during the famous siege of Troy, the great hero, Achilles, used yarrow leaves to heal his wounded warriors. This invasive herb is found growing all over the world in waste land, fields, and pastures. Though some gardeners consider it a weed – especially those who like to cultivate a perfect lawn – I find it useful in the organic garden. It makes a good compost accelerator (see page 37) and copper fertilizer. Copper is an indispensable constituent of all living tissues and is essential for the normal growth and wellbeing of plants and animals. It is not toxic like other metals, such as lead and mercury. In the kitchen, I add fresh young leaves, which have a light, warm flavor, to salads; and in the home the crushed leaves make a useful first-aid remedy for staunching the flow of blood. Despite its beneficial medicinal properties, the leaves and the flowers of this herb can cause minor skin irritation. It should not be taken in a medicinal form by pregnant women. Large doses can result in headaches or dizziness.

Achillea ageratum
ENGLISH MACE
Hardy perennial. Height 12–18in (30–45cm) and spread 12in (30cm). Clusters of small white flowers with cream centers appear in summer. The aromatic leaves are finely serrated, narrow, oval, and bright green. It prefers a sunny site and any soil except acid. The mildly flavored leaves are good with salads, rice, chicken, and fish.

FOR USE IN

The Garden | The Kitchen | The Home
PP. 21, 43, 49, 57, 58, 72, 73 | PP. 85, 93 | PP. 108, 109

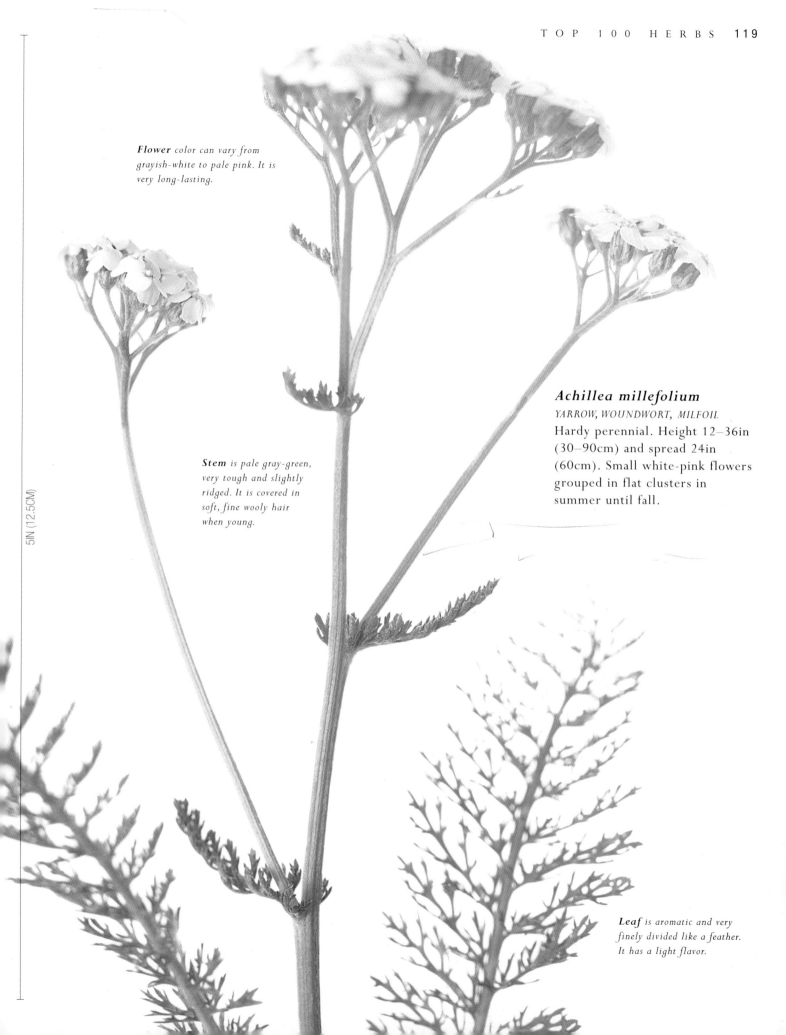

Flower *color can vary from grayish-white to pale pink. It is very long-lasting.*

Stem *is pale gray-green, very tough and slightly ridged. It is covered in soft, fine wooly hair when young.*

5IN (12.5CM)

Achillea millefolium
YARROW, WOUNDWORT, MILFOIL
Hardy perennial. Height 12–36in (30–90cm) and spread 24in (60cm). Small white-pink flowers grouped in flat clusters in summer until fall.

Leaf *is aromatic and very finely divided like a feather. It has a light flavor.*

Cultivation

Propagation Sow seeds in early spring under protection at 68°F (20°C). Germination takes 7–10 days. Or sow seeds in late spring into prepared open ground (see page 44), when the air temperature at night does not fall below 50°F (10°C). Germination takes 2–3 weeks. The plant will flower in the first year. Softwood cuttings can be taken in early summer. When the cuttings have rooted, pot them and place in a cold frame or cold greenhouse for the winter.

Site Plant in a warm, sunny site in any well-drained soil. Hyssop can withstand dry conditions, though it is less tolerant of clay soil – where it should be grown as an annual so its roots do not rot. When grown in a container, make sure the pot size can accommodate the mature plant. Use a standard loam-based substrate with grit added for drainage.

Maintenance Once established, this plant needs little maintenance. In the spring of the third season, it is advisable to dig it up and divide it (see page 57) to maintain its health and shape. Feed with a small amount of organic fertilizer such as comfrey or seaweed before replanting.

Harvesting Pick the leaves to use fresh in cooking or to conserve in oil or vinegar (see pp. 88–89) before the plant flowers in summer. Pick the flower spikes as they open. Remove the flowerets before use.

Uses The plant is used to treat coughs and wheezing. The fresh leaves and edible flowers can be used in leaf and fruit salads, or to make a refreshing infusion.

Agastache Anise hyssop LAMIACEAE

Renowned for its beautiful flower spikes that attract butterflies, this North American native has been introduced realtively recently to European herb gardens. Its medicinal healing properties were well known to many native North American tribes. In the kitchen, the young leaves and flowers offer a mild anise, minty flavor and taste good with fish and chicken dishes. This plant should not be confused with the Mediterranean *Hyssopus officinalis* (see page 170), which also has the common name "hyssop."

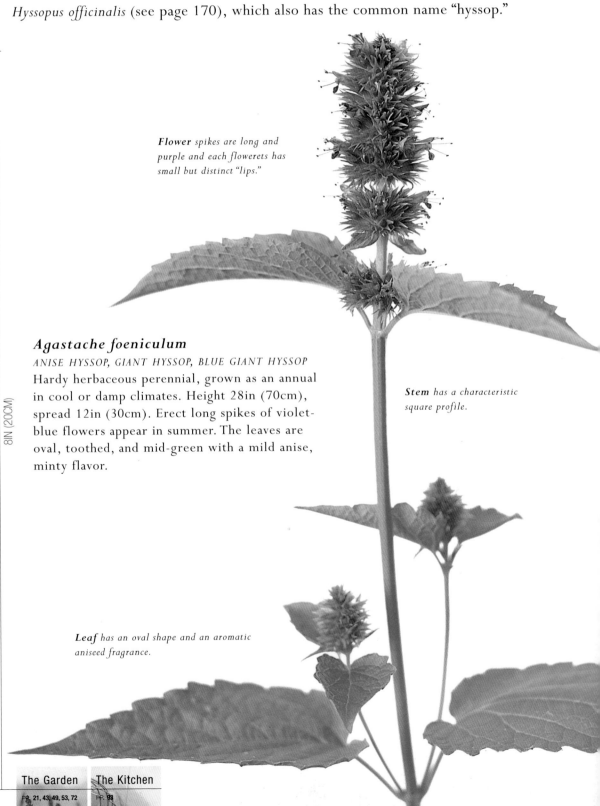

Flower spikes are long and purple and each flowerets has small but distinct "lips."

Agastache foeniculum
ANISE HYSSOP, GIANT HYSSOP, BLUE GIANT HYSSOP
Hardy herbaceous perennial, grown as an annual in cool or damp climates. Height 28in (70cm), spread 12in (30cm). Erect long spikes of violet-blue flowers appear in summer. The leaves are oval, toothed, and mid-green with a mild anise, minty flavor.

Stem has a characteristic square profile.

8IN (20CM)

Leaf has an oval shape and an aromatic aniseed fragrance.

The Garden | The Kitchen

PP. 21, 43, 49, 53, 72 | PP. 93

Cultivation

Propagation Self-seeds easily, or can be sown in pots in a cold frame. Germination takes 4–6 weeks, but this method is not always successful. Alternatively, sow into prepared ground in early spring. Germination takes 6–8 weeks, but again this can be erratic. Thin the seedlings to 12in (30cm) apart. Established plants can be divided in spring or fall (see page 57).

Site Lady's mantle will grow in sun or partial shade in all but excessively wet soils.

Maintenance This plant is prone to self-seeding, which can cause it to spread prolifically. To prevent seed dispersal, cut off the flower heads as soon as they die back. In the fall, cut out old growth. In spring, clear up around established plants. In containers, use a soil-based substrate and site in partial shade. Re-pot each fall. Containers can be wintered outside, but avoid water-logging or the roots will rot.

Harvesting From spring until early summer, cut very young leaves to use fresh in cooking and mature leaves for use in herbal medicine. The roots can also be used in herbal medicine and should be dug up in the second year. To make the plant dye, harvest mature leaves before flowering.

Uses An infusion of leaves helps alleviate menopausal discomfort and can be used to treat yeast and children's diarrhea. Young leaves have a mild, dry, bitter taste and can be added to salads.

Caution Do not use in pregnancy and seek professional advice on treating menstrual problems.

Alchemilla Lady's mantle ROSACEAE

This is one of the most attractive herbs in the garden. and I love to see the dewdrops form on the pale green lacy leaves. Native to Europe and Britain, it has special importance for women, and its attributes are said to include preserving a woman's youth and protecting her from dark forces. It was dedicated to the Virgin Mary and named "Our Lady's Mantle" because the leaf shape was thought to resemble Our Lady's cloak. This versatile plant is used to treat hormonal problems in people and animals, and produces a vibrant green dye for wool.

Flowers are greenish-yellow and appear in clusters in the summer.

8IN (20CM)

Alchemilla xanthochlora syn. *A. vulgaris*
LADY'S MANTLE
Hardy herbaceous perennial. Height 18in (45cm). Spread 20in (50cm). Profuse clusters of bright greenish-yellow, tiny, sweet-smelling flowers appear from late spring to summer. The pale green, slightly scalloped leaves are divided into seven or nine broad, shallow lobes with crinkled, fine-toothed edges. This species is very similar to *A. mollis*, but is thought to have more potent medicinal healing properties.

Leaf is round, pale green, and slightly scalloped at the edges.

Mature leaves are used to produce a green wool dye.

Cultivation

Propagation In early spring sow seeds under cover at 68°F (20°C). Germination takes 10–20 days. Alternatively, sow seeds in late spring into prepared open ground, when the air temperature at night stays above 45°F (7°C). Germination takes 2–3 weeks. Thin seedlings to 9in (25cm) apart and divide established clumps every 3 years in spring.

Site Plant in well-drained fertile soil. Keep well-watered throughout the growing season. In the fall, mulch with well-rotted manure.

Maintenance Onions are prone to disease. Keep the soil fertile and take care not to damage the roots or leaves when clearing around the plants in spring since the scent will attract the onion fly. Also, when thinning seedlings, remove all wilted ones and any seedlings not required. Take care not to damage the bulbs when hoeing or digging the site, or neck or bulb rot may occur.

Harvesting Dig up bulbs from early summer until early fall. Cut fresh leaves from late spring until early fall. Leaves do not dry well, but can be frozen.

Uses The fresh onion juice is antibiotic, diuretic, expectorant, and antispasmodic, and useful in the treatment of coughs, colds, bronchitis, and gastro-enteritis. Eating onion, especially garlic, helps lower blood pressure. Use bulbs raw in salads or add to pasta dishes, stews, and casseroles. Use fresh leaves in salads.

Allium Onion family ALLIACEAE

This popular and important medicinal herb family is grown throughout the world. Alliums have marvelous health-giving properties, and people believed that the stronger the smell, the more effective the healing powers of the plants. In the Middle Ages, people hung bunches of onions outside their front doors to absorb infections, the plague, and deter pests. The juice was used as a strong disinfectant and to heal gunshot wounds. Alliums make good companions in the organic garden; they help prevent leaf curl in trees, especially peaches; and planted next to roses, they ward off black spot.

Allium cepa **Proliferum Group**

TREE ONION, EGYPTIAN ONION, LAZY MAN'S ONION

Hardy perennial. Height up to 5ft (1.5m) and spread 24in (60cm). Small greenish-white flowers appear early in the second summer, followed by bulbs, which form at the top of the stem. These bulbs are edible. In fall or spring, propagate from the small stem bulbs, which have their own individual root system. Plant in an enriched soil.

Allium sativum

GARLIC

Hardy perennial, grown as an annual. Height up to 24in (60cm). Flat, solid green leaf. In warm climates, round white flowerheads appear in early summer. It is the strongest member of the onion family for medicinal and culinary uses.

Bulbs are harvested in midsummer. In winter, plant individual cloves taken from the bulb.

Flowers *are creamy-white, globe-shaped, and edible.*

Allium fistulosum

WELSH ONION, JAPANESE LEEK
Hardy perennial evergreen. Height and spread 20in (50cm). Large creamy-white, globe-shaped flowers appear early in the second summer. The leaves can be cut into rings and used in salads. The name Welsh comes from "walsch" meaning "foreign."

5IN (12CM)

Stem *is long, hollow, and cylindrical, and can easily bend in high winds or dry conditions.*

Cultivation

Propagation See page 122 for details.

Site Plant in rich, moist soil in a sunny position. Keep well-watered throughout the growing season. In the fall, mulch with well-rotted manure. Both chives and garlic chives grow well in containers. Use a soil-based substrate.

Maintenance To encourage new, lush growth, cut back after flowering and feed with comfrey liquid feed (see page 39). Chives can suffer from a rust virus. If it occurs, cut back diseased growth and burn it. Or, if your plant is well away from buildings or fences, cover the plant with straw and set it alight; this will burn the top growth and sterilize the soil. The plant should not be composted, as the virus will live on in the compost and transfer to the ground. In the fall, on cool, wet days, downy mildew can be a problem. If this is the case, cut back all the remaining growth, dig the plant up, divide it, and replant in a prepared new site.

Harvesting Cut fresh leaves during the growing season. Use fresh, or preserve in herb butter (see page 91). Use fresh flowers in early summer. Divide the flower head into individual bulbils.

Uses An excellent culinary herb. The leaves stimulate the appetite and aid digestion. They are also mildly antiseptic.

Allium Chive family ALLIACEAE

This herb is the only member of the onion family growing wild in Asia, Europe, Australia, and North America. Records of its medicinal use date back to 3000 B.C., and historically it was used as an antidote to poison and to staunch the flow of blood. I find chives indispensable in the kitchen: the leaves add a mild onion flavor to salads, and I like to mix them with sour cream to spice up plain baked potatoes. There is an old saying "chives next to roses creates posies" because the herb is believed to inhibit black spot. A decoction made from the leaves is also thought to prevent scab infection in animals.

Allium ursinum
WILD GARLIC, RAMSONS
Hardy perennial. Height up to 18in (45cm) and spread 24in (60cm). Clusters of star-shaped flowers appear in late spring. The mid-green leaves are elliptical. Plant in a moist, fertile soil in semi-shade. Sow the seeds and divide the rhizome in the fall. Flowers and leaves are edible. Eat the leaves before flowering. The leaves may also be boiled, and the resulting liquid used as a disinfectant wipe.

Allium tuberosum
GARLIC CHIVES, CHINESE CHIVES
Hardy perennial. Height and spread 12in (30cm). Clusters of white, star-shaped flowers appear in summer. The mid-green leaves are flat, solid, thin, and lance-shaped, and have a mild, sweet, garlic flavor.

Flowers *are pink or purple and globe-shaped. Edible, they have a mild onion flavor that is great in salads.*

3IN (8CM)

Allium schoenoprasum
CHIVES
Hardy perennial. Height and spread 12in (30cm). The purple globe-shaped flowers are composed of individual bulbils and flower all summer. Leaves are green, cylindrical, and hollow, and have a mild aroma and flavor similar to onion.

Stem *flavor is inferior to that of the leaf.*

Leaf *is hollow and cylindrical. It can be cut into rings with scissors and used in salads.*

Cultivation

Propagation Sow seeds on the soil surface, under protection at 70°F (21°C). Germination is erratic, taking anything from 4 months to up to 2 years. It is easier to propagate by division, simply remove the off-shoots that form at the base of a mature plant. Replant the off-shoots in a coarse loam substrate a day later to give them time to dry out slightly.

Site In tropical or sub-tropical climates only, plant outside in full to partial shade in a free-draining soil. In cooler climates, grow it in a container as a house plant. Use a soil-based substrate with extra grit. Although the foliage looks like a succulent, it is more closely related to the lily family and needs water in the growing season.

Maintenance If grown as a potted plant, feed monthly throughout the growing season with a liquid fertilizer like liquid seaweed. In winter, keep watering to a minimum, but do not let the substrate to dry out.

Harvesting Cut fresh leaves throughout the growing season and store in an airtight container in a refrigerator. Plants over 2 years old have stronger medicinal properties.

Uses Break the leaf to extract the soothing gel. Apply the gel to wounds and minor burns. It will form a protective seal over the wound and help the skin to regenerate (see page 107). It can also be used to treat eczema and fungal infections like ringworm and yeast. Used internally, under professional medical supervision, it can soothe peptic ulcers and irritable bowel syndrome.

Aloe Aloe ALOEACEAE

This tropical plant is an indispensable part of my natural first-aid kit, since it produces a soothing gel for treating burns. I always keep a pot growing on my kitchen windowsill so I can act quickly if I burn myself when cooking – I am notoriously clumsy. It has been identified in wall paintings of the ancient Egyptians, and it is said that Cleopatra was the first to use it as a beauty treatment. As a child, I remember having "bitter aloes" put on my fingers to stop me from sucking them – it didn't work. Do not take fresh aloe internally without seeking professional advice. The leaves are a potent laxative and should not be taken by pregnant women or young children.

Foliage is succulent, gray-green with spiny edges.

Aloe vera
ALOE VERA AGM syn.
A. BARBADENSIS
Half-hardy perennial grows at a minimum temperature of 50°F (10°C). Height and spread, when grown outside, 2ft (60cm). Yellow or orange bell-shaped flowers appear on mature plants only.

Foliage when young may have a lightly spotted appearance.

8IN (20CM)

Foliage is fleshy when broken to release its gel and will heal over within days.

The Garden
PP. 21, 43, 58, 67

The Home
PP. 104, 105, 107

Cultivation

Propagation In spring, sow seeds under protection at (60°F (15°C). Germination takes 10–20 days. When seedlings are large enough to handle, prick out into 3½in (9cm) pots, using a soil-based substrate with extra grit. Continue to grow in pots, under cover, for a minimum of 2 years before planting out. I do not advise sowing seed directly into the soil. In early summer, take softwood cuttings from new growth (see page 52).

Site This herb only tolerates outdoor temperatures above 40°F (4°C); below this, protection is needed. Plant in a light, free-draining soil in a warm sunny site (against a warm sunny wall is perfect). It grows well in containers using a soil-based substrate with extra grit. Place the container in a warm, light, airy spot, and water well during the growing season.

Maintenance In spring, trim back stems to a point where new growth is developing. (Some years, new growth does not appear until late spring or early summer). In late summer after harvesting the leaves, lightly prune the plant to remove dead flower heads and to reshape it.

Harvesting The best time to pick leaves is when the plant goes into flower. Dry the fresh leaves (see page 72) and store them in a dark glass jar. They will keep their scent for at least 3 years. Harvest fresh flowers and use them as required.

Uses Add leaves to flavor oils and vinegars (see pp.88–89), fruit desserts, gelatin, and cakes. Regular, long-term medicinal use of the herb may cause indigestion or upset stomach.

Aloysia Lemon verbena VERBENACEAE

The uplifting lemon scent of this South American herb can transport you to another world. It was imported into Europe in the eighteenth century by the Spaniards and used to make perfume until cheaper essential oils like lemon grass were substituted. The leaves were also used to perfume and sweeten the water in fingerbowls at banquets. Medicinally, a tea made from 3–5 leaves aids sleep if it is drunk at bedtime; it also helps digestion, and is a mild sedative and calmative.

Aloysia triphylla
LEMON VERBENA, LIPPIA
Half-hardy, deciduous shrub. Height up to 10ft (3m), spread up to 8ft (2.5m) in warm climates. Panicles of tiny white flowers tinged with lilac in summer. The flowers have a light lemon flavor when eaten. The rough-textured, lance-shaped, green leaves have a stronger lemon fragrance and taste.

7IN (17.5CM)

Flowers are white with a hint of lilac, and are slightly lemon-scented.

Leaves are very fragrant, lance-shaped, rough to the touch, and arranged in groups of three around the stem.

Stem is pale beige in color and ridged.

FOR USE IN

The Garden	The Kitchen	The Home
PP. 21, 43, 53, 65, 66	PP. 88, 89	PP. 101, 103, 107, 108, 111

Cultivation

Propagation Sow fresh seeds immediately because they only remain viable for 3 months after harvesting. In early fall, sow in the ground or into seed-plug trays (see page 44) that are placed outside, exposed to all weathers. Seedlings are hardy and do not need protection from frost. Mature plants do not transplant well.

Site Plant in deep moist soil, making sure the roots will be in shade and the flowers in sun. This is a good architectural plant, which gives structure to an herb garden. It is not an ideal potted plant because of its height – up to 8ft (2.5m).

Maintenance Make sure that seedlings and plants do not dry out. Keep well-watered in hot summers. Collect seeds for sowing in late summer. Cut the seedheads off before they drop onto the soil, or you will be inundated with seedlings. In exposed sites, stake long stems to prevent them from breaking.

Harvesting In late spring or early summer, pick young, soft leaves to use fresh. Cut the stems of second-year growth in late spring before the flower heads form to use fresh or preserve as a candy. Collect ripe seeds in early fall.

Uses Stems of second-year growth can be candied or cooked with stewed fruit. Young leaves can be chopped up and added to salads, soups, and stir-fry dishes. The seeds are used in Moroccan cooking.

Caution All angelica species may cause skin photosensitivity or dermatitis when touched. Do not take medicinally if you are suffering from diabetes.

Angelica Angelica APIACEAE

A native of continental Europe, this herb can be found along river banks and in other damp sites. Take care not to confuse it with poisonous hemlock (*Conium maculatum*), which has white flowers and purple spots on the stem. Hemlock leaves also produce a foul smell when crushed. The origin of the species name, *Angelica archangelica*, derives from the story of a monk who, when praying for a cure to the plague, was visited by St. Michael the Archangel, and shown this herb. Medicinally, angelica has antibacterial and antifungal properties, and is used to treat indigestion, anemia, coughs, and colds. A tea made from the young leaves helps alleviate nervous headaches. The stem of the plant is often candied and used to flavor desserts. Angelica is also one of the flavorings in alcoholic drinks, including vermouth, chartreuse, and gin.

Angelica gigas
KOREAN ANGELICA

Hardy, monocarpic (it dies after setting seed). Height up to 4ft (1.4m). It produces spherical crimson umbels with tiny white flowers from late summer until early fall, which are immensely attractive to butterflies. The leaves are shiny, dark green, and divided. It has many medicinal uses.

8IN (20CM)

Stem *is hollow and lightly ribbed. It is the second-year's growth that is used to make candied angelica.*

Flower *is sweetly scented and has a warm, mildly aniseed flavor.*

Leaf *is large, deeply divided, and bright green.*

Angelica archangelica

ANGELICA

Hardy, monocarpic (it dies after setting seed). Height up to 8ft (2.5m) and spread 3ft (1m) in second year. It produces round umbels of sweetly scented greenish-white flowers in late spring to early summer of the second season. It has large, deeply divided, bright green leaves around the base of the plant, which become smaller around the stem. The leaves have a dry flavor with a slightly bitter tang and a hint of aniseed. The leaves, stem, and seeds are all used in cooking.

Cultivation

Propagation In early spring, sow seeds under cover at 60°F (15°C). Germination takes 5–20 days. Or sow seeds in late spring into prepared, open ground, when the air temperature at night stays above 45°F (7°C). Germination takes 2–3 weeks. Thin seedlings to 9in (25cm) apart. In my experience, sowing the seeds directly into open ground is the best method because this plant dislikes being transplanted. Sow in small amounts at a time to provide a constant supply of leaves.

Site Dill favors a well-drained soil and a sunny position sheltered from high winds. Do not plant dill near fennel because they can cross-pollinate and produce an inferior plant. Dill can be grown in large containers, but bear in mind that it dislikes being transplanted. Place the container in a sheltered position in full sun. It does not seem to grow well on kitchen windowsills.

Maintenance After cutting, fertilize with comfrey liquid feed (see page 39) to promote new growth. In winter, dig up any remaining plants. Check that all the seeds have been removed to prevent self-seeding of this invasive plant, and then feed the remaining stalks with compost.

Harvesting In summer, cut back the leaves or the whole plant when it reaches about 1ft (30cm) high. Use the leaves fresh or dry. Preserve in butter, oils, or vinegars (see pages 88–9, 91). Harvest seed when it turns brown, dry well, and store in a dark glass jar (see page 74).

Uses This herb is used to treat dyspepsia, flatulence, and stomachache in adults.

Anethum Dill APIACEAE

Originating in the Middle East, dill can now be found throughout the world, and has naturalized in Europe, North and South America, Asia, and Scandinavia. There is evidence that it has been used for over 5,000 years, and it is mentioned in the Bible as a means of paying taxes. In the Middle Ages dill was used as a protection against witchcraft. Today it is well known as the active ingredient of gripe water, which is used to calm infants with colic or flatulence. Medicinally, a tea made from a teaspoon of dill seeds will ease dyspepsia, flatulence, and stomachache in adults.

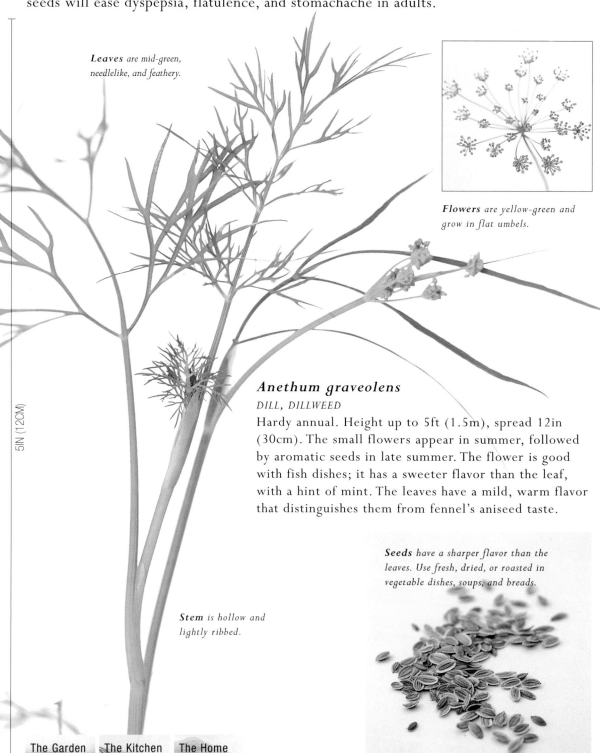

Leaves are mid-green, needlelike, and feathery.

Flowers are yellow-green and grow in flat umbels.

5IN (12CM)

Anethum graveolens
DILL, DILLWEED
Hardy annual. Height up to 5ft (1.5m), spread 12in (30cm). The small flowers appear in summer, followed by aromatic seeds in late summer. The flower is good with fish dishes; it has a sweeter flavor than the leaf, with a hint of mint. The leaves have a mild, warm flavor that distinguishes them from fennel's aniseed taste.

Seeds have a sharper flavor than the leaves. Use fresh, dried, or roasted in vegetable dishes, soups, and breads.

Stem is hollow and lightly ribbed.

FOR USE IN

The Garden
PP. 21, 43, 49, 62, 66

The Kitchen
PP. 85, 87, 89, 90, 91, 94

The Home
PP. 107, 109

Cultivation

Propagation Seeds are viable for one year. Sow in early spring under cover at 60°F (15°C). Germination takes 5–10 days. Or sow seeds in late spring into prepared open ground, when the air temperature at night stays above 45°F (7°C). Germination takes 2–3 weeks. Thin seedlings to 9in (25cm) apart. Chervil plants do not like being transplanted and will bolt and run to seed.

Site Plant in a well-prepared site in a light but not too dry soil, in partial shade. Too much sun in summer will make chervil plants bolt and go to flower; they will also discolor and lose flavor. Chervil can be grown as a container plant in a large pot. Place outside in partial shade and water regularly. This herb does not grow very well on kitchen windowsills.

Maintenance For fresh winter leaves, sow seeds in late summer. Cover with a cloche or horticultural fleece (see page 48) when the weather is wet or the temperature drops below -30°F (1°C).

Harvesting Pick fresh chervil leaves 6–8 weeks after sowing.

Uses This useful culinary herb is one of the four ingredients of "fines herbes;" which include parsley, chives, and tarragon. In winter, late-sown chervil makes a good substitute for parsley. Use fresh leaves in salads, soups, chicken, fish, egg dishes, and sauces.

Anthriscus Chervil APIACEAE

This herb, native to the Middle East and the Caucasus, has been cultivated throughout Europe, North America, and Australia where, in some areas, it has naturalized. It is advisable not to collect chervil from the wild because it is similar in appearance to other plants of the same family, like hemlock, which is deadly poisonous. Chervil was a popular Lenten herb and was eaten on Maundy Thursday for its blood-cleansing and restorative properties. Medicinally, the leaves are very high in vitamin C, magnesium, iron, and carotene. A tea made from the leaves can stimulate digestion.

Anthriscus cerefolium
CHERVIL
Hardy biennial, grown as an annual. Height up to 24in (60cm) and spread 12in (30cm). Clusters of tiny white flowers appear from spring until summer. It has light green leaves that can develop a purple tinge in early fall. The leaf flavor is light, sweet, and slightly aniseed, and resembles a mixture of parsley and myrrh.

Leaf has a slight aniseed flavor.

Leaf is light green and fernlike.

Flowers are tiny and white, very like its close relatives, cow parsley and myrrh.

6IN (15CM)

FOR USE IN

The Garden	The Kitchen	The Home
PP. 21, 43, 49, 62	PP. 84, 86, 90, 94	PP. 108

Cultivation

Propagation This plant is very easy to propagate from root cuttings, taken from spring up until late fall (see page 56). Either place the cuttings directly into a prepared site, 2in (5cm) deep and 12in (30cm) apart, or start the root cuttings off in individual pots, planting them out when the roots are established.

Site Horseradish is invasive and difficult to eradicate from the garden once established. It will tolerate all but the driest of soils. Plant in a light, well-dug, rich, moist soil in a sunny position, or dappled shade. To contain the roots and keep the plant under control, grow it in a container. Make drainage holes in the container, and fill with rich soil. Place in partial shade.

Maintenance In the fall of the third season, after harvest, established clumps benefit from being divided and replanted in well-prepared soil that has been fed with well-rotted manure before replanting.

Harvesting Pick young fresh leaves in spring and early summer. Dig up the root at any time between spring and early fall to use fresh. The strongest-flavored root is produced in the fall. Preserve the prepared root in vinegar.

Uses The fresh raw root is used as a condiment, but it loses all flavor when cooked. Medicinally, the root is a powerful circulatory stimulant with antibiotic properties. Horseradish is a good companion plant for root crops, helping build disease resistance. A spray made from an infusion of the leaves helps to prevent brown rot when applied to apple trees.

Armoracia Horseradish BRASSICACEAE

This robust herb – native of western Asia – has naturalized in many countries and is found on waste ground and roadsides in Britain, North America, and New Zealand. Its common name, "horse," is often used to mean a large, strong, or coarse plant. Horseradish has many excellent culinary and medicinal properties, and it played a major part in my childhood, as I watched my mother grate the fresh root to make horseradish sauce to accompany the Sunday roast. Medicinally, do not use it if your thyroid function is weak, or if you are taking thyroxin. Also avoid continuous dosage if you are pregnant or suffering from kidney problems.

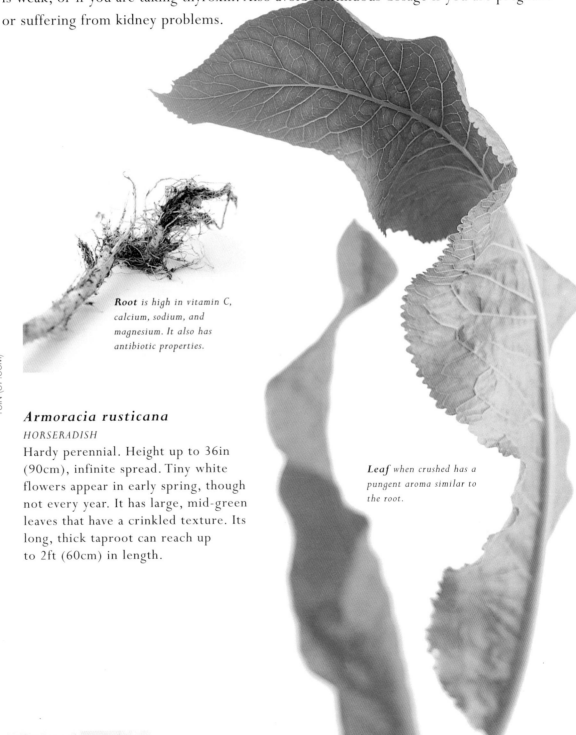

Root is high in vitamin C, calcium, sodium, and magnesium. It also has antibiotic properties.

15IN (37.5CM)

Armoracia rusticana
HORSERADISH
Hardy perennial. Height up to 36in (90cm), infinite spread. Tiny white flowers appear in early spring, though not every year. It has large, mid-green leaves that have a crinkled texture. Its long, thick taproot can reach up to 2ft (60cm) in length.

Leaf when crushed has a pungent aroma similar to the root.

FOR USE IN   The Garden   The Kitchen
PP. 21, 43, 56, 58   PP. 87

Cultivation

Propagation In the fall, sow fresh seeds into a loam-based substrate and place in a cold frame. Germination takes 3–4 weeks. If no germination occurs, place the container outside so the seeds are exposed to all weathers; germination can then take a further 5–7 months or up to 2 years. A more reliable method of propagation is to grow new plants from root cuttings taken from the rhizomes in the spring.

Site Plant in sun or partial shade in an acid or alkaline sandy soil that is rich in humus. Arnica is well suited to rock gardens or medicinal herb gardens and grows well in containers. Use an ericaceous potting substrate. Arnica has creeping roots. In the fall, repot container-grown plants to protect the roots from excessive wet.

Maintenance Dead-head flowers to prolong flowering. In the fall, collect fresh seeds for sowing immediately to provide quick germination.

Harvesting In summer, pick the flowers just before they are fully open for medicinal use. Pick leaves for drying in summer.

Uses In homeopathy, arnica is used to treat symptoms of shock and injury. Arnica cream soothes chilblains, but should not be used if the skin is broken. A tincture can be used to treat angina, but only under supervision from a qualified practitioner. A herbal tobacco can be made from dried arnica leaves.

Caution Arnica should not be taken internally except in a commercially available form or prescribed by a qualified herbalist.

Arnica Arnica ASTERACEAE

This plant is a native of the Rocky Mountains and the Selkirk Mountains of British Columbia. Its name most probably derives from the Greek word "arnakis" meaning "lamb's skin," because of the soft texture of the leaves. It has many medicinal uses and is particularly effective for treating bruises and sprains. The flowers of the species *Arnica chamissonis* are commonly used to make the first-aid remedy. The rhizomes of *A. montana* can also be harvested for the same purpose, which has contributed to *A. montana* becoming an endangered plant in Europe.

Flowers are lightly scented in summer and very attractive to bees.

Stem can be hairy or smooth, depending on planting situation and time of year. It is usually smoother toward the end of the growing season.

Leaf is lightly ribbed, lance-shaped, and slightly velvety to the touch.

5IN (12.5CM)

Arnica chamissonis

ARNICA, MOUNTAIN TOBACCO, NORTH AMERICAN ARNICA
Hardy herbaceous perennial. Height up to 2ft (60cm), spread 6in (15cm). Throughout the summer, it produces medium-sized, single, daisylike, golden-yellow flowers. Its light green oval leaves are slightly hairy. *A. chamissonis* is similar in appearance to *A. montana* — an endangered species.

FOR USE IN

The Garden — PP. 21, 43, 58
The Home — PP. 105, 106

Cultivation

Propagation In spring, sow fresh seeds, but do not cover with compost or perlite. Place under protection at 68°F (20°C). Germination takes 10–20 days. Take softwood cuttings from lush new growth in early summer. Divide established plants in spring every 3–4 years. Replant in a well-prepared site.

Site Plant in well-drained, light soil in a sunny position. Do not grow wormwood near culinary herbs as it can impair their flavor. Both wormwood and southern-wood can be grown in large containers – use a well-draining loam substrate and protect from excessive wet and cold in winter.

Maintenance Cut back wormwood stems to 6in (15cm) in the fall. Cut back southernwood to 12in (30cm). In climates where the temperature drops below 30°F (-2°C), wait until the spring to cut back. In winter, protect plants when the night temperature falls below 23°F (-5°C).

Harvesting In summer, pick the leaves for drying and the flowers just as they open.

Uses Wormwood is best used as a moth repellent (see page 103). Hang bunches of leaves in a chicken coop to deter fleas, lice, and flies (see page 112). The leaves and roots produce a yellow natural dye for textiles.

Artemisia Silver artemisias ASTERACEAE

Artemisia absinthium, a native of Asia and Europe, grows on waste ground, especially near the sea. In folklore, it was said to counteract the effects of poisoning by hemlock, toadstools, and a sea dragon's bite. Also known as wormwood, *A. absinthium* is one of the main ingredients of absinthe – the green, aniseed-flavored alcoholic drink. As its name suggests, wormwood has been used to expel worms for centuries but the pure oil is a strong poison and must be used only with professional guidance.

Artemisia annua
SWEET ANNIE, SWEET WORMWOOD
Hardy annual. Height up to 9ft (3m) and spread up to 4½ft (1.5m). It has tiny yellow flowers clustered in loose panicles in summer and aromatic, finely cut, bright green leaves. It is a very important medicinal herb that is used as an antimalarial agent. It is also a natural herbicide.

Artemisia abrotanum
SOUTHERNWOOD, LAD'S LOVE
Hardy semi-evergreen shrub. Height and spread up to 3ft (1m). Tiny, dull yellow flowers form dense panicles in late summer, though they are rarely present in cool climates. It has aromatic, very finely cut, gray-green leaves. The leaves make one of the best natural moth repellents and a good mosquito repellent when rubbed on the skin.

Artemisia absinthium

WORMWOOD, COMMON WORMWOOD
Hardy herbaceous perennial. Height
3ft (1m) and spread 4ft (1.2 m). It
has tiny, insignificant yellow flowers
in summer and aromatic, divided,
gray-green leaves. The leaves and
flowers are very bitter, with a
characteristic musky, aromatic smell.

Flowers *look like tiny yellow powder puffs.*

Leaf, *when looked at closely, is covered with soft gray down.*

Stem *is covered with fine silky hairs.*

6IN (15CM)

Cultivation

Propagation In summer take cuttings of French tarragon (*A. dracunculus*) and mugwort (*A. vulgaris*) from the growing tips. Alternatively, take root cuttings in spring. When you take root cuttings, make sure you include a growing nodule. Only hardy Russian tarragon (*A. dracunculoides*) can be grown successfully from seed in spring. French tarragon will not set seed in cold climates.

Site Plant in well-drained soil in a sunny position. Protect from excessive wet and cold in winter. It grows well in containers – use a soil-based substrate, and protect from excessive wet and cold. Cut watering down to a minimum in winter and place in a frostfree site.

Maintenance To maintain flavor, divide established plants every other year. Replant in well-prepared site. Trim the plant in early summer to produce new growth for late-summer cooking. It can suffer from a rust fungus called *Puccinia*. Easily identified, the leaves develop round rust-colored spots on the underside. Dig up the plant and burn it. The virus lives on in the soil, so do not plant chives, mint, or tarragon, which are all prone to the disease.

Harvesting In early spring, pick fresh leaves and stalks to make tarragon vinegar (see page 89). Pick leaves to use fresh throughout the growing season.

Uses An essential ingredient of Béarnaise sauce, tarragon combines well with chicken, fish, rice, and salads. Tarragon is a mild anesthetic and provides relief from toothache.

Artemisia Green-leaf artemisias ASTERACEAE

The great culinary herb *Artemisia dracunculus* was used excessively by Catherine of Aragon, and was cited as a reason for divorce by Henry VIII. A native of southern Europe, true French tarragon (*A. dracunculus*) has a unique, light aniseed flavor, with a hint of warmth. It is not the same as Russian tarragon (*A. dracunculoides*) which has a paler, larger leaf and a pungent, slightly bitter flavor. Medicinally French tarragon was used to heal snakebite and remove poisonous venom. A tea made from tarragon can help relieve insomnia and constipation, and aids digestion.

Artemisia vulgaris
MUGWORT

Hardy herbaceous perennial. Height up to 4ft (1.2m) and spread 18in (45cm). Panicles of tiny reddish-brown flowers appear in summer. The leaves are dark green, serrated, and downy. The Japanese use the leaves to make *Moxas*, a cure for rheumatism. It was one of the nine sacred herbs of the Druids and was believed to offer protection against evil and poisons.

Leaf *is covered in fine hairs — a characteristic of the* Artemisia *genus.*

5IN (12CM)

Stem *in early spring is lush and green, but as the season progresses, it turns woodier.*

Artemisia dracunculus
FRENCH TARRAGON
Hardy herbaceous perennial. Height 3ft (90cm) and spread 18in (45cm). Sprays of tiny yellow flowers appear in summer in warm climates, though rarely in cool climates. It has aromatic, long, narrow, and smooth green leaves, which when crushed release a warm aroma.

Cultivation

Propagation In early spring, sow seeds into pots under protection at 68°F (20°C). Germination takes 5–14 days. Alternatively, sow seeds in late spring into prepared open ground, when the air temperature at night does not drop below 45°F (7°C). Germination takes 2–3 weeks. Thin seedlings to 18in (45cm) apart. Once pot-grown seedlings are large enough to handle, plant them out in their final position; borage plants produce a long taproot and do not like being disturbed.

Site Borage tolerates most soils including clay, but prefers well-drained, light, poor soil in a sunny position. If the soil is too rich, it may grow tall and weak, and need staking. For this reason, it does not make a good container-grown plant.

Maintenance Borage self-seeds easily, especially in light soils. Once the petals of the flowers drop, the seeds appear. Collect those you want to propagate for next year's plants, and carefully remove any others.

Harvesting Pick fresh flowers just as they open fully. The best way to preserve the flowers is by freezing them in ice cube trays (see page 83). Pick fresh young leaves of *B. officinalis* throughout the season.

Uses Medicinally, the oil made from borage seeds is high in polyunsaturated fats. It is used to treat eczema, premenstrual complaints, and rheumatic problems. The fresh leaves of *B. officinalis* taste good added to salads, soups, and with cream cheese or yogurt.

Borago Borage BORAGINACEAE

This very pretty flowering herb originated in the Mediterranean, where it can be found growing on waste land. It has now spread and naturalized in North America and northern Europe. Historically, it was given to young Roman soldiers for courage and comfort, and borage flowers were given to the Crusaders – floated in stirrup cups – for the same reason. I am not sure about courage, but it raises the spirits to see these pretty summer flowers. It has several culinary and medicinal uses, but eaten excessively it can cause liver damage. The fresh leaves may cause contact dermatitis.

6IN (15CM)

Flower is blue or white and star-shaped, with black stamens that look like a bird's beak.

Borago officinalis
BORAGE, STAR FLOWER
Hardy annual. Height and spread 24in (60cm). Loose racemes of blue star-shaped flowers with black stamens in early summer until the first frosts. The mid-green leaves are bristly, oval or oblong in shape, and succulent.

Leaf is covered in tiny bristly hairs that dissolve when eaten.

Borago pygmaea
PROSTRATE BORAGE, CORSICAN BORAGE
Hardy perennial. Height and spread 18in (45cm). It has small, star-shaped, bright blue flowers that fade to pink with age, and very bristly, oval, dark green leaves, which grow in basal rosettes. Only the flowers of this species are edible.

Stem is hollow and covered with fine prickles.

FOR USE IN

The Garden — PP. 21, 43, 49, 62, 66

The Kitchen — PP. 83, 85

The Home — PP. 109

Cultivation

Propagation Take cuttings from new growth in spring and propagate in the shade. Rooting takes 3–4 months, but with warm 70°F (21°C) shady conditions, it takes only 6–8 weeks. Keep the cuttings moist but not over-wet. Alternatively, take semi-ripe cuttings in late summer and place in shade. Rooting should occur in 8–12 weeks.

Site Box favors an alkaline chalk or limestone soil, but it will adapt to all but water-logged conditions, in sun or partial shade. It grows well in containers. Use a soil-based substrate and feed with liquid fertilizer like seaweed or comfrey in the growing season. *B. sempervirens* makes a good hedge. Prepare a trench with well-rotted manure and plant 15–18in (37–45cm) apart.

Maintenance Cut box hedges in late spring, after the chance of frost has past, and again in early fall Slow-growing varieties only need trimming once, in summer. In fall, feed with well-rotted manure or a layer of fresh comfrey leaves (see page 37). If plants develop box blight, they will die back and leaves will become crisp and brown. Dig up infected plants and burn. Feed any remaining plants weekly with liquid comfrey (see page 39) – this can help to build up the plant's resistance.

Harvesting Cut sprigs from spring until late fall to use in floral arrangements.

Uses Box is used medicinally by homoeopaths, only under supervision, as a tincture to treat rheumatism and urinary tract infections. Boxwood is used by cabinetmakers and wood turners to make furniture and chess pieces.

Buxus BOX BUXACEAE

This ancient shrub was once widespread throughout Europe, eastern Asia, and North Africa. It was much in demand for its wood, which is close-grained and does not warp in adverse conditions, making it the ideal lumber for navigational instruments and printing blocks. Nowadays, box is better known as a traditional knot garden hedge, whose clipped leaves have a pungent smell. All parts of the plant are poisonous, especially the leaves and seeds, and animals such as goats, cows, and sheep have died from eating the leaves.

Buxus sempervirens
BOX, COMMON BOX
Hardy evergreen shrub, varying from bush to tree. Height up to 27ft (9m) and spread up to 15ft (5m). Small oblong, glossy, dark green leaves. Tiny, pale green flowers in early summer. This plant is slow-growing and long-lived. It makes an ideal hedging plant.

8IN (17.5CM)

Leaf is glossy on the upper surface, dull on the underside. It turns orange-brown when it is deficient in minerals.

Buxus sempervirens
'Latifolia Maculata' AGM
VARIEGATED GOLDEN BOX
Hardy evergreen shrub. Height and spread up to 3ft (1m). It has oval, shiny green leaves splashed with gold. All new growth is very golden in the spring. Good for hedging.

Cultivation

Propagation In early spring, sow seeds under protection at 68°F (20°C). Germination takes 5–14 days. Or sow seeds in late spring into prepared open ground when the air temperature does not fall below 41°F (5°C) at night.

Site Plant in any soil, except poor draining waterlogged soil, in a sunny position. They grow well in containers and combine well with other herbs.

Maintenance To encourage continuous flowering, dead-head regularly. In light soils, pot marigold will self-seed abundantly – otherwise, it is manageable. Beware of slug attack and remove them from the young plants. In late summer and early fall, leaves may contract powdery mildew. Destroy the affected leaves to prevent the disease from spreading.

Harvesting Pick fresh flowers as they open in early summer. Harvest young leaves to use fresh in salads.

Uses The flower petals are used to make a natural gold-colored food dye for butter, biscuits, and omelets. Add young leaves to salads – the term "pot" marigold, refers to its use in the cooking pot. Medicinally, marigold is known as a remedy for skin complaints; it is effective for most minor skin problems, cuts, grazes, wounds, inflamed skin including minor burns, sunburn, and fungal conditions like athlete's foot, yeast, and ringworm. It also helps to alleviate diaper rash. The sap from the plant stem has the reputation for removing warts, corns, and calluses.

Calendula Pot marigold ASTERACEAE

This well-known herb has been widely used in Arab and Indian cultures as a medicine, food colorant, and cosmetic. In medieval times, the flowers were considered an emblem of love; if marigolds appeared in your dreams, they were an omen of good things to come. Just looking at the sunny orange flowers was thought to cheer the spirits, which, in my opinion, they still do today. Excellent companion plants in the organic garden, pot marigolds (*Calendula officinalis*) deter asparagus beetles and tomato horn worms, but are not to be confused with *Tagetes* species see page 248.

Calendula officinalis
POT MARIGOLD, MARIGOLD
Hardy annual. Height and spread up to 24in (60cm). Large orange or yellow, daisylike, single or double flowers appear from spring until the first frosts. The light green, lance-shaped leaves are lightly aromatic. The flowers are sensitive to temperature variation and dampness – open flowers forecast a fine day ahead.

8IN (20CM)

Leaf *has a mild aromatic scent when crushed.*

Flower *petals have a warm flavor when used in cooking.*

Pot marigold *deters pests like asparagus beetle, and tomato horn worms.*

The Garden	The Kitchen	The Home
PP. 21, 43, 49, 62	PP. 85	PP. 105, 106, 107

Calomeria Incense plant ASTERACEAE

I was given my first incense plant by a passionate plant collector. It has become rare in Britain, for it is no longer grown in parks or large private estates. It is a most fantastic plant for scent – in flower, it will perfume the whole glasshouse and surrounding area – though, in full flower, its perfume can cause breathing difficulties. Historically, the plant arrived in England from Australia with the plant collector Sir Joseph Banks who gave some seed to Lady Hume (hence its former name *Humea elegans*). The leaves and bracts can cause skin irritation and burns.

Cultivation

Propagation To achieve a very high germination rate, I suggest placing the dry seeds in a pillowcase and tumble drying them on high for 10–15 minutes. In late fall, sow the seeds on the surface of the substrate. Do not cover. Place in a light, well-aired, frostfree position. Germination takes 16–20 weeks. When the seedlings are large enough to handle, plant in a pot and grow to 12in (30cm) tall. Then pot up one size at a time, or plant out when the night temperature does not fall below 41ºF (5ºC). Take care not to transfer the plant to a larger pot size, or plant it outdoors too early, or you may cause it to "damp off." This Madagascan plant is difficult to propagate in a cool climate.

Site Plant in well-drained soil in a sunny position. Choose a site where people will not brush against this plant, as it may burn their skin. It also grows well in a container, using a soil-based substrate. Feed the young plant regularly from the appearance of the first bract.

Maintenance This plant is very popular with whitefly aphids when grown as a container plant. At the first sign of this pest on the leaf (look for slight curling), treat with a commercial horticultural soap according to the manufacturer's instructions.

Harvesting Pick the coral bracts for drying as soon as the flowers appear.

Uses The dried flowers look wonderful and last a long time in dried floral displays. They are also very useful in potpourri (see page 102).

Caution The fresh leaves and bracts can cause skin irritation and burns. The flowers do not trigger an allergic reaction.

FOR USE IN

The Garden
PP. 21, 43, 49, 67

Calomeria amaranthoides (Humea elegans)
INCENSE PLANT, PLUME BUSH
Half-hardy biennial. Height up to 6ft (1.8m), spread 3ft (90cm). Aromatic, delicate, coral bracts surround small, cream daisylike flowers and cascade from thin branches in summer. The mid-green leaves are large and oblong in shape, and aromatic.

Flowers are cream-colored, surrounded by coral bracts.

Stem is strong, slightly sticky, and green.

Leaves are highly aromatic, lightly textured, and larger around the plant base.

16IN (40CM)

Cultivation

Propagation Sow fresh seeds in early fall into prepared ground, when the air temperature does not fall below 45°F (7°C) at night. Germination takes 2–3 weeks. Or sow fresh seeds in early spring under protection at 60°F (15°C). Germination will take 5–10 days. Plant out as soon as possible with minimal root disturbance. It is important to use fresh seed because it only remains viable for one year.

Site Plant in a fertile, well-drained soil, in a sunny position. Thin to 8in (20cm) apart. Caraway is not suited to container growing.

Maintenance In the fall, clear weeds from around first-year plants. When the seeds have been harvested in the second fall, dig over the area well. If planting out young plants in spring, cover the plants with horticultural fleece to protect them from carrot-root fly. Always rotate this crop to prevent attack from carrot-root fly.

Harvesting Pick fresh young leaves of the first-year crop to use in salads. Harvest seeds in late summer from the second-year crop and dry well.

Uses The young leaves have a mild aniseed flavor and taste good in salad and soup. Use seeds sparingly or they may dominate other flavors. A small dish of seeds at the end of a spicy meal both sweetens the breath and aids digestion. Medicinally, caraway is an antispasmodic, diuretic, and expectorant. It is a mild remedy and is suitable for children, especially in cough remedies or to relieve colic.

Carum Caraway APIACEAE

I find it reassuring that this small biennial herb has survived and is still grown today for use in the kitchen and as a medicinal herb. Records show that it was used in the Stone Age, and it has been found in Egyptian tombs and at the ancient caravan stops along the Silk Road trade route. In Elizabethan feasts, eating caraway seeds became a traditional way to finish the banquet, and the herb was also reputed to ward off witches and to prevent lovers from straying. I like using the seeds and leaves in the kitchen for their flavor, and I love to grow the herb for its delicately pretty flowers.

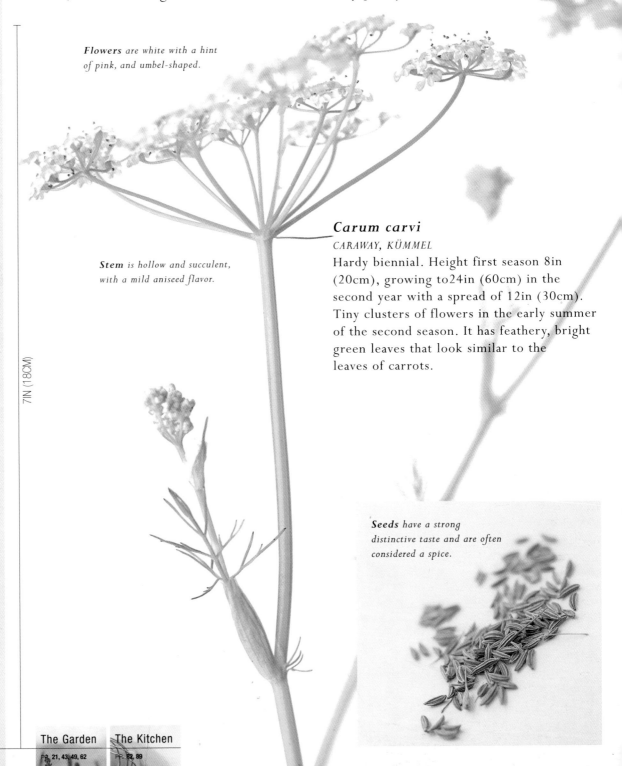

Flowers are white with a hint of pink, and umbel-shaped.

Stem is hollow and succulent, with a mild aniseed flavor.

7IN (18CM)

Carum carvi
CARAWAY, KÜMMEL
Hardy biennial. Height first season 8in (20cm), growing to 24in (60cm) in the second year with a spread of 12in (30cm). Tiny clusters of flowers in the early summer of the second season. It has feathery, bright green leaves that look similar to the leaves of carrots.

Seeds have a strong distinctive taste and are often considered a spice.

Cultivation

Propagation Sow seeds in spring under protection at 68°F (20°C). Germination takes 14–20 days, but can be erratic. Take softwood cuttings in early summer. When the cuttings have rooted, pot up, and winter in a greenhouse or cold frame. Plant out the following spring at 3ft (1m) intervals.

Site Plant in a warm sunny site against a south-facing wall in well-drained soil. In cool climates, when the night temperature falls below 29°F (-2°C), cover the plant with horticultural fleece, or bring it into a cool greenhouse or conservatory. In cold climates, it grows well as a container plant. Use a soil-based substrate. Trim the container plant to maintain its shape and to prevent it from becoming too tall.

Maintenance Cut back after flowering to keep the plant's shape and encourage new growth. Protect from hard frost. When grown as a container plant, the leaves can be prone to aphids. Treat by introducing a predator or with horticultural soap, according to the manufacturer's instructions.

Harvesting Pick leaves for drying before the plant flowers. Harvest the flowers for drying as soon as they appear. Pick the seedheads when the flower petals have dropped. Dried, they look good in flower arrangements.

Uses Balm of Gilead leaves can be used in hot water to make an infusion to clear the head or blocked nasal passages. An infusion of the leaves added to bath water has an invigorating effect. The leaves can be rubbed directly onto the skin as a mosquito repellent. Dried leaves can be added to potpourri (see page 102).

FOR USE IN

The Garden
PP. 21, 43, 53, 66

Cedronella Balm of Gilead LAMIACEAE

Known as "Balm of Gilead," *Cedronella canariensis* is native to the Canary Islands. It has a strong eucalyptus scent similar to other plants with "balsam" as part of their name (such as *Populus balsamifera* or *Commiphora opobalsamum*), which may be the explanation for why they share the same common name. When passing a plant, take the chance to rub some of the leaves between your hands and then sniff their head-clearing scent. Allow the plants to form seedheads to hear the seeds rattling in the breeze. This lovely aromatic herb also has the reputation of being an aphrodisiac.

Flower varies in color from pale pink to mauve and is followed by black seedheads.

The crushed leaf clears the head if you have a cold or are suffering from sinus problems.

Cedronella canariensis syn. *C. triphylla*

BALM OF GILEAD, CANARY BALM
Half-hardy herbaceous perennial. Height 3ft (1m), spread 2ft (60cm). Pink to pale mauve two-lipped flowers appear in summer, followed by black seedheads. The leaves are three-lobed and tooth-edged, and have a strong eucalyptus scent.

Leaf has a distinct scent of eucalyptus.

2IN (5CM)

Cultivation

Propagation For best results, sow seeds in open ground, when the air temperature does not fall below 50°F (10°C) at night. Germination will take 14–21 days.

Site Plant in well-drained soil in a sunny position. If you wish to create a natural meadow effect, clear all grasses and weeds and leave a 12in (30cm) square area for each plant. Sow 5 seeds per patch but thin out once established, leaving 2 plants per area. In the fall, let the plants die back and self-seed naturally. Bachelor's buttons can be grown in large containers using a soil-based substrate. Tie the fragile stems together for support and to minimize damage from high winds or heavy rain.

Maintenance To produce straight stems for drying or flower arranging, you will need to support bachelor's button stems with sticks or, if the plants have been sown in a row, with netting.

Harvesting Bachelor's buttons mature and fade within a few days of flowering. Pick the flowers when they are half open, and before the center stamens are visible. When drying flowers, tie bunches of ten stems together and dry them fast; otherwise, the color will fade and their petals disintegrate.

Uses The flowers are edible. Medicinally it is a tonic and stimulant.

Centaurea Bachelor's buttons ASTERACEAE

This European wildflower almost became extinct in Britain in the 1970s as a result of the introduction of chemical weed controls in farming. The French eyewash "Eau de Casselunettes" was made from these flowers, because of their eye-brightening properties. Juice extracted from the petals makes a blue ink and a watercolor pigment. I adore the stunning blue flowers of this herb. They have little scent but dry very well, and can be added to potpourri for their attractive appearance. The bright blue blooms also attract bees into the garden, which helps with pollination.

Centaurea cyanus
BACHELOR'S BUTTONS, CORNFLOWER, BLUE BOTTLE

Hardy annual. Height 24in (60cm) and spread 6in (15cm). Single and double blue daisylike flowers in summer. The gray-green leaves are lance-shaped. The lower leaves are often toothed and covered with fine hairs. There are hybrids with the same habit that have pink, white, or purple flowers.

Flower bud is covered in tiny hairs.

Flower is such a striking color that "cornflower blue" has become the commonly used term for this shade of blue. They have very little scent.

Stem is narrow but surprisingly tough — in the days of harvesting by hand, it was known to make a sickle blunt.

6IN (15CM)

FOR USE IN

The Garden
PP. 21, 43, 49

The Home
PP. 111

Cultivation

Propagation Gotu kola is easily grown from cuttings. Take the cutting at the point where the leaf joins the stem, from spring until late summer. Or propagate it by division (see page 57) in summer. It cannot be grown from seed in cold climates.

Site In tropical or sub-tropical climates, it will grow outdoors all year round. In cooler and cold climates it will tolerate temperatures down to 50°F (10°C) before it needs protection. It will grow in a container. Plant in a soil-based substrate in partial shade.

Maintenance Protect from cold rain, frost, and snow. Repot every season and do not let the substrate dry out in the growing season. In warm summer weather, place the container outside. Container-grown plants are prone to red spider mite. Introduce *Phytoseiulus persimilis* – its natural predator – or treat the whole plant, stem included, with a commercial horticultural soap according to the manufacturer's instructions.

Harvesting From spring until late summer, cut very young leaves to use fresh in cooking, and mature leaves for use in herbal medicine.

Uses A rejuvenating diuretic herb that clears toxins and reduces inflammation. It is used in the treatment of rheumatism and rheumatoid arthritis. In India the fresh leaves are given to children for dysentery. It is also used there to help concentration and to treat leprosy. As a beauty aid, it stimulates the production of collagen and helps improve the tone of veins near the surface of the skin. It is an ingredient in manufactured face creams.

Centella Gotu kola APIACEAE

Leaves *can vary from bright green to rusty orange, depending on air temperature and soil type.*

Stem *is thin and creeping.*

Flowers *are small and magenta-colored, resembling powder puffs.*

8IN (20CM)

Centella asiatica

GOTU KOLA, PENNYWORT, SPADELEAF
Tender perennial. Height 3½in (8cm). A creeping plant with an indefinite spread. Tiny magenta flowers appear in summer, but you have to look carefully under the leaves to see the small flowers. The leaves are bright green and kidney-shaped with indented margins. Although edible, the leaves are slightly dry and tough in texture, and have a bittersweet flavor. They are used in Sri Lanka and India as a vegetable.

This is an important medicinal herb, native to subtropical and tropical India, Pakistan, Sri Lanka, and South Africa, where it can be found growing in swampy areas including paddy fields. It was traditionally used to help wound healing and slow the progress of leprosy. In India, it is a key herb in Ayurvedic medicine, but it did not become important in western medicine until the 1800s.

Caution: Excessive use of this herb taken internally or externally can cause itching, headaches, and even unconsciousness. Avoid if you are pregnant or nursing, using tranquilizers or sedatives, or have an overactive thyroid.

FOR USE IN

The Garden
PP. 21, 43, 67

The Home
PP. 107

Cultivation

Propagation Chamomile has very fine seeds, which may wash away when sown in the ground, so it is best started in early spring under protection at 65°F (18°C). Germination takes 14–20 days. Take cuttings in spring and fall from the offsets. Divide established plants in spring, replanting in a well-prepared site.

Site Although chamomile adapts to most soils, except wet, it favors well-drained soil in a sunny position. All *Chamaemelum* species grow well in containers in a soil-based substrate.

Maintenance Cut back after flowering to encourage new growth and to prevent the plant from becoming straggly. If you are making a chamomile lawn, do not let the plants dry out in summer. Roll once a week through the growing season.

Harvesting Pick the flowers just as they open fully, to use fresh or to dry.

Uses Renowned for its sedative properties, a tea made from the fresh or dry flowers relieves insomnia, digestive disorders, travel sickness, and hyperactivity in children. Use a chamomile infusion as a gargle for mouth ulcers or as an eyewash. This infusion can also be applied to the skin to soothe burns. A hair rinse made with chamomile flowers lightens fair hair. Chamomile is known as the "Physician Plant" – because when planted next to sick plants, it helps them revive. A spray made from the leaves and flowers helps prevent "damping off" of seedlings. Fresh chamomile leaves can also be added to the compost heap to help activate the process of decomposition (see page 37).

Chamaemelum Chamomile ASTERACEAE

Chamomile species can be a bit confusing because a number of different plants share the same common name. There is dyers' chamomile (*Anthemis tinctoria*), which produces bright yellow through to olive natural dye colors for textiles; wild chamomile (*Matricaria recutita*), which is principally used in medicine; and there is chamomile (*Chamaemelum nobile*), which is one of our most favorite old garden herbs. The delicate flowers are used fresh or dried to make a calming herbal tea that can be taken for insomnia and digestive disorders.

Chamaemelum nobile 'Treneague'
LAWN CHAMOMILE

Hardy evergreen perennial. Height 2in (6cm) and spread 6in (15cm). Non-flowering, it has finely divided, highly aromatic leaves. It is ideal for creating a chamomile lawn because it spreads to form a ground cover that does not need mowing. If grown as a lawn, roll once a week throughout the growing season, to encourage the creeping stems to root into the ground, avoiding brown patches. Lawn chamomile can only be propagated from cuttings.

Chamaemelum nobile 'Flore Pleno'
DOUBLE-FLOWERED CHAMOMILE

Hardy evergreen perennial. Height 3in (8cm) and spread 12in (30cm). Produces small, double daisylike flowers throughout the summer and dense, aromatic, finely divided foliage. It can provide good ground cover for lawn areas and between paving stones. Harvest the flower heads just as they open in summer and use fresh.

FOR USE IN | The Garden PP. 21, 43, 49, 53, 58 | The Kitchen PP. 82 | The Home PP. 105, 106, 107, 108, 109, 110, 111, 113

Flower *is daisylike with a yellow center and a light scent.*

8IN (20CM)

Stem *of the flower has individual leaves spaced along its length.*

Leaf *is finely divided and very aromatic when crushed.*

Chamaemelum nobile
CHAMOMILE, ROMAN CHAMOMILE
Hardy evergreen perennial. Height 4in (10cm) in the green and 12in (30cm) when in flower. Spread 18in (45cm). It produces large, single, white daisylike flowers throughout the summer months. The finely divided foliage is green and sweet-smelling when crushed underfoot or between the fingertips.

148

Cultivation

Propagation Sow seeds in early spring, under cover at 65°F (18°C). Germination takes 14–20 days. Or, sow seeds in late spring, when the air temperature at night does not fall below 45°F (7°C). Sow seeds into prepared open ground, in ½in (1cm) drills. Leave 18in (45cm) between rows, and cover the seed with ¼in (6mm) soil. Germination takes 2–3 weeks. Thin seedlings to 12in (30cm) apart. In spring, divide established plants of perennial species only. Replant into a prepared site that has been fed with well-rotted manure.

Site For a good leaf crop, plant in soil that has been fed the previous fall with rotted manure. It will tolerate most soil conditions except waterlogged soils, but it favors free-draining soil and a sunny position. It will grow well in containers in a loam-based substrate.

Maintenance Keep well-watered in the summer months. Feed the soil in the fall with well-rotted manure. Renew perennial species every 3–4 years. Collect seeds or cut back in late summer to early fall to prevent self-seeding.

Harvesting Pick leaves to use fresh in spring until late summer. Pick seeds in late summer, just as they ripen. Dry and store (see page 74).

Uses The young leaves are rich in iron, calcium, and vitamin B1 and C, and can be added to salads. Treat mature leaves like spinach. Steam the flowers and eat like asparagus. Ground seeds can be used as flour. The seeds, ground and made into a tea, also have a gentle laxative effect.

FOR USE IN

The Garden
pp. 21, 43, 49, 58, 62

Chenopodium Goosefoot CHENOPODIACEAE

When I first came across "Good King Henry," I was intrigued by its unusual name and wanted to find out more – it is one of the reasons I became an herb farmer – so I have a special affection for this plant. I wondered whether there was a "Bad Henry" and how this herb that looked like spinach could be used in cooking. I have since discovered that this unassuming plant is rich in vitamins and that the "Bad Henry" is, in fact, *Mercurialis perennis* (Dog Mercury), a poisonous woodland plant.

Chenopodium bonus-henricus
GOOD KING HENRY
Hardy herbaceous perennial. Height 24in (60cm) and spread 18in (45cm). It produces tiny greenish-yellow flowers in summer. The leaves are mid-green, large, and arrow-shaped. Like spinach, you can eat the young leaves raw or cook them. The plant is also used to fatten poultry and as a remedy for coughs in sheep.

Leaf is typical of Chenopodium *species. It is arrow-shaped with serrated edges.*

6IN (15CM)

Stem becomes coarse with age.

Young leaves at center are magenta in color.

Chenopodium giganteum
TREE SPINACH, GIANT GOOSEFOOT
Hardy annual. Height up to 6ft (2m), spread 18in (45cm). Tiny greenish flowers appear in summer. The leaves are arrow-shaped with serrated edges. The young leaves in the center of the plant are a wonderful magenta color and fade to green with age. The young leaves can be eaten raw in salads or cooked like spinach, when the leaf color reverts to green.

Cichorium Chicory ASTERACEAE

Chicory was first used by the ancient Egyptians as a medicinal herb, vegetable, and salad plant. In the Napoleonic era, roasted chicory roots were found to make an ideal coffee substitute. The leaves of chicory have a mild, bitter flavor and are excellent in salads. In winter, leaves are often blanched, a way of forcing the plant to produce leaves at that time of year. The edible flowers are pretty and can add visual interest to a salad or rice bowl.

Cultivation

Propagation Sow seeds in spring under cover at 60°F (15°C). Germination takes 5–10 days. Or sow seeds in summer into prepared open ground. Germination takes 2–3 weeks. Thin seedlings to 4–12in (10–30cm) apart, closer together for leaves, farther apart for flowers as it needs space to run to flower.

Site Chicory prefers a light, alkaline soil, though it will adapt to all but heavy clay. Plant in a sunny site. This tall plant is not suited to growing in containers.

Maintenance In the fall, cut down the flowering stems and collect seeds for next year's sowing. Dig in well-rotted manure. If you want substantial roots, do not allow the plant to flower. To force the plant to produce leaves in winter, dig up some of the roots in late fall, and cut off the plant tops to just above ground level. Plant the roots in a box filled with loam-based substrate so the crowns sit at soil level. Water well and keep the plants in the dark with the temperature above 50°F (10°C). In 4–6 weeks the root will produce 6–8in (15–20cm) long chicons (blanched leaves).

Harvesting Pick leaves to use fresh from summer on. Pick fresh flowers from midsummer from second-year plants. Pick fresh chicons (blanched leaves) to use in salads as required. After one hour in daylight, they become limp.

Uses Chicory is a gentle tonic that increases the flow of bile. A tea made from the leaves is good for the liver and digestive tract.

Caution Medicinally, it should be used with care as excessive use impairs the function of the retina.

FOR USE IN

Bract is coarsely toothed.

Flowers open to the sun and close five hours later. They are usually blue, but can be pink or white.

8IN (20CM)

Cichorium intybus

CHICORY, SUCCORY

Hardy perennial. Height 3ft (1m) and spread 1ft (30cm). In the second season, it produces clear, blue, single flowers from summer until early fall. The oval, mid-green leaves are coarsely toothed with tiny hairs on the underside.

The Garden   The Kitchen

PP. 21, 43, 49, 62   PP. 83

Cultivation

Propagation Sow seeds in early spring under protection at 65°F (18°C). Germination takes 5–10 days. Or sow seeds in late spring into prepared open ground when the air temperature at night remains above 45°F (7°C). Germination takes 2–3 weeks. Thin seedlings to 2in (5cm) intervals for a leaf crop, or 9in (23cm) apart for a seed crop (seed plants need more space). In my opinion, sowing the seeds direct into the open ground gives the best crop. Coriander does not like to be transplanted, and may bolt and run to seed. Sow in small amounts at weekly intervals to give a constant supply of leaves.

Site Plant in light, well-drained soil in a sunny position. This plant dislikes damp and humid conditions. *Coriandrum sativum* 'Leisure' is the one variety of coriander that grows well in containers. It produces a good amount of leaves and is slow to run to seed.

Maintenance As the coriander seeds ripen, support plant stems with stakes because they become top-heavy. Once the seed is harvested, pull up the plant and dig over the plot.

Harvesting From late spring until late summer, cut the fresh leaves and eat as required – they do not store well. Pick flowers to use fresh throughout the summer. Harvest seeds from summer on.

Uses Medicinally, coriander stimulates the appetite. Add the larger leaves only at the end of cooking as a condiment and garnish.

Coriandrum Coriander APIACEAE

This important culinary and medicinal herb has been cultivated for over 3,000 years and is mentioned in the Old Testament. The Chinese believed it bestowed immortality, and in the Middle Ages, it was an ingredient of love potions. Coriander is an interesting culinary plant because its seeds and leaves have two distinctly different flavors, and the whole plant is edible. The seed is warm, aromatic with a hint of orange, whereas the leaf is pungent and oily, with a hint of earth in its distinctive taste. *Coriandrum sativum* has wonderful leaf flavour and is a good species to grow for cooking.

Coriandrum sativum
CORIANDER, CILANTRO
Annual. Height 24in (60cm) and spread 9in (23cm). It bears white flowers in summer followed by round seeds. The first and lower leaves are broad and scalloped, with a strong scent and flavor; the upper leaves are finely cut with a pungent taste.

6IN (15CM)

Flowers are white and appear in the summer.

Seeds are aromatic with a mild orange flavor. Use whole or crushed.

Stem is weak and needs staking when seeds begin to form.

Leaf of the first growth, before flowering, is the one used in cooking. It is pungent, oily with a hint of earth.

The Garden | The Kitchen
PP. 21, 43, 49, 62 | PP. 91, 92

Cultivation

Propagation Sow fresh seeds in the fall under protection at 50°F (10°C). Germination takes 2–3 weeks. If there is no germination within that period, place the container in a refrigerator for 4 weeks to stratify the seeds, then return to a protected environment. Germination should occur within 4–6 weeks. During winter, keep seedlings in a frostfree environment and plant out the following spring. Propagate established plants by division (see page 57) in spring. Replant in a well-prepared site.

Site Sea fennel favors a well-drained site with extra grit added to the soil. Plant in a sunny position and protect from cold winds. Protect from hard frosts and temperatures below 23°F (-5°C). Do not mulch or feed with well-rotted manure. This plant grows well in containers in a soil-based substrate mixed equally with grit.

Maintenance In the fall, collect seeds for immediate sowing. Protect from frosts.

Harvesting Pick the leaves in early summer to use fresh or to pickle.

Uses This plant is rich in sulfates, iodine compounds, and pectin. Medicinally, it relieves flatulence, eases digestion, and is a diuretic. There is research into its uses for treating obesity. The leaves can be eaten in salads, cooked in butter, or used to make sauces and a pickle that is very aromatic. The leaves also have a high vitamin C content, and contain a fragrant oil which is rich in eugenol and other fragrant substances that are widely used in modern perfumery and medicine.

Crithmum Sea fennel APIACEAE

This seaside herb, found growing in cliffs, rocks, and at the water's edge, is a native of the Atlantic, Mediterranean, and the Black Sea, where it has been dedicated to Saint Peter, the patron saint of fishermen. It has been used as a vegetable for centuries. I first saw it growing wild on a beach vacation with my children. Having crushed the salty, succulent leaves between my fingertips, I was sure it was an herb and was delighted to find that I could use it in cooking. I now grow it successfully away from its natural habitat.

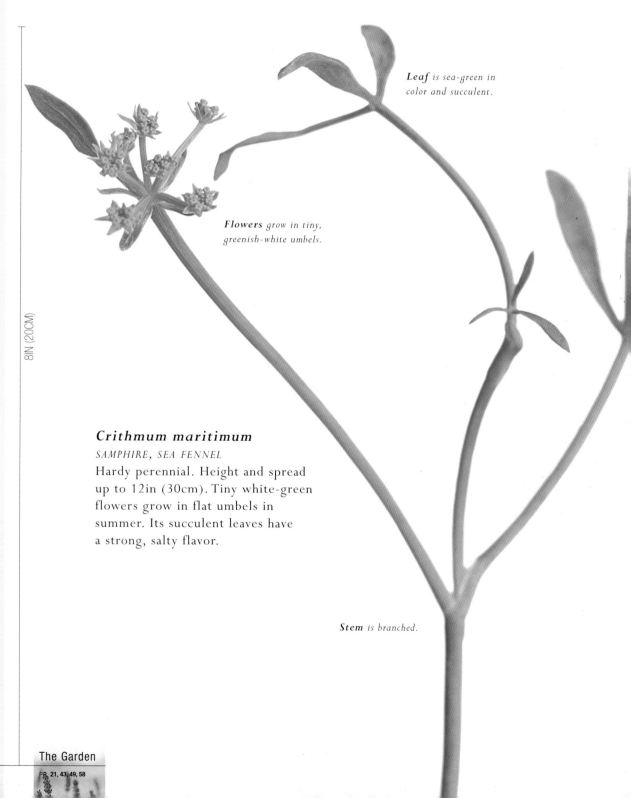

Leaf is sea-green in color and succulent.

Flowers grow in tiny, greenish-white umbels.

8IN (20CM)

Crithmum maritimum
SAMPHIRE, SEA FENNEL
Hardy perennial. Height and spread up to 12in (30cm). Tiny white-green flowers grow in flat umbels in summer. Its succulent leaves have a strong, salty flavor.

Stem is branched.

FOR USE IN

The Garden
PP. 21, 43, 49, 58

Cultivation

Propagation Sow seeds in spring under cover at 68°F (20°C). Germination takes 15–25 days. Pot in a loam-based substrate, and grow on until well established. In warm climates, plant out in the garden, but in cooler regions, grow as a container plant. In spring, propagate established plants by division. Keep at least two crowns per clump. In warm climates, replant into the ground, or into containers in cool climates.

Site In regions where temperatures at night do not fall below 48°F (8°C), the summer days are hot and wet, and the winters warm and dry, lemon grass will grow outside in any soil. In cool climates, grow as a potted plant in soil- or loam-based substrate.

Maintenance When light levels drop, this plant becomes dormant. In the fall, move to a frostfree site with a temperature no less than 40°F (5°C). Reduce watering to a minimum. In early spring, as the plant starts to produce shoots, increase the heat and light, and cut back all dead growth and stalks to 2in (5cm). Repot if necessary and liquid-feed once a week.

Harvesting The best-flavored leaves are obtained from the lower 4in (10cm) of the plant. Pick throughout the growing season to use fresh or dry. The lower white section of stem also has a concentrated lemon flavor. Harvest the stem during the summer months.

Uses A tea made from fresh leaves is a stomach and gut relaxant. The essential oil is antiseptic and deodorizing, and is used in perfume, in poultices to ease pain and arthritis, and as an insect repellent.

Cymbopogon Lemon grass POACEAE

This important culinary and medicinal herb grows in tropical regions and is used extensively in Asia, India, and Thailand. I have been lucky enough to see it growing and flowering naturally in the Caribbean, where it is used primarily for reducing fever. This useful plant has a strong lemon flavor and can be grown successfully outside in temperate climates, although it rarely flowers in cooler regions or when cultivated. It is now grown commercially for its widely used essential oil.

Cymbopogon citratus
LEMON GRASS, FEVER GRASS
Half-hardy perennial. Evergreen in warm climates. Height 5ft (1.5m) and spread 3ft (1m). It has lemon-scented, linear leaves that grow up to 3ft (90cm) in length, and robust, canelike stems.

7IN (18CM)

Leaves are sharp and rough to the touch, with a lemon scent when crushed between the fingers.

Stems are cut at ground level; they have an intense lemon flavor, and are used in cooking and medicine.

FOR USE IN

The Garden   The Kitchen

PP. 21, 43, 49, 58, 67   PP. 94

Cultivation

Propagation Sow seeds in early spring under cover at 65°F (18°C). Germination takes 5–10 days. Or sow seeds in late spring into prepared open ground, when the air temperature at night does not fall below 45°F (7°C). Germination takes 2–3 weeks. Alternatively, in spring or fall, take the suckers (side shoots) off the main stem and set them in pots filled with loam-based substrate. When they have taken root, plant out (after all threat of frost has passed).

Site Plant in a sunny site in well-drained, deep, fertile soil that has been fed the previous fall with well-rotted manure. Space young plants at 36in (90cm) intervals.

Maintenance When grown in hot, dry conditions, cardoon leaves and stalks become pithy and tough, and the flower bud hardens, making all parts inedible. To prevent this, maintain a good supply of water throughout the growing season. In the fall, feed the soil around established cardoon plants with well-rotted manure.

Harvesting To produce edible blanched artichoke leaves, tie the mature outer leaves together, and wrap the whole plant in sacking to shield it from the light. Leave for 4–5 weeks. Then, unwrap and harvest the blanched leaves around the heart. Pick flower buds before the outer green bracts start to open. Collect seeds in early fall as the flowers drop. When harvesting, wear gloves and beware of prickles.

Uses A detoxifier that helps the liver regenerate and stimulates the gall bladder. The blanched leaves, ribs, and stalks are used as a winter vegetable.

Cynara Cardoon ASTERACEAE

This large, attractive herb has been in cultivation for thousands of years as a vegetable and as a gentle laxative. It is currently popular as an ornamental plant for adding structure and height to the garden. In Australia, where it is classed as a weed, its potential is being researched as winter fodder for livestock, a vegetable oil (extracted from the seed), and as an environmentally friendly energy source. The flower buds and blanched leaves, roots, and stalks are the edible parts, but I consider the taste inferior to the more familiar globe artichoke, *Cynara scolymus*.

Cynara cardunculus
CARDOON
Perennial. Evergreen in warm climates. Height 6ft (2m) and spread 4ft (1.2m). The large, thistlelike, blue-violet flowers are very attractive to bees and butterflies. The seeds that follow the flowers are also a good food source for garden birds like finches. The stems are thick and fibrous. The leaves are silver-gray-green, deeply cut and leathery with a silvery, downy underside.

6IN (15CM)

Flower, which appears in summer, is violet and thistlelike.

***Bud** is edible before the outer bracts start to open. Eat in the same way as its cousin, globe artichoke.*

FOR USE IN   **The Garden**
Pp. 21, 43, 49

Cultivation

Propagation Sow fresh seeds in the fall. The seed is very fine, so mix it with flour to make the dark seeds more visible as you sow them. Do not cover the seed. Place the seed tray outdoors or in a cold frame. Germination takes 5–7 weeks.

Site Foxgloves adapt to most conditions, except for dry, exposed sites. They prefer partial shade in a moist but well-drained acid soil, enriched with leaf mold. They also grow well in containers, in a soil-based substrate. Place the container in partial shade and shelter the plant from high wind – they grow very tall in the second year.

Maintenance Water well in dry weather. During the first winter, protect the plants if the temperature at night falls below 14°F (-10°C). Use leaf mold to enrich the soil around established plants (see page 37). In the second season, remove the main flowering spike (after flowering) to increase the size of the others. Foxgloves self-seed, so if you want to keep plants under control, pick out seedlings. Pot a few seedlings as insurance against hard winters. Thin out plants if they are overcrowded. Wear gloves, because just touching the plant may cause rashes, headaches, and nausea.

Harvesting In summer, the pharmaceutical industry harvests the leaves to make the drug to treat heart conditions.

Uses Glycosides is extracted from the leaves to make a drug used to treat heart disease.

Caution The whole plant, including the seeds, is highly poisonous.

Digitalis Foxglove SCROPHULARIACEAE

This plant is native to both North America and Europe it became very important medicinally in the late eighteenth century when William Withering developed the use of *Digitalis* in the treatment of heart disease. Despite the high toxicity of the plant and its seed, infusions made from the leaves of foxgloves were often used in traditional country medicine to treat sore throats, rhinitis, and as a compress for swellings and bruises.

Digitalis purpurea
FOXGLOVE, FAIRY GLOVES
Hardy biennial. Height up to 6ft (1.8m), spread 2ft (60cm). Purple or white tubular flowers with purple spots on the throat. They first flower in the spring of the second season. The green leaves are large, textured, and lance-shaped.

Flower is purple or white with irregular-shaped purple spots in the throat.

Stem is round and green with a velvet texture.

Flowerbud is sealed at end.

14IN (35CM)

Cultivation

Propagation Sow seeds in early spring under protection at 65°F (18°C). Germination takes 5–10 days. For the best results, sow seeds in late spring when the air temperature at night does not fall below 45°F (7°C). Sow into prepared open ground. Germination takes 2–3 weeks. Thin plants to 8in (20cm) apart.

Site This herb will grow anywhere, taking off like a "rocket" – hence its name. It has adapted to the poorest of sites, growing in crevices and walls, but poor sites produce tough and bitter-tasting leaves. To produce a lush tender leaf crop, grow rocket in light shade in a well-prepared, well-fed soil. It is not ideal as a container plant because it produces a long taproot.

Maintenance For a good leaf crop, sow annually in spring. Later in the year, cover young plants with horticultural fleece to extend the picking season until the temperature falls below 30°F (-1°C). The following spring, dig up old plants and sow a new crop. This herb is prone to flea beetle attack. To prevent attack, you can cover the young crop with fleece from mid-spring on.

Harvesting Pick the leaves and flowers to use fresh as required throughout the growing season.

Uses Rocket is a digestive stimulant and is high in sulfur, which is good for healthy skin, hair, and nails. The leaves are delicious in salads. Dress the leaves with salt, lemon, oil, and vinegar, or simply serve rocket leaves with a little fresh parmesan cheese.

Diplotaxis Wild rocket BRASSICACEAE

A form of this herb can be found growing wild throughout Europe, Asia, and North and South America. For hundreds of years it has been collected in the wild and sold in markets, and both the leaves and seeds of rocket were used as flavoring by the Romans. Today rocket is popular as a fresh salad herb, and adds a distinctive peppery flavor; it has a much stronger taste than its close relative, arugula (*Eruca vesicaria* subsp. *sativa*) and can be distinguished by its more deeply divided leaf shape.

Diplotaxis muralis
WILD ROCKET, RUCOLA
Perennial often grown as an annual. Height 12in (30cm) and spread 6in (15cm). Yellow four-petaled flowers appear in summer. The green, deeply divided aromatic leaves form a rosette as the plant matures.

4IN (10CM)

Flower *is bright yellow with four petals. It has little scent.*

Leaves *become more deeply divided and pungent as the plant matures.*

Stem *is narrow and edible when young, adding bite to a fresh green salad.*

Cultivation

Propagation In early spring, sow seeds into a container under cover at 65°F (18°C). If germination does not occur within 28 days, place outside for a further 21 days, then re-cover the container, and place out of direct sunlight. Germination should occur within a further 20 days. When the seedlings are large enough to handle, plant into a prepared site, 12in (30cm) apart. In winter, divide established plants while they are still dormant, or take root cuttings in late winter or early spring. When the roots take, plant out into a prepared site in the garden.

Site Plant in a sunny site in a rich, free-draining soil. Excessive wet causes roots to rot. (*E. purpurea* is not as sensitive to wet soils as other species.) Echinacea will grow well in a large container. Use a soil-based substrate and repot each winter.

Maintenance After flowering, cut back the plant and collect the seeds. In spring, lightly mulch established plants with well-rotted manure. Spring growth in mature plants and young plants attract snails. Check plants and remove snails on a daily basis.

Harvesting Pick flowers and leaves during flowering before the seedheads (cones) are fully formed. When the petals are dead, pick the seed heads and dry. In the fall, harvest roots and rhizomes from four-year-old plants.

Uses Echinacea raises the body's resistance to infection by stimulating the immune system. It is very effective in preventing colds and flu. A decoction of juice extracted from flowers can also be used to treat minor wounds, burns, and boils, and as a gargle for throat infections.

Echinacea Echinacea ASTERACEAE

This marvelous North American herb suggests that we should hold folk medicine in higher regard. For many years, Native Americans have known that echinacea increases resistance to infection, but only in the past decade that modern research has confirmed these properties. Now demand for echinacea almost exceeds supply. *Echinacea angustifolia*, *E. pallida*, and *E. purpurea* all have similar medicinal properties, and are becoming increasingly rare in the wild due to over-collection; today, only cultivated herb plants grown by reputable sources should be purchased.

Echinacea angustifolia
NARROW-LEAFED ECHINACEA, BLACK SAMPSON

Hardy herbaceous perennial. Height 24in (60cm) and spread 12in (30cm). From summer to early fall, it bears single flowers with long thin purple or, rarely, white petals, and a spiky central cone. It has mid-green linear leaves. In its natural habitat it is an endangered species.

Echinacea pallida
ECHINACEA, CONEFLOWER

Hardy herbaceous perennial. Height 33in (80cm) and spread 18in (45cm). The flower is single with long mauve-pink, narrow, drooping petals, with a spiky central cone in summer to early fall. The leaves are oval, narrow, dark green, and veined. *E. pallida* is not as medicinally effective as other species of echinacea, but it is a very pretty plant that looks attractive growing in an herbaceous flowerbed.

Flower is lightly honey-scented and very long lasting. It is excellent as a cut flower when grown in cultivation.

Stem is ridged, finely ribbed, and textured.

13IN (33CM)

Echinacea purpurea

ECHINACEA, PURPLE CONEFLOWER

Hardy herbaceous perennial. Height 4ft (1.2m) and spread 18in (45cm). It bears large daisylike purple-pink flowers with a central golden brown spiky cone that becomes more pointed as the plant matures. The leaves are oval and deeply veined. This species of *Echinacea* is the simplest to grow successfully, and it is the species that is grown on a commercial scale.

Leaf is oval and deeply veined.

Cultivation

Propagation In late fall, sow fresh seeds under protection at 75°F (24°C). An additional light source may be need to encourage germination. Germination takes 14–21 days. Seed-raised plants will take 5 years before they flower. It is much easier to propagate plants by the division of rhizomes in spring. In warm climates, they will take 3 years to flower.

Site Plant in rich moist soil in partial shade, where temperatures do not fall below 50°F (10°C). It will only produce flowers and fruit under tropical conditions. In subtropical or cool regions, it is best grown as a foliage plant in a container using a loam-based substrate. Place in a warm conservatory or greenhouse in partial shade; full sun will make the leaves turn yellow.

Maintenance In hot climates, it can be invasive. In spring, dig up its creeping rhizomes to control it. In spring, repot container-grown plants. Feed container-grown plants regularly from spring until early fall with liquid seaweed or comfrey.

Harvesting In hot climates, seeds are harvested by hand, which makes them an expensive crop to produce. In cool climates, pick the leaves to use fresh as required.

Uses Seeds, extracted from the pod and chewed, freshen the breath and aid digestion. Some varieties have green and others brown pods. The bright green pods are best for culinary use. Use the leaves to add flavor to steamed fish, chicken, and vegetable dishes by lining the steamer with leaves.

Elettaria Cardamom ZINGIBERACEAE

This tropical plant was originally found growing wild in the Ghat Mountains on the Malabar Coast of southwest India, in an area known as the Cardamom Hills. Today, it is cultivated for its lemon-flavored seeds in India, Sri Lanka, Guatemala, and Tanzania. Aromatic cardamon seeds are used to flavor sweet and nonsweet foods, and drinks such as coffee and wine. In cool temperate climates, cardamom plants will grow successfully in a conservatory or greenhouse. They will not flower or produce seed pods in these conditions, but, in my opinion, their beautiful leaves more than make up for it.

Leaf is highly aromatic when crushed or steamed.

Elettaria cardamomum

CARDAMOM
Tropical evergreen perennial. Height up to 10ft (3m) and spread indefinite. Orchidlike white flowers with a striped purple-pink lower lip are followed in tropical climates by 15–20 aromatic seeds. The smooth, lance-shaped, dark green leaves have a silky, paler underside. They are highly aromatic when crushed or heated.

Stem is smooth and ridged. The leaves unfurl from the growing tip.

10IN (25CM)

Pods contain are approximately 12–18 black seeds. The seeds have a warm spicy lemon flavor.

Cultivation

Propagation Sow fresh seeds in spring under protection at 68°F (20°C). Germination takes 10–15 days. In cool climates, place young plants in a frostfree environment over winter. In late spring, take softwood cuttings from the growing tips. In cool climates, grow the young plants under protection for the first year.

Site This plant grows wild on granite and clay slopes and by the sea. In the garden, it prefers full sun and well-drained soil. In warm climates, it can be grown as a hedge or clipped into ball shapes. In temperatures below 45°F (8°C), it grows well as a container plant in a loam-based substrate.

Maintenance Prune after flowering in late spring to encourage bushy growth. Protect from frosts and, more importantly, from damp, wet conditions.

Harvesting Pick the leaves to use fresh or to dry after flowering from spring until early fall. Pick aromatic branches as required, and harvest seeds when they become fluffy.

Uses Wild rosemary has been used to treat coughs and colds, flatulence, and colic. It is also used as a diuretic. For relaxation, add an infusion of leaves to the bath. Make a foot bath of leaves to relieve swollen legs or to stimulate the onset of menstruation. An infusion of the leaves and twigs is used to control dandruff and to stimulate hair growth. In cooking, the leaves are used in meat dishes and vegetable stews. Dried leaves can be added to potpourri (see page 102).

Eriocephalus Wild rosemary ASTERACEAE

I have been growing this plant for more than ten years, but for a long time, I was unaware of its herbal properties – I only knew that the leaves smelled lovely, and that, in winter, it produced attractive flowers followed by fascinating fluffy white seeds. When my neighbors brought back a medicinal plant book from South Africa, I discovered that this plant grew wild in the Western Cape, and that it was an important medicinal and culinary herb. Its colloquial name, "kapokbos," derives from the Afrikaans word for snow, which is "kapok," and refers to the appearance of the downy seeds.

3IN (7.5CM)

Seed is covered in *fluffy white hairs, which look like snow.*

Leaves have silvery hairs that trap moisture.

Eriocephalus africanus
WILD ROSEMARY, SNOWBUSH, KAPOKBOS
Half-hardy evergreen shrub. Height and spread 3ft (1m). Clusters of small white flowers with magenta centers in winter. The small, silver-haired, slightly succulent leaves grow in tufts along the branch and reflect sunlight, which reduces leaf temperature.

The Garden
PP. 21, 43, 55, 64

Cultivation

Propagation In the fall, sow fresh seeds in pots and place them in a cold frame. If no germination occurs within 28 days, place the container outside to expose it to all weathers, especially frost. After 21 days, move it back to the cold frame. After germination, keep seedlings in a cold frame over winter before planting out the following spring in a well-prepared site. Take root cuttings in spring. Divide established plants in fall and replant in a well-prepared site.

Site Plant in moist, fertile soil in full sun or light shade. This plant is not ideal for growing in containers because it grows too big too quickly.

Maintenance In late spring, pinch back the stems to make a shorter, bushier plant. In the fall, prevent self-seeding by cutting back as soon as the seeds have set.

Harvesting In spring, cut the flowering stems in bud. Lift roots in the fall.

Uses Medicinally, the roots are the most potent part of the plant. As the common name "gravel root" indicates, it helps treat bladder stones (gravel) and urinary problems. An infusion of flowers makes a diuretic tea to alleviate fluid retention. A tea made from the fresh leaves is used to bring down high fevers, and to treat rheumatism. To make a fly repellent, crush dried leaves and burn them. The flowers and seeds yield a pink or red textile dye.

Eupatorium Joe Pye weed ASTERACEAE

This herb, native of North America, can be found growing in low moist ground, wooded slopes, savannas, and along streams. It is said to have taken its name from a Native American named Joe Pye, who reputedly used it to cure fevers and typhus. It is still considered an aphrodisiac by some Native American tribes. I think it looks lovely growing in drifts, either at the back of a bed or around a pond, where it will attract butterflies.

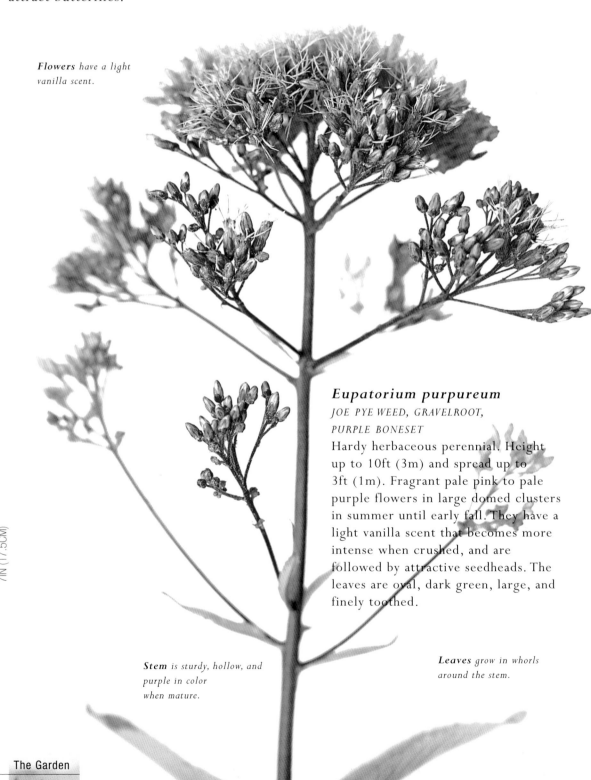

Flowers have a light vanilla scent.

7IN (17.5CM)

Eupatorium purpureum
JOE PYE WEED, GRAVELROOT, PURPLE BONESET
Hardy herbaceous perennial. Height up to 10ft (3m) and spread up to 3ft (1m). Fragrant pale pink to pale purple flowers in large domed clusters in summer until early fall. They have a light vanilla scent that becomes more intense when crushed, and are followed by attractive seedheads. The leaves are oval, dark green, large, and finely toothed.

Stem is sturdy, hollow, and purple in color when mature.

Leaves grow in whorls around the stem.

Cultivation

Propagation Sow seeds into a container in early spring and place in a cold frame. Germination usually takes 1–3 months, but can be erratic. Divide established plants in early fall. Replant 12in (30cm) apart.

Site Plant in moisture-retentive soil in sun or partial shade. It is a good plant for growing in clay soils, and close to or in water. It grows well in containers, in a soil-based substrate. Place the container in partial shade and do not let it dry out.

Maintenance To encourage new leaf growth, cut back after flowering in late summer. Queen-of-the-meadow is prone to mildew. If it occurs, cut off the diseased leaves. If it is very serious, cut the plant down to the ground and destroy all the contaminated leaves.

Harvesting Pick young leaves to use fresh or to dry before flowering. Harvest the flowers just as they open to use fresh or to dry. Dig up the roots of 3-year-old plants to dry or use fresh.

Uses Both the leaves and flowers are edible. The flowers have a mild almond flavor and can be added to stewed fruits, jelly, and jam. They are also good for flavoring mead and beer, and make an interesting wine. Young spring leaves have a dry flavor and can be added to salad or soups. The flowers make a good tea, which is ideal for those suffering from aches or pains. The roots of the plant make a black textile dye.

Filipendula # Queen-of-the-meadow ROSACEAE

When I first moved to my farm, I was brought a housewarming present of "meadowsweet" vinegar, which had been made from the flowers that grow wild along the lane. In the nineteenth century, queen-of-the-meadow's reputation grew when salicylic acid was isolated from the stem sap. This was later synthesized as acetylsalicylic acid and forms the basis of Aspirin. Queen-of-the-meadow is not recommended for children or adults who are sensitive to this painkiller.

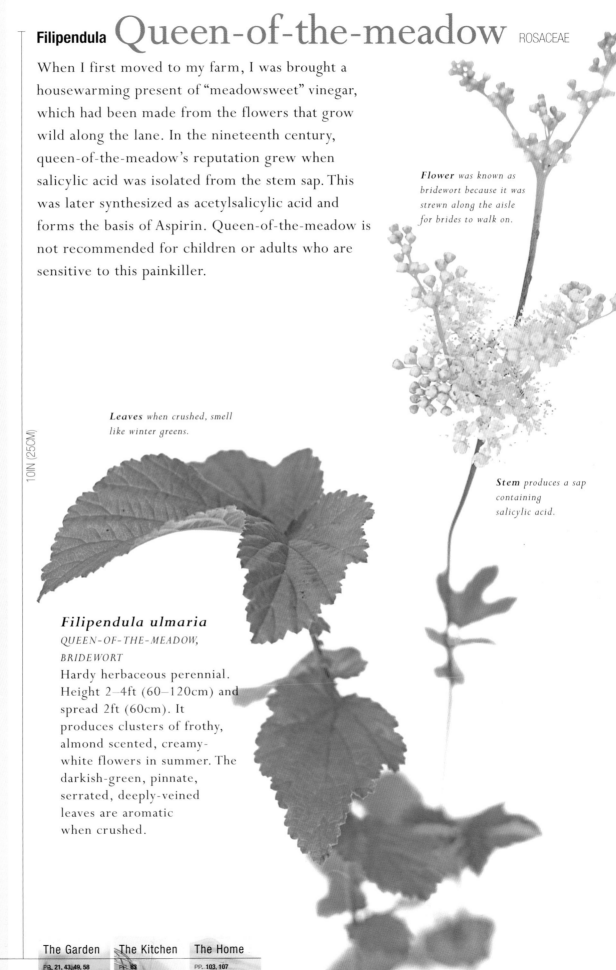

Flower was known as bridewort because it was strewn along the aisle for brides to walk on.

Leaves when crushed, smell like winter greens.

10IN (25CM)

Stem produces a sap containing salicylic acid.

Filipendula ulmaria
QUEEN-OF-THE-MEADOW,
BRIDEWORT
Hardy herbaceous perennial.
Height 2–4ft (60–120cm) and spread 2ft (60cm). It produces clusters of frothy, almond scented, creamy-white flowers in summer. The darkish-green, pinnate, serrated, deeply-veined leaves are aromatic when crushed.

FOR USE IN | The Garden | The Kitchen | The Home
PP. 21, 43, 49, 58 | PP. 83 | PP. 103, 107

Cultivation

Propagation Sow seeds in spring under protection at 68°F (20°C). Germination takes 7–10 days. Continue to grow under protection until all threat of frost has past. Or sow seeds in late spring into prepared open ground when the air temperature at night remains above 41°F (5°C). Germination takes 14–20 days. If you have light soil, divide established plants in spring.

Site Plant in a warm, sunny site in well-drained, fertile soil. If grown in poor soil or arid conditions, fennel will taste bitter. Also, do not plant fennel near dill or coriander – the former may crosspollinate with fennel, and the latter alters the flavor. Fennel grows well in containers in a loam-based substrate.

Maintenance Harvest the seeds and then cut back the plant to promote new leaf growth. Replace plants every 3–4 years to maintain a good flavor. In the fall, when the plant has died back, mulch the soil around the plant with well-rotted manure. In winter, protect the plant from wet conditions because it is susceptible to mildew and/or rot.

Harvesting Pick leaves to use fresh in summer prior to flowering. Pick flowers to use fresh as they open. Harvest seeds just as they change color from green to brown, and dry well.

Uses The seeds have the best medicinal properties. An infusion of seeds eases flatulence and colic in young children and prevents heartburn and indigestion in adults. A mild infusion can be used as an eyewash.

Foeniculum Fennel APIACEAE

This beautiful aromatic herb has been in cultivation for thousands of years. The Greeks ate fennel to suppress hunger, and in the Middle Ages it was used to deter insects. Today nearly all parts of the fennel plant are used for culinary purposes: the leaves for salads, the fennel stems on barbecues to add flavor to meat and fish, and the seeds ground as spice for use with lamb, pork, and vegetables. However, taken in large doses, oil made from the seed can cause convulsions and disturb the nervous system.

Foeniculum vulgare 'Purpureum'
BRONZE FENNEL
Hardy herbaceous perennial. Height 4–7ft (1.5–2.1m) and spread 18in (45cm). Large flat umbels of small yellow flowers appear in summer, followed by aromatic seeds. The feathery, threadlike foliage is a soft bronze color. This fennel looks very striking in a mixed flowerbed as well as in the herb garden.

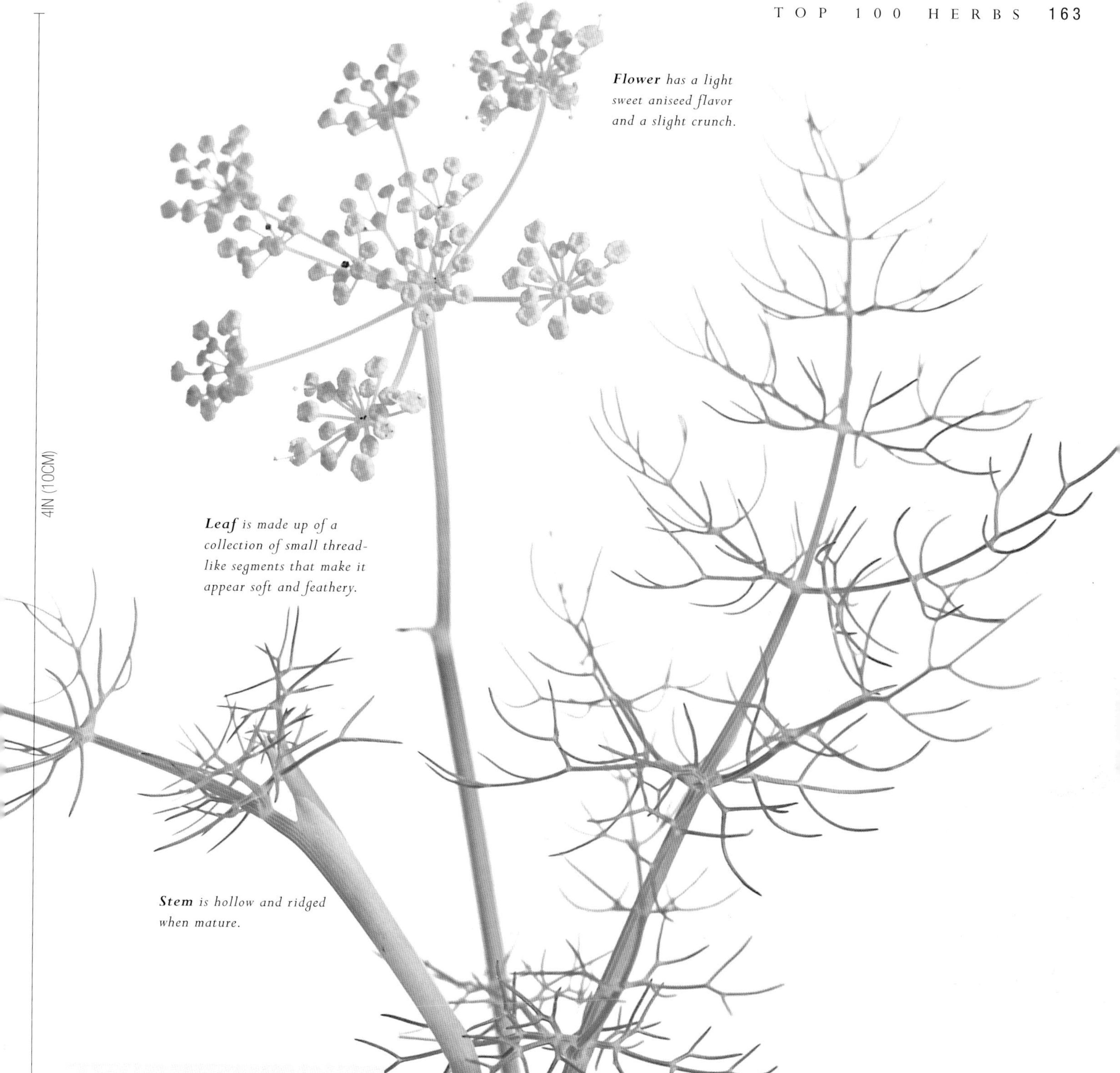

Flower has a light sweet aniseed flavor and a slight crunch.

Leaf is made up of a collection of small thread-like segments that make it appear soft and feathery.

Stem is hollow and ridged when mature.

4IN (10CM)

Seed are very aromatic. You can chew them to freshen the breath.

Foeniculum vulgare

FENNEL

Hardy herbaceous perennial. Height 4–7ft (1.5–2.1m) and spread 18in (45cm). Large flat umbels of small yellow flowers in summer, followed by aromatic seeds. The feathery foliage is soft green. This herb is often confused with *Foeniculum vulgare* var. *dulce* (Florence fennel), which produces a bulb and is grown as a vegetable.

Cultivation

Propagation In late summer, pick fresh fruit and leave to dry on cheesecloth. Rub the seeds off the dried fruit and sow fresh in early fall, on the surface of the substrate. Place in a cold frame, but do not cover. Germination takes 6–10 weeks. Alternatively sow in spring on the surface. Do not cover. Place under protection at 68°F (20°C). As soon as the seeds have germinated, remove them from heat and grow on under protection at 60°F (15°C). Plant out when they are large enough to handle and there is no chance of frost. Established plants produce runners. As each runner has a small root system, plant out where required in a prepared site.

Site Plant in sun or partial shade in fertile soil that does not dry out in summer. This herb is good ground cover and grows well in containers in a soil- or loam-based substrate.

Maintenance Feed regularly with liquid comfrey fertilizer throughout the fruiting season. Cut back runners if the plant becomes too invasive. As insurance against an extreme winter, pot a few runners in the fall.

Harvesting Pick leaves to use fresh or to dry in late spring before the fruit sets. Pick ripe fruit from summer until early fall. Harvest the fruit to dry for seed collecting in early summer.

Uses Medicinally, the leaves are mildly astringent and can be made into a gargle for sore throat. The fruit is a diuretic. They are a useful addition to the diet for those suffering from rheumatic gout. The fresh fruit can help remove tooth discoloration.

Fragaria Wild strawberry ROSACEAE

This herb grows in the cool temperate climates of Europe, Northern Asia, Australia, and North America. For me, picking wild strawberries on walks in the forest, bringing them home carefully, and then eating them the following morning with my cereal is a vivid childhood memory. The strawberry fruit was dedicated by the ancient Romans to Venus and the Virgin Mary – possibly because of its medicinal properties, or maybe just because it is so heavenly to eat. Some people, however, are allergic to strawberries.

Flower has five white petals, and a yellow center and stamen.

Fragaria vesca
WILD STRAWBERRY
Hardy perennial. Height 6–12in (15–30cm) and spread 7in (18cm), or indefinite if you include the runners. Small white flowers with yellow centers followed by small, scarlet, sweet fruit appear throughout the summer. The trifoliate, mid-green, toothed leaves can also be eaten, and taste good mixed with other herbs in a salad or as a tea.

Fruit is edible, small and scarlet, and smells and tastes sweet.

Leaves have a musky scent and flavor.

2IN (5CM)

Galium Sweet woodruff RUBIACEAE

Formerly known as *Asperula odorata*, this herb is a native of Europe and was introduced into North America and Asia, where it became naturalized. Woodruff is ideal ground cover, under deciduous trees, and by hedges or on banks, and is one of the few herbs to grow well in dappled shade. It has a pretty, star-shaped flower and attractive foliage. The leaves can be dried and used like lavender to scent fresh laundry.

Cultivation

Propagation This plant happily self-seeds in the wild, but in controlled conditions it may be a challenge to grow from seed. In the fall, sow fresh seeds in a pot and cover with coarse horticultural sand. Place outside. Germination takes 1–6 months. Alternatively, it may be easier to propagate established plants by division or take root cuttings in spring (see pp.56–7). Once divided or rooted, plant in a prepared site 12in (30cm) apart.

Site Plant in moist fertile soil in partial shade. (It will adapt to most soils, but in hot or dry conditions it will need extra water.) It can be mildly invasive if grown in its optimum conditions. It will adapt to containers, but leave enough room for seasonal growth or the roots may rot in wet conditions.

Maintenance In hot, dry conditions, this herb may exhibits seasonal dieback, causing the leaves to turn yellow. Cut it back, and it will revive with watering and the cooler temperatures of late summer. If the plant becomes invasive, dig it up before the flowers have set.

Harvesting Pick the leaves and flowers together in early spring. Its scent of new mowed hay is strongest after the plant has been dried.

Uses Fresh leaves are used as flavoring agents in nonalcoholic and alcoholic drinks (see page 83). Dried leaves are used as a fabric freshener (see p103). As a medicinal plant, woodruff has been used as an antispasmodic and diuretic.

2IN (5CM)

Galium odoratum
SWEET WOODRUFF
Hardy herbaceous perennial. Height 6 in (15cm) and spread 12in (30cm) or more. Small white star-shaped flowers appear from spring until early summer. The leaves are narrow and lance shaped. 6–8 leaves grow around each stem in a complete circle.

Stem is trailing. It often forms roots at the nodes, which increase the spread of the plant.

Leaves, when crushed, smell sweet like freshly mown hay.

The Garden   The Kitchen   The Home
PP. 21, 43, 49, 58   PP. 83   PP. 103, 107

Cultivation

Propagation In the fall, remove the pith from around the seed and wash in mild detergent to remove the protective coating around the seed. Sow one seed per pot. Cover with coarse grit and place in a cold frame. Germination takes 4–6 months or longer. Grow on in a pot for a further 5 years before planting out. Take cuttings from new growth in summer. When rooted, grow on as a container plant for at least 5 years before planting in the final growing position. Fruits will only be produced in a warm climate when a male and female tree are planted near one another.

Site Plant in full sun to partial sun in light, fertile, deep soil. It is adaptable and tolerates air pollution. Young specimens grow well in containers in a loam-based substrate.

Maintenance Little maintenance is needed for trees in the open ground. When grown as a container plant, remove the leaves from around the plant in autumn after leaf fall. Repot each year in the spring.

Harvesting Pick fresh leaves as they turn from green to yellow in the fall, and dry. The small plums are picked when ripe. The kernel (nut) is extracted and dried in the fall.

Uses The nuts from the ginkgo fruit are roasted, and used in soups and stir fries. In western medicine, the leaves are taken to improve the circulation and the memory and to relieve tinnitus and vertigo.

Caution If taken in excess, it can cause a toxic reaction.

Ginkgo Ginkgo GINKGOACEAE

This fascinating tree is thought to be one of the oldest trees on the planet, and is one of the most well-researched herbs in the world. In Chinese medicine, the nuts are used to treat asthma, bronchial congestion, and coughs. The name "ginkgo" is derived from the Japanese word "ginkyo," meaning "silver apricot," which refers to the fruit. "Biloba" translates as "two-lobed," referring to the split in the middle of the fan-shaped leaves. I think it is wonderful to be able to still grow one of the oldest trees on earth.

9IN (23CM)

Leaf blade is sometimes whole, but often has a characteristic slit in the center. The veins are slightly raised.

Ginkgo biloba
GINKGO, MAIDENHAIR TREE
Hardy deciduous tree. Height 130ft (40m), spread 70ft (20m). It is dioecious, which means it bears male and female flowers on different trees in early summer. The flowers are followed by small fruit on the female tree. The leaves are fan shaped.

Cultivation

Propagation Seeds collected in cool climates tend not to be viable. Sow seeds in spring under protection at 68°F (20°C). Germination takes 10–14 days, but can be erratic. Grow on for 2 years in a container before planting out in the open ground. Divide established plants in the fall after the plant has died back. Make sure there is a growing bud visible in each division, replanting into a well-prepared site.

Site Plant in fertile, deep, well-cultivated soil in a sunny position. Plant pot-grown plants or divided roots, at a depth of 6in (15cm), and place 3ft (1m) apart. Licorice is not well suited to growing in containers unless they are very deep, like a trash can.

Maintenance To produce a good crop of roots, mulch the soil in the fall with well-rotted manure. In spring, cut back old leaf growth.

Harvesting In early winter, dig up the roots for drying from established 3- or 4-year-old plants. Since this plant is slow growing, dig up one third of the root now and leave the rest to harvest in subsequent years. Fill in with well-rotted manure to encourage more root growth.

Uses Licorice root is used to flavor black treacle and Guinness beer. Medicinally, it is one of the most prescribed herbs in China. It is used to treat the spleen, liver, and kidney. The Japanese use a licorice preparation to treat hepatitis. In western medicine, it is used to alleviate sore throats, coughs, and bronchitis.

Caution Do not take medicinally if pregnant, or suffering from kidney disease.

FOR USE IN The Garden PP. 21, 43, 49, 53, 58

Glycyrrhiza Licorice PAPILIONACEAE

One of the most popular and widely-consumed herbs in the world, licorice is native to southern Europe, Asia, and the Mediterranean, and is commercially cultivated in Russia, Spain, Iran, and India. It has been used medicinally for over 3,000 years. The ancient Egyptians and Greeks recognized its benefits in treating coughs and lung disease. It was introduced into Britain in the sixteenth century, but is now no longer grown as a commercial crop. I used to eat licorice whips as a child and just loved the flavor; I still find it a fascinating old herb today.

Root is dried before use as a flavoring for confectionery (known as licorice sticks) or as a medicine.

Growing bud

Glycyrrhiza glabra
LICORICE
Hardy herbaceous perennial. Height 4ft (1.2m) and spread 3ft (1m). Short spikes of pea-like white flowers tinged with mauve-purple in late summer followed by long pods. The large green leaves are divided into oval leaflets.

6IN (15CM)

Leaf is composed of between 9 and 17 oval leaflets.

Cultivation

Propagation Obtain seeds from a specialized supplier to avoid hop wilt disease. Sow in the fall and cover with horticultural sand and coarse grit. Place the container outside. Germination usually takes 4–6 months, but may take up to one season. Take softwood cuttings from the female plants in spring or early summer – it is difficult to identify the gender of plants grown from seed until they are 2–3 years old. In spring, divide root stems of established plants. Replant 3ft (1m) apart in well-prepared soil, and support.

Site Plant in a sunny position in a soil that is rich in leaf mold and has been deeply dug. Grow hops in containers in a soil-based substrate. Provide support for the plants to climb or to cascade over the edge.

Maintenance In the fall, cut back the plant to the ground, clear away any leaf or stem debris, and feed with well-rotted manure or compost. Hops are prone to hop wilt, which is very contagious. Dig up the plant and burn it. Do not plant hops in that area again. Leaf miner and powdery mildew are also problems. Remove infected leaves and burn.

Harvesting In spring, pick young side shoots to use fresh. Harvest hop flowers in early fall. Dry well, and use quickly – the flavor fades rapidly.

Uses Medicinally, the female flower is good for insomnia and intestinal cramps. A pillow stuffed with female flowers aids sleep. To eat, steam or lightly boil side shoots, and parboil the male flowers to eat in salads. Blanch young leaves to remove bitterness, and use in soups and salads.

Humulus Hops CANNABACEAE

This herb is native to Britain and was originally eaten as a vegetable – the young shoots are similar in taste to asparagus. In the reign of Henry VIII, hops revolutionized the brewing of beer in Britain, enabling it to be kept longer by replacing traditional bitter herbs such as alecost (*Tanacetum balsamita*). Hops have been used medicinally for hundreds of years as a sedative, and a pillow stuffed with dried hops cured George III's insomnia – a method that is still used today.

Humulus lupulus
COMMON HOP
Hardy herbaceous perennial vine. Height up to 20ft (9m). It is dioecious, which means that male and female flowers grow on separate plants in summer. The female flower is conelike and hidden by papery scales. The male flower grows in clusters without sepals. The leaves have 3–5 lobes with sharply toothed edges.

Flowers in bud. Open flowers of the female plant have a scent of ripening apples and yeast.

Leaves have sharply toothed edges.

Stem is hollow and covered with tiny hooked prickles that enable it to climb and cling to trees, walls, and trellis.

8IN 20CM

The Garden | The Home
PP. 21, 43, 53, 58, 66 | PP. 107, 110, 111

Cultivation

Propagation In spring, mix the very fine seeds with sand or flour for even sowing. Do not cover. Place under protection at 68°F (20°C) or in a cold frame. Germination takes 10–20 days with warmth; 15–30 days in a cold frame. Divide established plants in early fall, replanting 12in (30cm) apart in a prepared site.

Site Plant in a sunny position in well-drained chalky soil, although it will adapt to partial shade and all but water-logged soils. If grown in a light soil, it may become invasive. It will grow well in a container with a soil-based substrate. Please note that in some countries, notably Australia, this herb is subject to statutory control as a weed.

Maintenance After flowering and harvest, cut the plant down to the ground to allow the green growth to form a semi-evergreen mat in winter.

Harvesting Harvest the flowers in summer as they open. Remove green parts, then dry or preserve in oil.

Uses This important medicinal herb acts as tonic for the nervous system and as an antidepressant. An oil infused with the flowers stimulates tissue repair and is used to treat wounds, burns, and shingles. It is also good for sciatic pain, sunburn, ulcers, and varicose veins. It is used in homeopathy for pain and inflammation caused by nerve damage.

Caution High doses may cause photosensitivity. Do not mix with other drugs. Always check with your doctor or herbalist before using. It can poison livestock.

Hypericum St. John's Wort CLUSIACEAE

I love the fascinating stories associated with this herb. According to the old saying, whoever treads on St. John's Wort after sunset will be swept up on the back of a magic horse! In a more practical vein, however, it has many medicinal properties. Today, it is used in the treatment of neuralgia and varicose veins, and is famous as "nature's Prozac" in the treatment of depression. However, it should not be taken by people who are chronically depressed. It is a lovely herb to grow, with stunning yellow flowers in midsummer, which are followed by prolific seedheads.

Hypericum perforatum
ST. JOHN'S WORT
Hardy semi-evergreen perennial. Height 12–36in (30–90cm) and spread 12in (30cm). Lightly scented yellow flowers with tiny black gland dots appear in summer. The small, oval, green leaves are covered with tiny translucent spots, which are resin glands. When crushed or on a hot day, they give off an unpleasant foxy scent.

Leaves are oval and stalkless.

4IN (10CM)

Flower has bright yellow petals that contain hypericin, a red pigment that is the active ingredient.

Stem exudes a blood-red juice.

FOR USE IN

The Garden The Home
PP. 21, 43, 49, 58 PP. 104, 105, 106

Cultivation

Propagation In spring, sow seeds under protection at 68°F (20°C). Germination takes 5–10 days. Take softwood cuttings in early summer from non-flowering shoots. In early fall, divide established plants that are under 3 years old. Dig up and gently pull the plant apart to obtain pieces of stem with both roots and leaf attached. Re-plant into a prepared site.

Site Plant in a sunny position in well-drained neutral-to-alkaline soil – good drainage is essential to the health of this plant. Hyssop makes a very pretty short-term hedge. It grows well in containers using a loam-based substrate.

Maintenance A short-lived perennial, hyssop lasts for 4–5 years. In mild areas, cut back to 8in (20cm) in early fall, or wait until after spring frosts in cold areas.

Harvesting Pick young fresh leaves throughout the growing season. Harvest leaves for drying from non-flowering stems in summer. Pick flowers just as they open. The scent is more intense when dried.

Uses Hyssop is a good companion plant; planted near cabbages, it lures away the cabbage white butterfly. Planted near grape vines, it attracts bees and increases pollination. The leaves have a strong flavor, so use them sparingly. The flowers are delicious in green salads. Medicinally, an infusion helps relieve bronchial congestion. It is also a tonic for the digestive, and nervous systems.

Caution Hyssop essential oil can cause epileptic fits. Hyssop should not be taken medicinally when pregnant.

Hyssopus Hyssop LAMIACEAE

This delightful Mediterranean herb not only looks lovely in the garden, but is also a great culinary and medicinal herb. It was used by the Greek physician Hippocrates (460–377 B.C.), who recommended it for chest complaints, for which it is still used today. The wonderful blue flowers, which have a sweet anise/minty flavor, are great for attracting pollinating insects into the garden. Use the flowers in salads.

Hyssopus officinalis 'Roseus'
PINK HYSSOP

Hardy semi-evergreen perennial. Height 32in (80cm) and spread 36in (90cm). Dense spikes of small pale sugar-pink flowers appear from summer until early fall. It has small, narrow, lance-shaped, aromatic green leaves.

5IN (12.5CM)

Hyssopus officinalis
BLUE HYSSOP

Hardy semi-evergreen perennial. Height 32in (80cm) and spread 36in (90cm). Dense spikes of small dark blue-violet flowers appear from summer until early fall. The small lance-shaped leaves have a slightly bitter but minty and sage-like flavor.

Leaves *are small, narrow, and lance shaped.*

Flower *is tubular and lightly scented, with double "lips."*

Stem *becomes woody as the plant matures.*

Cultivation

Propagation In spring, sow seeds and place under protection at 68°F (20°C) or in a cold frame. Germination takes 1–3 weeks with heat, or 3–4 weeks cold. The cold method can give better results with home-collected seeds, although both can be erratic. In the fall, when established plants have died back, propagate by division. It may be easier to remove offshoots that grow around the parent plant since the main root can be tough. Remove carefully, maintaining the root system. Replant in a well prepared site 3ft (1m) apart or pot and plant out in spring.

Site Plant in moist, fertile soil in full sun. Since it grows so tall, it is not ideal for planting in containers.

Maintenance In windy or exposed sites, the flowers may need staking. In hot, dry summers, the plant will need extra water. In fall, after the plant has died back, mulch with well-rotted compost or leaf mold.

Harvesting Pick flowers when fully open and dry for medicinal use, or pick just before the seeds turn brown for use in dried flower displays (later, and the seeds will float everywhere). Dig up roots of two- or three-year-old plants in the fall to be used fresh in cooking or dried for medicinal use.

Uses The roots were once used to flavor desserts. The flowers are used in decoctions, the roots to make syrups, powders, and tinctures for treating chest complaints. Recent research has shown that it is effective against bacterial and fungal infections, and can expel intestinal parasites. It is also said to make a good facial wash for the complexion.

Inula Elecampane ASTERACEAE

This is a magical herb and a must if you have space in the garden. I love the sunflower-like flowers in summer. Historically, Helen of Troy was believed to be gathering this herb when she was whisked off by Paris. The Romans used to candy the roots and dye them red with cochineal. In Tudor times, candy made from elecampane was used for coughs and chest complaints, which is still its main medicinal use today.

Inula helenium
ELECAMPANE, ELFWORT
Hardy herbaceous perennial. Height 5–8ft (1.5–2.4m), spread 3ft (1m). Large bright yellow ragged daisylike flowers in summer. Large green, oval, lightly toothed leaves that have a fine down on the underside.

5IN (13CM)

Flower is a large ragged yellow daisy about 3in (7cm) in diameter when fully open.

Stem is fibrous and covered in fine down.

Cultivation

Propagation In the fall, sow seeds in pots and place in a cold frame. Germination takes 3–4 weeks. Or sow seeds in late spring directly in a well prepared site at 12in (30cm) intervals.

Site Plant in a sunny position in well-drained, well-fed soil. Woad grows wild on chalky wasteland, but will adapt to any soil. It is not an ideal container plant; it looks dull for the first year and then grows too tall in the second.

Maintenance To increase leaf production and extend the life of the plant over another season, cut off the flowering stems as soon as they appear. Collect seeds before they fall; it does not self-seed naturally very well.

Harvesting In late summer, pick the leaves of the first-year growth to dry for medicinal use or for dyeing. The dye is extracted by a process of fermentation in water and urine from fresh or dry leaves. In the fall, dig up the roots of second-year growth and dry. Harvest the seeds as they turn dark brown; dry well.

Uses It is difficult to grow sufficient quantities for dyeing purposes. In Chinese medicine, they extract "qing dai" from the leaf pigment and prescribe large doses with apparently no ill effects, even though it is highly astringent and poisonous. The Chinese also use the root to treat meningitis, mumps, and sore throats. Woad is classed as a noxious weed in Australia and the U.S.

Caution Do not take internally except under supervision.

Isatis Woad LAMIACEAE

This ancient blue dye plant is undergoing a huge revival because of the current interest in natural plant pigments. The desirable blue colouring comes from the leaves, especially those of the first year's growth. It is also now popular with gardeners for its rich honey scent and attractive yellow flowers. I fell in love with woad when I first grew it with my children for a school project.

15IN (38CM)

Isatis tinctoria
WOAD, DYER'S WOAD
Hardy biennial. Height in the first year 18in (45cm), growing to 48in (1.3m) in the second, spread 18in (45cm). Clusters of numerous small bright yellow flowers in the second summer, followed by pendulous black seeds. Lance-shaped, lightly toothed, blue-green leaves.

Flower bud cluster turns into a 4-petaled flower with a sweet honey perfume.

Stem grows up in the second year.

Leaves in the second season grow more lance-shaped and blue-green in color.

Root is known as "ban lang gen" in Chinese medicine. It is used to treat meningitis.

Cultivation

Propagation This is not the easiest tree to grow from seed and requires patience. In early fall, collect ripe berries and remove the seed from the pith (see page 75). Use a loam-based substrate and cover with coarse grit. Place the pot outside. Germination can take 2–5 years. Do not let the seed dry out in summer. Alternatively, take semi-hardwood cuttings from the fresh new growth in spring. With both methods, grow on for 2 years in a container before planting out into a prepared site.

Site Plant in a sunny position in alkaline or neutral soil. This slow-growing plant looks attractive grown in a container. Use a soil-based substrate. It likes being pot-bound, so do not pot on too often.

Maintenance To maintain the plant shape, trim and remove any leader shoots growing out of line in late spring or early summer. Do not cut back into old growth.

Harvesting Both male and female plants are necessary to produce berries. The berries grow on the female bush. The best flavor is from those berries grown in warm climates. Pick berries in late summer, dry them on cheesecloth (see page 75).

Uses The flavor of the crushed berries is warm and spicy, and combines well with strong-flavored meat and marinades. Medicinally, juniper is used internally to treat cystitis, kidney inflammation, and rheumatism. Juniper oil, which is distilled from the berries, is used in fragrances and aromatherapy oils. It also makes a good massage oil to treat aching joints and muscles.

Juniperus Juniper CUPRESSACEAE

This attractive conifer can be found in many different forms growing throughout the world; from the Arctic to the Mediterranean, from the West Himalayas to North America, on heaths, moorlands, coniferous forests, and mountain slopes. Historically, it was used to cure snakebite and protect against infectious diseases. It was also burned in the hearth to guard against evil spirits and to ward off plague from the home. The berries are famous for giving gin its distinctive flavor.

Juniperus communis
JUNIPER
Hardy evergreen conifer. Height 20ft (6m) (and spread 10ft (3m). It is dioecious, bearing small male (yellow) and female (green) flowers on different trees in early summer. Berries form on the female tree. Spiky blue-green aromatic needle shaped-leaves.

Leaf is aromatic and needlelike.

8IN (20CM)

Berry turns from blue to black as it ripens over a period of 3 years.

Stem is woody.

FOR USE IN

The Garden	The Kitchen	The Home
PP. 21, 43, 53, 66	PP. 82, 90, 94	PP. 102, 109

Cultivation

Propagation Before sowing seeds in the fall, scarify them (see page 46). Then place in a pot, cover with coarse horticultural sand, and keep under protection at 68°F (20°C) for one month before moving to an area with a minimum temperature at night of 55°F (13°C). Germination takes 5–12 months. Grow on in the pot for 2–3 years before planting out. Take cuttings from new growth in late summer. High humidity is essential for successful propagation which takes 3 weeks to 6 months. Or propagate by division in spring or fall.

Site In hot, dry climates, plant in well-drained soil in partial shade. In cool climates, with temperatures at night above 23°F (-5°C), plant in a sheltered, sunny position in well-drained soil. In cold climates, grow in a container with a soil-based substrate. They prefer to be pot bound. Protect in winter.

Maintenance In cold climates, prune into shape in spring, or prune in the fall in warm climates. Check leaves regularly for sooty mold, caused by scale insect. To treat sooty mold, wash the leaves with horticultural soap or rub them with cotton swabs dipped in brandy.

Harvesting Since this is an evergreen herb, the leaf can be picked for use fresh all year round. Pick the berries in the fall.

Uses Bay leaves in cooking promote digestion, especially of meat. You can use the leaves fresh or dried (I prefer fresh). They are an ingredient in a bouquet garni (see page 94). A leaf in a jar of flour or rice will deter weevils.

Laurus Bay LAURACEAE

To the Greeks and Romans, bay was a symbol of wisdom and glory, and wreaths of laurel were once used to adorn the heads and necks of victorious athletes and leaders. A full-grown bay tree certainly has a regal shape in the garden. I love cooking with the fresh leaves and find bay a versatile herb that goes well with main dishes as well as milk and rice puddings. However, do not take the essential oil made from the berries or leaves internally. Also, an allergic reaction can occur when used externally.

Laurus nobilis 'Aurea'
GOLDEN BAY
Perennial evergreen tree. Height up to 18ft (5m) and spread 6ft (2m). Small, pale yellow flowers blossom in spring, followed by oval berries, which are black when ripe. The golden, oval, and pointed leaves are aromatic when crushed. This bay needs shelter from the wind, frosts, and full sun to prevent leaf scorch.

Laurus nobilis f. *angustifolia*
WILLOW LEAF BAY
Perennial evergreen tree. Height up to 23ft (7m) and spread 8ft (2.5m). Small pale yellow flowers appear in spring, followed by oval berries, which are black when ripe. The dark green leaves are aromatic, oval, and much narrower than *Laurus nobilis*. They are pointed, with a shiny upper surface. This is a hardier variety than *L. nobilis* 'Aurea.'

FOR USE IN | The Garden | The Kitchen | The Home
PP. 21, 43, 46, 63, 64, 66 | PP. 92, 94, 95 | PP. 102, 111

Laurus nobilis

BAY, SWEET BAY

Perennial evergreen tree. Height up to 26ft (8m) and spread 12ft (3m). Small, pale yellow flowers appear in spring and are followed by oval berries, which are black when ripe. The oval, dark green leaves have a shiny upper surface. When crushed, they give off a sweet aromatic scent. They can be used fresh or dried.

8IN (20CM)

Leaf *when held to the light becomes translucent, showing all its veins.*

Flower *is waxy in appearance, with very little scent.*

Stem *becomes woody as it matures.*

Cultivation

Propagation In spring, sow seeds under cover at 65°F (18°C). Germination takes 18–28 days. Lavenders grown from seed rarely produce identical plants. For a lavender hedge, where symmetry is important, grow plants from softwood cuttings taken from non-flowering stems in late spring.

Site These plants are hardy to 5°F (-15°C) – it is wet conditions and high humidity that kill, not cold. Plant in a sunny position, in fertile free-draining soil. These species will adapt to most soils, except heavy and wet ones, and will tolerate semi-shade. It grows well in containers using a soil-based substrate.

Maintenance Trim plants each year, either after flowering in early fall or in spring in cold, wet climates. Do not cut into the old wood since it will not produce new growth.

Harvesting Cut the flowers in summer just as they open, to use fresh or to dry. Dry loose on a flat tray or make small bunches to hang up and dry. Pick leaves to use fresh or dry before flowering.

Uses Use flowers and leaves sparingly in cooking. The flowers are used to flavor sugar for making cookies and cakes. A few leaves can add flavor to baked lamb. Lavender essential oil is used to treat burns, stings, or cuts, or added to the bath to calm children and relax adults. Rubbed into the temples, the oil can help ease headaches. It is also a good mosquito, gnat, and fly repellent. Sprinkle a few drops on bed linen to repel mosquitoes. Place sachets of dried lavender flowers and leaves with clothes to deter moths (see page 103).

Lavandula Hardy lavender LAMIACEAE

For many people, this is the quintessential herb: it smells good, looks good, and does you good. It was first taken to Britain by the Romans, who used it in their bathwater for its scent, to promote the healing of cuts and wounds, and as a flea and lice repellent. In France, hardy lavenders have been grown since the seventeenth century for their essential oil, which was, and still is used in the perfume industry. Lavender's soothing and calming properties are well known. A tea made from lavender flowers can help you sleep.

Lavandula angustifolia 'Hidcote'
HIDCOTE LAVENDER

Hardy evergreen perennial. Height 22in (55cm) and spread 18in (45cm). It has richly scented, short, rounded spikes of deep purple-blue flowers in summer and short aromatic gray leaves. An ideal lavender for hedges, it should be planted at a distance of 12in (30cm) apart.

Lavandula 'Sawyers'
LAVENDER SAWYERS

Hardy evergreen perennial. Height 27in (70cm) and spread 18in (45cm). Richly scented, long, conical spikes of purple flowers appear in summer. The aromatic leaves are soft and silvery gray. This lavender is a hybrid of *L. lanata* and *L. angustifolia,* and can only be grown from cuttings.

FOR USE IN

The Garden | The Home
PP. 21, 43, 49, 53, 55, 65, 67 | PP. 100, 102, 105, 107, 108, 110, 111

The classic flower for drying and using in lavender bags.

Lavandula x *intermedia*
Old English Group
OLD ENGLISH LAVENDER

Hardy evergreen perennial. Height 36in (90cm) and spread 24in (60cm). Aromatic, long, pointed spikes of clear pale blue-purple flowers appear in summer. The silver-gray-green leaves are aromatic. *L.* x *intermedia* is a hybrid of *L. latifolia* and *L. angustifolia*, and has been bred to produce a high yield of essential oil.

Flower is a clear, pale blue-purple, clustered on a tapering, pointed spike.

Leaf is long, narrow, and silver-gray-green.

8IN (20CM)

Cultivation

Propagation See pp. 176–77 for details. (Bract lavenders grown from seed produce plants with different colored and sized bracts.) If you want identical plants, see pp.176–177 for details.

Site Bract lavenders are hardy to 23°F (-5°C). See pp.176–77 for details.

Maintenance Bract lavenders have a long flowering period from late spring until early fall. Regular deadheading encourages new young growth; the plant will bush out and not become too woody. In the fall, cut back the plant to just above the old wood. Feed it well with liquid seaweed and protect from frost. In very cold climates, cut back in spring.

Harvesting See pp.176–77 for details.

Uses French lavender was probably one of the first lavenders to be used for its oils. It was used to alleviate nausea and as a mild sedative. An infusion made from the flowers of all kinds of *L. stoechas* is good as a gargle, or for washing minor grazes to stop infection. Lavender water, with its mild antiseptic properties, can also be used to wipe down kitchen work surfaces. To prevent a horse from being annoyed by flies, rub some lavender water around its head and ears.

Lavandula Colorful bract lavender LAMIACEAE

The first time I saw these lavenders with their colorful bracts, or "ears" as they are commonly called, I thought they looked wonderful, like small colorful bees or even butterflies. Each year, a new variety is discovered, and there are flowers with not only purple but, now, deep red bracts. Traditionally, bract lavenders were grown for their oil, which was used to repel insects, as an antiseptic agent, and as a relaxant. *L. stoechas* is found growing wild throughout the Mediterranean area and is often confused with *L. pedunculata*, which is a native plant of central Spain and Portiugal.

Lavandula stoechas 'Kew Red'
LAVENDER 'KEW RED'

Tender evergreen perennial. Height 16in (40cm) and spread 12in (30cm). Unique cerise-crimson flowers clustered around small stalks topped with short pale pink bracts are borne from late spring to early fall. It has narrow, aromatic, green leaves. This variety needs to be protected from wet winters.

Lavandula stoechas 'Helmsdale'
LAVENDER HELMSDALE

Frost-hardy evergreen perennial. Height 36in (90cm) and spread 24in (60cm). Lovely deep burgundy-purple flowers clustered around medium tapered stalks, topped with short burgundy bracts, appear from late spring until early fall. Its narrow green-gray leaves are camphor-scented. This variety originated in New Zealand.

Lavandula stoechas
FRENCH LAVENDER
Frost-hardy evergreen perennial. Height 20in (45cm) and spread 24in (60cm). Attractive small deep purple flowers are clustered around small flowering stalks, topped with short mauve-purple bracts from late spring until early fall. Its narrow green-gray leaves are camphor-scented.

Leaf *is narrow, gray-green and highly scented.*

Flower *comprises small dark-purple flowers topped with short mauve-purple bracts.*

Leaves *are camphor-scented.*

5IN (13CM)

Cultivation

Propagation Grow from cuttings taken in spring from non-flowering stems. Once rooted and well established, you can pot up, but not too often; it prefers being pot bound. Protect from frost.

Site Tender lavenders make a fine display when grown outside from late spring to fall. Plant in fertile, well-draining soil, in full sun, protected from cold wind. In cold climates, they need to be brought in before the first frosts, ideally into a heated glasshouse or conservatory, and kept warm at around 40°F (5°C). They do not thrive in over-wet or humid conditions, but are ideal for growing in containers, using a soil-based substrate.

Maintenance These lavenders have a very long flowering period from spring until early fall. I have known *L. christiana* to flower year-round in a container. Keep dead-heading to encourage more blooms and to prevent the plant from becoming over-woody and straggly. Cut back hard (not into the hard wood) and repot in spring. Feed container plants regularly throughout the growing season using a liquid feed. Keep the plants well-ventilated throughout the season to prevent rot.

Harvesting Cut flowers for drying when the third part of the trident starts to flower. The best time is summer when the air is drier. Dry on open trays or by hanging in small bunches.

Uses Essential oils.

Lavandula Tender lavender LAMIACEAE

These tender lavenders, which originate from North and South Africa, the Canary Islands, and Madeira, are truly worth collecting and should not be ignored because they are less hardy than other lavender species. They can make excellent summer bedding, are wonderful when grown in containers, flower all year round, and produce attractive foliage. Both *L. candicans* and *L. allardii* are high in essential oil, which can be used for burns and cuts, as a sedative, and as a fly and mosquito deterrent. *L. christiana* looks stunning in flower, but does not produce a useful oil.

Lavandula dentata var. candicans
LAVENDER CANDICANS, FRINGED LAVENDER

Tender evergreen perennial. Height 30in (75cm) and spread 24in (60cm). Attractive pale purple flowers clustered around medium stalks topped with short pale blue-purple bracts appear in early summer. The soft, silver leaves are serrated and aromatic. It can be grown as a lavender hedge in mild climates. Its leaves are used to make essential oils.

Lavandula x allardii
LAVENDER ALLARDII, GIANT LAVENDER

Tender evergreen perennial. Height 48in (1.2m) and spread 30in (75cm). Very long, pointed spikes covered in small blue and pale blue flowers appear in summer. The leaves are broad, green-gray, slightly toothed, and camphor-scented, and are used to make essential oils. This lavender originated in South Africa.

Lavandula x christiana

LAVENDER CHRISTIANA,
FEATHERED LAVENDER

Tender evergreen perennial. Height
30in (75cm) and spread 24in (60cm). It
has scented, lacy foliage and stunning
blue flowers from spring to early fall.
The flowers are not scented. A sterile
hybrid of *L. canariensis* and *L. pinnata*,
this lavender is often sold as the latter. It
was found in a Moroccan garden
in the 1930s.

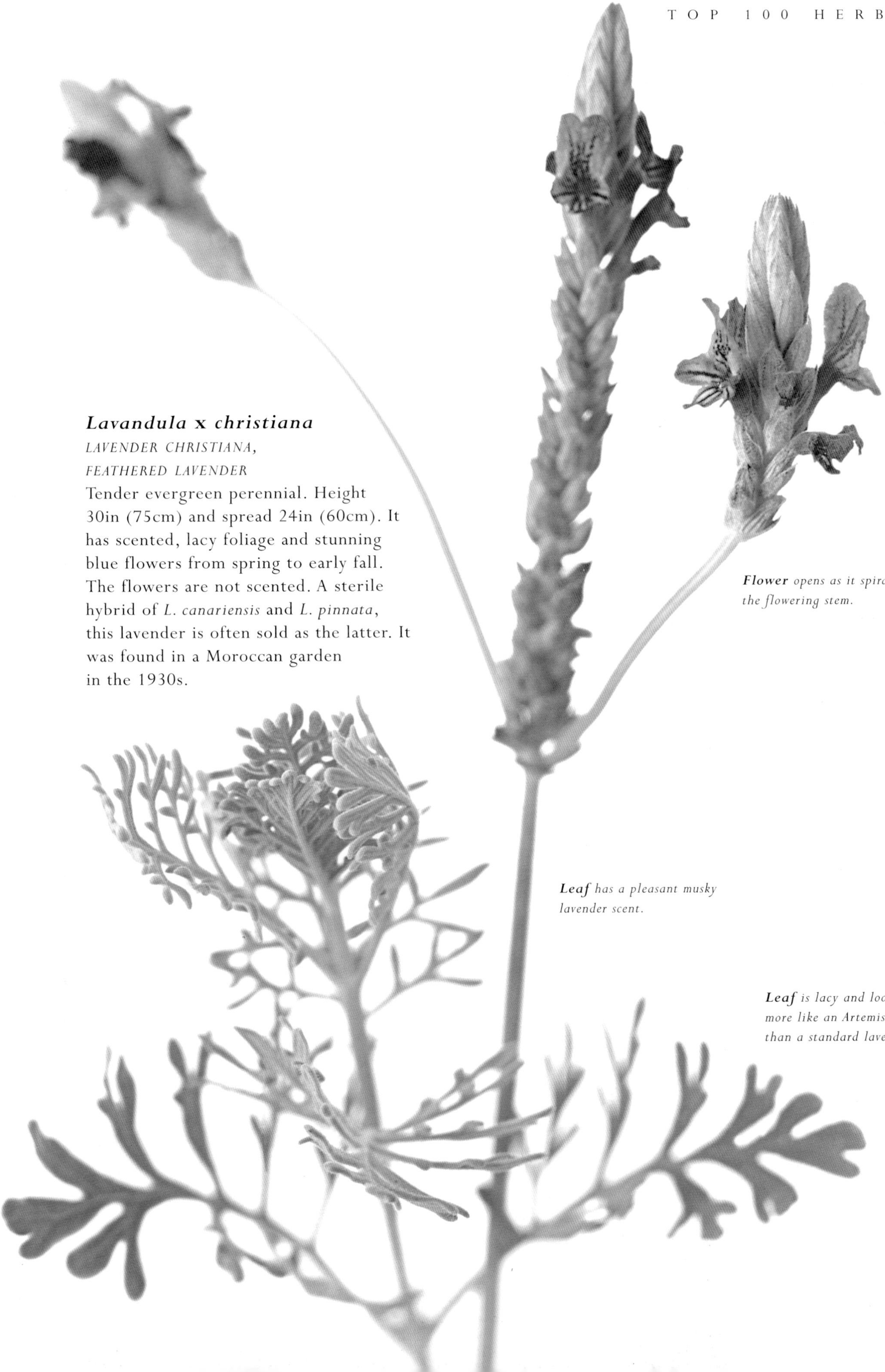

5IN (13CM)

Flower *opens as it spirals up
the flowering stem.*

Leaf *has a pleasant musky
lavender scent.*

Leaf *is lacy and looks
more like an Artemisia leaf
than a standard lavender.*

Cultivation

Propagation Sow seeds in spring or late summer under protection at 65°F (18°C). Germination takes 6–10 days. Or sow seeds in early summer into prepared open ground, when the air temperature at night does not fall below 50°F (10°C). Divide established plants in spring, replanting into a well-prepared site 24in (60cm) apart.

Site Lovage is a large plant, so choose the position carefully, bearing in mind that it takes 3–5 years to mature fully. Plant in a rich, well-fed, well-drained soil in full sun or partial shade. It grows well in large containers in a soil-based substrate. Do not let the container dry out in summer and feed with liquid comfrey (see page 39) during the growing season.

Maintenance To keep the leaves young and tender, pick regularly and cut back all leaves in succession to encourage new growth. In the fall, after the plant has died back, feed well with well-rotted manure.

Harvesting Pick the main crop of fresh young leaves before flowering. Harvest the seeds as they turn brown, dry well, and store (see page 74).

Uses Add tender young leaves to salads. Use crushed seeds in bread or on salads and rice. Use the root as a vegetable, but remove the skin. The leaf and seed can be used in celery salt. Medicinally, an infusion of the seed or leaf reduces water retention.

Caution Do not take medicinally if pregnant or if suffering from kidney disease. Do not eat in large amounts since it may cause nausea.

Levisticum Lovage APIACEAE

Lovage, as its common name indicates, was used as an aphrodisiac in the sixteenth century. It has many other historical claims: the ancient Greeks used it to aid digestion and relieve flatulence, while travelers in the Middle Ages used it as an early "odor eater" by lining their boots with the leaves. The French call it "*céleri bâtard*" (false celery) because of its flavor and appearance. In my opinion, lovage is a forgotten culinary delight, which adds a meaty flavor to dishes – and makes wonderful soup.

Seeds ripen to light brown and have a warm, meaty, celery flavor.

Levisticum officinale
LOVAGE
Hardy herbaceous perennial. Height up to 6ft (2m) and spread 3ft (1m). Flat clusters of tiny, pale greenish-yellow flowers appear in summer followed by brown seeds. The deeply divided, toothed leaves smell of celery when crushed. Old leaves become tough and bitter.

5IN (13CM)

Leaves are green, soft, and lightly veined, but darken in color with age.

Stem is hollow and ribbed.

The Garden PP. 21, 43, 49, 58, 65, 69   The Kitchen PP. 83, 94   The Home PP. 107, 111

Cultivation

Propagation Flax does not transplant well, so it is best to sow it directly into a prepared site. Sow it in late spring when the air temperature at night does not fall below 48°F (9°C). Thin to 12in (30cm) apart.

Site Plant in fertile (rich in humus), well-draining soil, in a sunny, sheltered position.

Maintenance If growing as a crop, weed the soil constantly to prevent flax from being choked by perennial weeds.

Harvesting Flax is ripe when stems turn yellow and the seed capsules turn brown. In wet summers the stems may remain green and the plants continue to flower long after the early seed capsules ripen. If so, harvest when the majority are ripe. For fiber, harvest as the stems turn yellow, and dry thoroughly.

Uses The seed can be grown as a nutritious sprouting seed in seed trays, or added direct to bread, salads, or breakfast cereals. A vegetable oil is also obtained from the seed, though it needs to be refined before use. Medicinally, the oil is valuable for maintaining a healthy heart and circulation. The plant has a long history of use in the treatment of cancer and contains anticancer agents. It is also used to treat constipation and in poultices to treat boils and draw out splinters. Seeds and oils are used as an animal fodder. The oil is used in paint production as an emulsifier.

Caution The seeds of some strains contain toxic glycosides, which become more toxic in drinking water. These cyanogenic glycosides have caused poisoning in livestock.

Linum Flax LINACEAE

Flax has been grown for at least 7,000 years and was one of the first crops to be cultivated. In the Stone Age, it was used to produce textile fiber and seed, and in ancient Egypt, linen cloth made from flax was used to wrap mummies. The Greeks used it to make sails for their boats. Linen, linseed, and rope are all made from this plant. An excellent companion plant in the organic garden, flax grown among vegetables increases pollination and therefore the vegetable yield, because bees are attracted to its lovely blue flowers.

Linum perenne
FLAX, LINSEED
Hardy annual. Height up to 4ft (1.2m), spread 12–24in (30–60cm). Sky blue flowers in summer are followed by capsules which contain the seeds. Pointed linear leaves grow on long, thin stems. Cultivars of this herb have been developed to produce high yields of linseed oil, edible seed, and fiber production for the textile industry.

Flower is sky blue with petals that droop in the early afternoon.

Stem is thin and tough.

Leaves are narrow, small, linear, and lance-shaped.

4IN (10CM)

FOR USE IN

The Garden
PP. 21, 43, 49, 58

The Home
PP. 109

Cultivation

Propagation Remove the outer pith of the berry and sow fresh seeds in spring. Place under protection at 60ºF (15ºC). Germination takes 1–2 months, but can be longer. Grow on in a container, with winter protection for a minimum of 2 years, before planting out into a prepared site. Take softwood cuttings from the new growth in early summer, and treat the cuttings in the same way as seedlings.

Site Plant in well-drained soil in a sunny position. A hardy plant to 23ºF (-5ºC) in dry cold winters, it needs protection in wet, cold, damp winters. It is ideal for growing next to a wall, where it will be sheltered from excessive wet. This tree makes an attractive large container plant. Use a soil-based substrate and do not allow it to dry out in summer. Keep fairly dry in winter.

Maintenance In cold climates, trim in early fall or spring. Prune back to the main branches in spring. Do not let it dry out in summer.

Harvesting Pick the leaves to use fresh as required. Pick the berries in the fall to use fresh or to dry.

Uses The leaves and berries have a warm spicy flavor and taste good in stews, soups, and marinades. The leaves are a good alternative to bay leaves. In Chile, the wood is used to make tools and charcoal. Medicinally, the seeds produce an aromatic oil that has antibiotic properties and is used in the treatment of respiratory diseases. Ferment leaves in mild olive oil for one month to make a treatment for dandruff and hair loss.

Luma **Luma** MYRTACEAE

This wonderful aromatic tree is native of Chile and is a great addition to any sheltered herb garden. I have grown it very successfully in containers as an exhibit plant, and often show it off to the public in my herb display gardens at flower shows. When grown as a container plant, it only reaches 10ft (3m) tall, which is far short of its tree height of 50ft (15m). The common name "Arrayán" comes from the Arabic "ar-rayhan" or "rihan," which translates as "the aromatic one" and refers to its fragrant leaf.

Luma chequen

LUMA, ARRAYÁN
Hardy evergreen tree. Height 50ft (15m) and spread 20ft (6m). It produces pretty, white flowers with delicate stamens in summer, followed by dark blue-purple berries. Its aromatic, dark green, oval leaves are slightly pointed and have a lighter green underside.

Flower is slightly aromatic, with white petals and masses of delicate stamens.

Leaf is aromatic, fairly tough, and shiny on the upper surface.

Stem is covered in red bark, which, as it matures, flakes off to reveal white areas.

6IN (15CM)

Cultivation

Propagation Sow fresh seeds in the fall, in a soil-based substrate. Place in a cold frame. Germination takes 3–4 weeks. If no germination occurs during this time, place the container outdoors. Germination can take a further 5–7 months. When germinated, winter the young plants in a cold frame before planting out into open ground. Divide established plants either in the spring or the fall.

Site Plant in water-retentive soil in sun or partial shade. It grows well in or around ponds. Wherever you choose to plant it, please remember it can be invasive. Gypsywort is not well suited to growing in containers.

Maintenance Cut back after flowering in late summer to prevent self-seeding and dig up plants that have escaped from their designated area in the fall and/or spring.

Harvesting Both the leaf and stem of this herb are best used fresh. However, they may be preserved in a tincture made from the fresh plant only. Harvest just before the flower buds open.

Uses Only the fresh leaf or a tincture made from the fresh plant has medicinal properties. It is used to calm heart palpitations caused by excessive thyroid activity. Tea made from the dried herb has practically no effect. The plant contains a black pigment for dyeing textiles, especially wool or silk.

Caution Take medicinally only under medical supervision, and do not take during pregnancy if you suffer from hypothyroidism.

Lycopus Gypsywort LAMIACEAE

The common name for this herb originates from an old belief that gypsies used the juice of this plant to darken their skins so that they could pass for Egyptians. This practice also led to another common name, "Egyptian Wort." Traditionally this herb was used to calm nerves and was considered a mild narcotic. *L. virginicus* is the native North American species, which looks similar and has similar medicinal properties.

Lycopus europaeus
GYPSYWORT, BUGLEWEED
Hardy herbaceous perennial. Height up to 40in (1m) and spread up to 24in (60cm). Close whorls of tiny, creamy-white flowers with a hint of pink appear from mid-summer until early fall. The leaves are faintly mint-scented, deeply toothed, and lance-shaped.

Leaf is rough to the touch.

Stem is square and slightly hairy.

Flowers are bell-shaped and grow in clusters close to the stem.

8IN (20CM)

The Garden

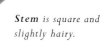

PP. 21, 43, 49, 58

Cultivation

Propagation Sow seeds in spring and place in a cold frame. Germination takes 2–4 weeks. When well established, plant out into open ground 24in (60cm) apart. Divide established plants in fall or spring. Replant in a prepared site.

Site Plant in any garden soil that holds moisture during summer. The ideal site is close to a pond in partial shade. Or plant it in a small water-barrel garden, but do not let it take over.

Maintenance An incredibly invasive plant, it not only self-seeds prolifically, but also spreads on creeping rhizomes, and has been known to swamp shorelines. In summer, cut back after flowering to prevent self-seeding. In winter and/or spring, dig up the plant and reduce the creeping rhizomes by half.

Harvesting Pick the leaves to use fresh or to conserve in oil or vinegar (see page 88) before the plant flowers in summer. Pick the flower spikes as they open. Remove flowerets before use.

Uses Although this herb is not used frequently by modern herbalists, it is still used in folk medicine to calm horses and cattle. Or, tie plant stems and leaves around a horse's bridle to deter flies. It is also a good insect repellent for the home or outdoors. Burn the dried stems and leaves, and the smoke will not only deter all flying insects but snakes. It is still used as a hair dye, highlighting blond hair and restoring graying hair to fairly blond.

Caution This herb is considered a pernicious weed because it is so invasive.

Lysimachia Yellow loosestrife PRIMULACEAE

This tall, handsome European herb can be found growing in fens and wet woodland, along lake shores, and on the banks of rivers. It adapts well to damp gardens or pond sites. It was named "Lysimachia" in memory of King Lysimachus of Sicily, who promoted its medicinal benefits as a wound-healing herb. When fresh young leaves were bound around a wound, it was said to stem bleeding immediately. This herb is often confused with purple loosestrife (*Lythrum salicaria*), see page 187 – both thrive in similar damp habitats and are invasive – but they are not related.

Lysimachia vulgaris
YELLOW LOOSESTRIFE,
WILLOW WORT
Hardy herbaceous perennial. Height up to 5ft (1.5m) and spread 3ft (90cm). Bright yellow, five-petaled flowers grow in pyramidal spikes in summer. It only flowers when the plant is well established. The mid-green, lance-shaped leaf is dotted with either black or orange glands, or occasionally both. The flower can attract dragonflies to the garden, especially when grown close to water.

Flowers are cup-shaped and grow in pyramidal spikes at the top of the plant.

Leaf is long and lance-shaped.

Leaf is soft to touch and, like the stem, covered with fine hairs.

4IN (10CM)

Lythrum Purple loosestrife LYTHRACEAE

The name "lythrum" means "gore" in Greek and was coined by a doctor who used loosestrife to heal warriors' battle wounds and stem bleeding. Later, the plant leaves were used for tanning leather because of their high tannin content. The first time I saw it growing in profusion was at the water's edge at the Wildfowl Trust at Slimbridge, in England, where it looked magnificent. It is highly rated by beekeepers, who consider it a good plant for over-wintering colonies of bees, which collect pollen from its flowers right up until late summer.

Cultivation

Propagation The seeds are very small and prolific – a mature plant can produce over 2.7 million seeds. Before sowing, mix fresh seeds with fine sand or flour to make them easier to manage. Do not cover. Place the container outside to expose it to all weathers, including frost. Germination takes 5–7 months. Pot up when the seedlings are large enough to handle. Plant in a prepared open site when the root ball is well formed. Established plants can be divided in the fall. Replant into a prepared, open site.

Site Plant in damp marsh soil in full sun or partial shade. An ideal location is by water. It is not suited to growing in containers.

Maintenance This invasive herb needs controlling to prevent it from competing with and replacing native grasses, sedges, and other flowering plants. In fall and spring, dig up spreading plants to maintain control. If it is out of control, use the beetle *Galerucella calmariensis* to strip the leaf and flower. In the fall, cut plants back before the seed sets and starts dispersing.

Harvesting Pick leaves before flowering to use fresh or to dry. Harvest the flowers in summer just before they are all fully opened to use fresh or to dry.

Uses It was once used to treat chronic diarrhea and dysentery, to clean wounds, and as a gargle and an eyewash. Currently, it is being researched for its healing properties relating to intestinal illnesses.

Lythrum salicaria
PURPLE LOOSESTRIFE
Hardy herbaceous perennial. Height 4ft (1.2m) and spread 30in (75cm). Beautiful tall spires of small magenta flowers appear all summer. The mid-green leaves are stalkless and lance-shaped, with either a rounded or heart-shaped base where the leaf joins the stem. The flowers attract not only bees and butterflies, but also dragonflies and hoverflies.

Stem is square and becomes woody with maturity.

Leaves are lance-shaped and covered with fine hairs.

Flowers are very attractive to bees.

8IN (20CM)

FOR USE IN | The Garden
PP. 21, 43, 49, 58, 66

Cultivation

Propagation Sow seeds in the fall. Place the container outside to expose it to all weathers. Germination is erratic. In early summer, when young plants are well-established, plant out in a prepared site at 24in (60cm) intervals. In late spring or summer, take cuttings from firm lower shoots.

Site Plant in well-drained, fertile soil in a sunny position. If the soil is damp, the plant stems will become soft and need staking in summer. *M. moschata* is suitable for growing in containers in a soil-based substrate but has a tall, messy habit.

Maintenance Cut back stems after flowering to clear up, and to promote new growth and a second flowering. In the fall, cut stems back to the lower leaves.

Harvesting Pick young fresh leaves as required throughout the spring. Harvest fresh flowers throughout the flowering period. Dig up the roots of the second year's growth to dry for medicinal use.

Uses The tender young leaves and flowering tips can be used in salads or steamed as a vegetable. A decoction made from the roots and leaves can be added to bath water to ease skin rashes, boils, and ulcers. Medicinally, this herb is thought to be inferior to marsh mallow (*Althea officinalis*), which is higher in mucilage and therefore better for coughs, but there is current research into its abilities to alleviate urinary complaints.

Malva Mallow MALVACEAE

In the Middle Ages, mallow was used as a calming antidote to aphrodisiacs and love potions. Before this, the Romans ate the young shoots as a vegetable delicacy. The ancient Celts believed that placing the disk-shaped fruit over a dead holy man's eyes would keep evil spirits from entering his body and help him on his journey to heaven. According to the sixteenth-century Doctrine of Signatures, the hairs on the plant meant that it would help hair growth. The root was also used as a sort of toothbrush, or peeled and given to teething children to chew. In the garden it is attractive in a rather wild way, and can be grown in either flowerbeds or the vegetable garden, where it attracts insects. It is edible and mildly medicinal.

Malva moschata
MUSK MALLOW

Hardy herbaceous perennial. Height up to 32in (80cm) and spread 24in (60cm). Scented pinkish, sometimes white, flowers from late summer to early fall. The mid-green leaves are musk-scented, and kidney shaped at their base but deeply divided at the stem. Plant in a sunny position in well-drained soil. This species has milder medicinal properties than common mallow (*M. sylvestris*).

Leaf *is lobed and downy with prominent veins on the underside.*

Malva sylvestris

COMMON MALLOW

Hardy herbaceous short-lived perennial. Height up to 36in (90cm) and spread 24in (60cm). It has pretty, pale purple-pink flowers with dark-colored veins throughout the summer until the first frosts. The mid-green leaves are a similar shape to ivy.

Flower *petals are each thinly veined in a darker color.*

7IN (17.5CM)

Root *can be cut into slices and used to draw out splinters and thorns.*

Stem *is thick, rounded, and strong.*

Cultivation

Propagation Sow seeds in the fall in a free-draining substrate. Place in a cold frame. Germination can take from 4 months to 2 years. In fall, carefully take root cuttings from established plants since it does not respond well to being disturbed. In cold, wet climates grow on for 2 seasons in a container, protected from adverse weather, until the plant is well established. In spring, plant out in a well prepared open site.

Site Plant in deep, well-drained, fertile soil in full sun or partial shade. It does not like chalk or gravel soils, and is prone to rot in clay or cold, wet soils. It has a long root system – up to 4ft (1.2m) – and is not well-suited to container growing. Grown in pots in a soil-based substrate, plants remain small and do not set fruit.

Maintenance This herb is very prone to attack from slugs, which will totally obliterate the plant. Mark the spot where it is planted; it will reappear in late summer.

Harvesting Dig up roots in the fall when the plant is dormant. Use the root fresh for juice extraction or dried in decoctions.

Uses Mandrake root is widely used in homeopathy as a treatment for coughs and asthma. Modern-day witches still hold it in high regard for its magical properties. Do not confuse it with American mandrake (*Podophyllum peltatum*).

Caution Mandrake is toxic and should only be taken under medical supervision. Avoid during pregnancy.

Mandragora Mandrake SOLANACEAE

Mandrake has close links with magic ritual and is regarded by some as evil. In folklore, it was thought fatal to dig up the plant, which would then scream piercingly and drive a person to suicide. Mandrake root was thought to have anesthetic properties, and a piece was given to patients before operations. This plant is toxic and should only be taken under professional supervision, however, it bears beautiful flowers in early spring and is an asset in any herb garden for this reason.

Mandragora officinarum

MANDRAKE, SATAN'S APPLE
Hardy herbaceous perennial. Height 2in (5cm) and spread 12in (30cm). Small, bell-shaped, white-blue flowers in spring, followed in late summer by aromatic, round, yellow fruits (in warm climates only). The large oval leaves have a rough, slightly prickly texture.

8IN (20CM)

Leaves become darker and rougher as they mature.

The Garden
PP. 21, 43, 49, 58

Cultivation

Propagation Sow seeds in early spring and place under protection at 65°F (18°C). Germination takes 1–2 weeks, but can be erratic. Alternatively, take softwood cuttings in summer from new growth. In cold and wet climates, grow on seedlings or cuttings in a container for the first winter. Plant out the following spring in a well-prepared site. Propagate established plants by division in spring (see page 57), re-planting in a prepared site.

Site Plant in a sunny position in well-drained alkaline soil. Protect from cold winds. This plant can be grown in a container. Do not overwater and use a free-draining soil-based substrate mixed with extra grit to improve drainage further.

Maintenance In summer, cut back after flowering to prevent the plant from becoming straggly and self-seeding.

Harvesting Gather the leaves and flowering tops in late spring, just before the plant flowers, when the plant oils are at their richest.

Uses This useful medicinal herb treats bronchitis and whooping cough, and is used in most cough mixtures to clear phlegm. The leaves and stems are boiled and used in candied products, cough drops, and syrups. Extracts of white horehound are used in traditional ale-making and is brewed to make Horehound Ale in Britain. An infusion of the leaf can be used as an organic spray to deter cankerworm in fruit trees.

Caution Do not take during pregnancy or if you suffer from stomach ulcers.

Marrubium # White horehound LAMIACEAE

I am fascinated by the thick silvery hairs that grow on the young stem and the underside of the young leaves of white horehound. It creates the impression that a silvery spider's web has spun them together. The Roman physician Galen used this herb to treat chest complaints, and it is still used for this purpose. Quite apart from its medicinal benefits, it is well worth growing as an unusual ornamental. It is not to be confused with black horehound (*Ballota nigra*), which has an unpleasant scent and is a de-wormer.

Flowers grow in clusters.

8IN (20CM)

Stem is square and covered in fine silvery hairs, making it appear wooly.

Marrubium vulgare
HOREHOUND, WHITE HOREHOUND
Hardy herbaceous perennial. Height 18in (45cm) and spread 12in (30cm). Clusters of small creamy white flowers in summer from the second season. The oval green leaves are wrinkled and lightly toothed with a wooly, silky, silver underside. They are aromatic.

Leaf is wrinkled on the upper surface and wooly on the underside.

Cultivation

Propagation Sow seeds (*Melissa officinalis* only) in spring under cover at 68°F (20°C). Germination takes 1–2 weeks. Do not over-water the seedlings as they are prone to "damping off" – a fungal disease. Take softwood cuttings in early summer. Plant out when the plants are well established. Divide established plants in early fall or early spring, replanting into a well-prepared site.

Site This plant will grow in all soils except waterlogged. It is invasive in light, fertile soils. The best situation is well-drained soil in a sunny position. All forms of this plant grow well in containers. Use a soil-based substrate.

Maintenance To maintain a supply of fresh leaves, and to prevent the plant from becoming woody or straggly, cut back after flowering. This will also stop self-seeding. This plant is invasive, so dig up roots as necessary. This herb is related to mint and, like mint, is prone to the rust virus (see page 194). If affected, dig up and burn.

Harvesting Pick fresh leaves before the flowers open to use fresh or to dry. This is when the highest yield of leaf oil is available.

Uses The lemon scent of the leaves is lost in cooking. Use the leaves fresh in green or fruit salads. Medicinally, it is antiviral and antibacterial, helps lower fevers, and improves digestion, as well as being a mild antidepressant. It helps heal and prevent canker sores. Rub the leaf into the skin for a good natural insect repellent. Applied in this way, it also helps to reduce skin irritation caused by insect bites.

Melissa Lemon balm LAMIACEAE

In ancient times, lemon balm was planted beside the front door to drive away evil spirits. Then in the Middle Ages it was used to prevent baldness, as a lucky love charm, and to help cure mad-dog bites, toothache, and even neck problems. Currently, research shows that it can be beneficial in the treatment of canker sores by, on average, halving the healing time and reducing the chance of further outbreaks. The scent of lemon balm is a delightful asset in the garden – there is nothing nicer than going outside on a summer's evening and gently rubbing lemon balm leaves to fill the air with lemon fragrance.

Melissa officinalis 'All Gold'
GOLDEN LEMON BALM

Hardy herbaceous perennial. Height 30in (75cm) and spread 18in (45cm) or more. Clusters of small, cream-colored flowers in summer. The lemon-scented golden-yellow leaves are oval-shaped and textured. Since the leaves are prone to scorching, plant this variety in partial shade. Cut back in summer to encourage new growth and therefore fresh leaf color. This variety can only be propagated successfully by softwood cuttings or root division.

Melissa officinalis 'Aurea'
VARIEGATED LEMON BALM

Hardy herbaceous perennial. Height 24in (60cm) and spread 12in (30cm) or more. Clusters of small pale cream flowers in summer. The leaves are lemon-scented, oval, toothed, textured, and variegated green and gold, but revert to pure green in summer. To maintain variegated leaves, cut back in summer before flowering to promote new growth. This variety can only be propagated successfully from softwood cuttings or by root division.

FOR USE IN

The Garden	The Kitchen	The Home
PP. 21, 43, 49, 53, 58, 68	PP. 82, 88, 94	PP. 100, 101, 102, 105, 107, 108, 110

Leaves *taste better raw than cooked. When crushed, they have a very good lemon scent.*

Stem *has fine hairs.*

Melissa officinalis

LEMON BALM, SWEET BALM

Hardy herbaceous perennial. Height 30in (75cm) and spread 18in (45cm) or more. Clusters of small cream-colored flowers in summer. The flowers have a light lemon flavor when eaten. The leaves are lemon-scented, oval, toothed, and textured. Add leaves to stewed fruit to help reduce the tartness.

Flowers *grow in clusters around the stem. They have a sweet lemon flavor and are rich in nectar, making them a very good bee plant.*

Leaf *is covered in fine hairs with toothed edges. It is highly lemon scented when crushed.*

4IN (10CM)

Cultivation

Propagation In fall or early spring, take root cuttings (see page 56). Spring cuttings take 2 weeks before new growth emerges. Softwood cuttings can be taken in late spring from new non-flowering growth. Divide mature plants in spring or fall. Only pennyroyal grows true from seed; others set seed, but are variable.

Site The healthiest plants are those that are left to spread naturally. Plant in rich, well-drained soil in a sunny position. It grows well in containers in a soil-based substrate. Repot each year in the fall to prevent root rot and to encourage abundant leaf the following season. Never plant two different mints together: they will intermarry and their flavors will become inferior.

Maintenance Cut hard back in summer and feed with liquid comfrey (see page 39). Tender new growth will be ready to pick in 6–8 weeks. A fungus, *Puccinia mentha,* is a common problem. Known as "mint rust," it is identified by its small rusty spots, which cover the leaf, starting on the underside. The only organic way to get rid of this disease is to either dig up the plant and destroy it, or cover it with straw and set it alight. This dramatic action will sterilize the soil and burn the contaminated leaves.

Harvesting Pick leaves before flowering, or after it has been cut back and the plant has started to regrow.

Uses Medicinally, it relieves indigestion, nausea, stomach gas, diarrhea, and colic. Mint tea soothes colds, and cold mint tea can be used as a wash to bring fever down, or as a throat gargle.

Mentha Classic mints LAMIACEAE

Mints are promiscuous herbs. They have successfully interbred, crossbred, and hybridized, which is wonderful for the plant collector, but difficult for me when having to decide which examples to write about. I have chosen to divide the mints up into classic mints and peppermints (see page 196). Spearmint (*Mentha spicata*) is without doubt the best-known of the classic mints. It was introduced to Europe by the Romans. It is still highly regarded and in demand as a culinary herb, as a source of leaves for refreshing mint tea, and as a useful home herbal remedy to aid digestion.

Mentha pulegium 'Upright'
PENNYROYAL UPRIGHT

Hardy, semi-evergreen perennial. Height 6in (15cm), spread indefinite. Small mauve flowers grow in terminal globular clusters around the stem in summer. The small oval leaves are highly peppermint scented. Use this herb sparingly in cooking. It is an excellent insect repellent and gives relief from stings. Pennyroyal should not be taken internally, when pregnant, or when suffering from kidney disease. It can be raised easily from seed and comes true (and is the only mint to do so), but is best propagated from cuttings.

Mentha spicata **var.** *crispum*
CURLY MINT

Hardy herbaceous perennial. Height up to 24in (60cm), spread indefinite. Small, lilac-pink flowers grow in terminal, globular spikes in summer. The spearmint-scented and flavored leaves are bright green, oval, and very crinkled – the first time I grew this plant, I thought that the leaves were diseased. It matures into an attractive plant and can be used in exactly the same way as *M. spicata*.

Mentha spicata

SPEARMINT, GARDEN MINT
Hardy herbaceous perennial.
Height up to 24in (60cm) and
spread indefinite. Small, purple-
mauve flowers grow in cylindrical
spikes in summer. The spearmint-
scented and -flavored leaves are
mid-green, oval shaped, and
wrinkled. Spearmint can vary in
flavor and leaf color,
depending on the soil in
which it is grown.

Flower *has a lovely sweet
minty flavor.*

Leaf *is lance-shaped with
a strong spearmint-scented
leaf when crushed. The leaf
flavor is very minty.*

Leaf *has a
distinctly
serrated edge.*

8IN (20CM)

Cultivation

Propagation Peppermint is a hybrid of water mint *(Mentha aquatica)* and spearmint *(Mentha spicata)*. It does not set viable seed, so is best propagated from root cuttings (see page 56) taken in spring and fall, or from softwood cuttings taken in late spring from new non-flowering growth. Alternatively, propagate established plants by root division (see page 57) in fall or spring.

Site For maximum leaf flavor and oil production, plant in full sun in well-drained fertile soil. See page 194 for more details.

Maintenance To maintain healthy plants, divide established plants every few years. Cut back after flowering to encourage new leaf growth, and feed with liquid comfrey (see page 39). New growth will be ready for picking in 6–8 weeks. In winter when the plant has died back, feed with well-rotted manure. Peppermints are prone to mint rust (see page 194). If plants become invasive, dig up root runners with care — any root left behind will grow into a new plant.

Harvesting Pick fresh leaves before flowering, or after cutting back when the plant has started to regrow up until the first frosts.

Uses Strongly flavored, peppermint can overwhelm more subtle flavors, but it tastes good in desserts like chocolate mousse. It is the key ingredient in remedies for indigestion and irritable bowel syndrome, and is a decongestant for colds and rhinitis. The oil is antiseptic and is used to treat itching skin and as a mosquito deterrent.

Mentha Peppermints LAMIACEAE

Peppermint is the quintessential herb: it attracts beneficial butterflies and flies to the garden, smells lovely, aids digestion, and eases headaches. It has been used medicinally for thousands of years. The ancient Egyptians knew its medicinal properties, and the Japanese have been extracting menthol oil from the leaves for at least 2,000 years. Today, peppermint oil is found in toothpaste, indigestion tablets, and confectionery. There are many different varieties available and some are more invasive than others. Variegated species tend to be weaker and therefore more easily contained.

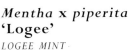

Mentha x piperita f. *citratus*
EAU-DE-COLOGNE MINT

Hardy herbaceous perennial. Height up to 32in (80cm) and spread indefinite. Small, pale purple flowers grow in terminal oval spikes in summer. The eau-de-cologne-scented and lightly peppermint-flavored leaves are dark brown-tinged with green, round, smooth, and toothed. You can add fresh mint leaves to bath water for a refreshing effect.

Mentha x piperita 'Logee'
LOGEE MINT

Hardy herbaceous perennial. Height up to 18in (45cm), spread indefinite. Small, pale purple flowers grow in terminal cylindrical spikes in summer. Its leaves are green and white variegated, pointed, oval, toothed, and peppermint-scented and flavored. This mint can be used in the same way as standard peppermint *(Mentha x piperita)*.

Mentha x *piperita*

PEPPERMINT, BLACK PEPPERMINT

Hardy herbaceous perennial. Height up to 24in (60cm) and spread indefinite. Small, pale purple flowers grow in terminal cylindrical spikes in summer. The edible leaves have a strong peppermint flavor and scent; the flowers taste of sweet peppermint. The leaves are dark plum-brown tinged with green, pointed, oval, and toothed.

Flower *is pale purple and clustered in spikes.*

Leaf *is oval and pointed with the veins in a darker color.*

Mentha x *villosa* var. *alopecuroides* 'Bowles'

BOWLES MINT

Hardy herbaceous perennial. Height up to 36in (1m) and spread indefinite. Small, pale mauve flowers appear in terminal cylindrical spikes in summer. The large, round, hairy, soft green leaves have a hint of peppermint mixed with strong spearmint. This wonderful culinary mint is particularly good for making mint sauce.

Stem *is square and dark plum-brown in color.*

7IN (18CM)

Cultivation

Propagation First stratify the seeds (see page 46) before germination. In the fall, sow in a container and place outdoors. Germination should occur the following spring, but can be erratic. In early fall, propagate established plants by root division. Replant into well-prepared open ground.

Site Plant in full sun in fertile soil that holds its moisture in summer. It adapts to most soils, except waterlogged or arid. It can be grown in a deep container, using a soil-based substrate, but its long taproot does not respond well to being too confined. Each fall, repot using a soil-based substrate.

Maintenance To grow meu as a root vegetable, mulch with well-rotted manure in the fall. If you want a leaf crop, feed with liquid comfrey (see page 39) in early spring. Feed once only, or the leaves and root will grow soft and lose flavor.

Harvesting Pick fresh either before or after flowering. The root of 3-year-old plants can be dug up in early fall and used fresh.

Uses Fresh leaves taste similar to lovage (see page 182), but are spicier and taste good with omelets and cheese, and in salads and soups. If cows eat the leaves mixed with grass, it makes their milk and butter taste spicy. A member of the carrot family, the roots have a strong spicy flavor, and are good in casseroles and soups. The roots can also be used to make a spicy wine. Medicinally, meu leaves and roots were used for curing snakebite, coughs, and flatulence. Today it is little used, but it is good for digestive problems.

Meum Meu APIACEAE

This attractive aromatic plant grows in mountain grasslands and is, in my opinion, underused in the modern herb garden. The spicy root was once eaten by Scottish Highlanders as a vegetable, and the fresh leaves also offer a delicious spicy flavor similar to lovage (see page 182). Traditionally it is reputed to spice up a flagging love life and has been used to treat a variety of medicinal problems. I think it is a good aid to digestion, and that it is high time this beautiful plant became more high profile.

Leaf resembles a soft green feather.

7IN (17.5CM)

Meum athamanticum
MEU, SPIGNEL
Hardy herbaceous perennial. Height 12in (30cm) and spread 8in (20cm). Umbels of small white flowers with a hint of pink around the edges in early summer. The bright green leaves are feathery, with a light, spicy scent.

Root is long and fibrous, with a strong spicy flavor.

FOR USE IN   The Garden   The Kitchen
PP. 21, 43, 46, 49, 58   PP. 93

Cultivation

Propagation Sow seeds in early spring under protection at 65°F (18°C). Germination takes 1–2 weeks. Do not overwater the seedlings because they are prone to "damping off"– a fungal disease. In cool climates, take root cuttings from the creeping rhizomes in spring. Take cuttings from the growing stems in early summer. Divide established plants in the fall.

Site There is some difference regarding site preference. *M. fistulosa* likes well-drained soil and a sunny position, *M. didyma* rich fertile soil that retains moisture in the summer and partial shade. Neither likes cold wet soil. Bergamot grows well in a large pot with some shade from the midday sun. Use a soil-based substrate.

Maintenance Dig up plants over 3 years old, remove the dead center, and replant in a prepared site. All *Monarda* species are susceptible to mildew and rust fungus. If either appear, cut the plant back to ground level, remove contaminated parts, and burn them.

Harvesting Pick fresh leaves to use as required. For drying, pick off the flowers and leaves from second-year plants just as they start to bloom.

Uses The leaf has a strong culinary flavor that goes well with meat. The flowers have a milder, sweeter flavor. Medicinally, a decoction of leaves makes a steam inhalant to soothe bronchial complaints. Bergamot essential oil is used in aromatherapy to treat depression and to fight infection. It is also used as a natural fragrance by perfume and soap manufacturers.

Monarda Wild bergamot LAMIACEAE

This herb is worth growing for its flower alone, which reminds me of a rather flamboyant lady's hat feathers. A native of North America, the Oswego Indians used wild bergamot medicinally to treat colds and bronchial complaints. It is still drunk as a refreshing tea, called Oswego tea after the tribe. In 1773, following the Boston Tea Party, wild bergamot was introduced to North American settlers. It became a popular substitute for India tea. Although the leaves smell similar, do not confuse wild bergamot with bergamot orange (*Citrus bergamia*) – which give Earl Grey its distinctive scent and taste.

5IN (12.5CM)

Flower tastes strongly herby with mint overtones.

Flower is tubular and lipped, and grows in clusters. The name fistulosa means "tubular" in botanical Latin.

Monarda fistulosa
WILD BERGAMOT, OSWEGO, HORSEMINT
Hardy, herbaceous perennial. Height up to 4ft (1.2m) and spread 18in (45cm). Lovely lilac-mauve bracts with a pink tinge in summer that last until early fall. The aromatic green leaves have a scent similar to bergamot orange (*Citrus bergamia*), hence its common name. Look out for hybrid crosses of *M. fistulosa* and *M. didyma*, which have produced a host of stunning hybrids for the herb garden or herbaceous bed.

Leaf is toothed and slightly hairy.

Cultivation

Propagation Sow seeds in spring under protection at 72°F (22°C). Germination takes 2–4 weeks, but can be erratic. An easier method of propagation is to lift and replant the small suckers that grow around the base of a mature shrub. Grow on the suckers in small pots. Do not plant out for at least 2 seasons.

Site Plant in fertile, light soil in full sun or partial shade. Young plants need watering once a day for the first three years. It will adapt to hot, dry climates, though the plant will be less productive and smaller. This tropical plant needs protection when temperatures fall below 55°F (13°C). In cool climates, grow as a container plant using a soil-based substrate.

Maintenance In the fall, feed the curry tree with well-rotted manure. If grown in a container, feed once a week throughout the growing season with liquid comfrey (see page 39). Mature plants can be cut back in winter. Young plants are prone to aphid attack. Treat with liquid horticultural soap.

Harvesting Pick fresh leaves as required. Dry leaves quickly lose their flavor.

Uses To flavor vegetable and lentil curries in southern India, and chicken and meat curries in Sri Lanka. Medicinally, it is used to treat digestive disorders, diarrhea, dysentery, and piles. Leaves are used as a poultice to treat burns, bruises, and skin eruptions, and have weight-reducing properties. The juice of the leaf makes an eye-brightening wash.

Murraya Curry tree RUTACEAE

When I first started herb farming, the only species of curry plant that was available was *Helichrysum italicum* – an evergreen shrub with silver foliage that fills the air with a curry scent. Today, the leaf from the native Sri Lankan curry tree (*Murraya koenigii*) is available as a culinary delight. In Asian cooking, the curry leaf itself is rarely eaten, but is used as a flavoring in dishes before being thrown away before the dish is served. Interestingly, there is an old Indian saying that compares a curry leaf to a person who is only wanted for a particular use before being discarded.

Leaf is large, oval, and dark green.

7IN (17.5CM)

Murraya koenigii
CURRY TREE, KAHDI PATTA
Tropical, evergreen shrub. Height up to 20ft (6m) and spread up to 15ft (5m). Clusters of pretty, fragrant, star-shaped, white flowers in summer, followed by edible black berries. The large, oval, dark green leaves have a bitter, pleasant, aromatic flavor when eaten, and produce a curry aroma when brushed against or crushed between the fingertips.

The Garden
PP 21, 43, 53

Cultivation

Propagation These large seeds need stratifying to germinate (see page 46). In cold climates, sow the seed fresh in the fall. Use garden soil, and place the container outside. Germination occurs the following spring. Take root cuttings in fall and spring. Divide established plants in the fall.

Site Plant in a soil rich in humus, in light shade. It will not grow in humid or hot climates. It is not an ideal potted plant because it has a long taproot. In light, fertile soil, contain the root to prevent it from becoming invasive; grow it in a large container, using loam-based substrate, in partial shade.

Maintenance To prevent self-seeding, collect unripe green seeds to use in salads, and then cut hard back. Remove the whole taproot if you wish to prevent it from rooting.

Harvesting Pick leaves to use fresh before or after flowering. Pick flowers just as the cluster opens and harvest seeds green when required. Store seeds when they have ripened to a dark brown color. Make sure they are dry.

Uses Add leaves to soups, stews, and as a natural sweetener and flavoring for stewed fruit and fruit salads. Cook the root as a vegetable or grate it raw to add to salads. The seeds when green add crunch to a salad. Brown seeds add aniseed flavoring to fruit. The root also makes a good wine. Medicinally, it is used for digestive complaints, coughs, and as a pick-me-up tonic.

Myrrhis Myrrh APIACEAE

The frothy, cream-colored flowers are one of the earliest to appear in the herb garden, and herald the arrival of spring. Originally, the roots of this herb were boiled and chewed as a breath sweetener. The flavor is like a mix of aniseed and parsnip. *Myrrhis odorata* is closely related to *Osmorhiza longistyli*s, which was used extensively by Native American tribes. Both species of myrrh, or sweet cicely, were used as an herbal tonic for the young and elderly. In the past, the seeds were crushed and used to make a furniture polish that was particularly good for oak.

Seed is edible when green and can be added to salads. When dark brown and ripe, it has a sweet aniseed flavor.

Myrrhis odorata

MYRRH. SWEET CICELY

Hardy herbaceous perennial. Height up to 3ft (90cm) and spread 2ft (60cm). Flat umbels of sweetly scented white flowers in early spring that last until early summer. The flowers are followed by long, angular seeds that ripen to black. The flowers have a sweet aniseed flavor and, like elderflower (see page 83), can be made into a refreshing cordial drink. The leaves are fernlike, very divided, and smell of sweet aniseed when crushed.

4IN (10CM)

Flower forms in flat white umbels.

Leaf is a natural sugar substitute. It has a sweet aniseed flavor.

Root is cream-colored and tastes strongly of aniseed.

FOR USE IN

The Garden   The Kitchen

PP. 21, 43, 46, 49, 58, 69.   PP. 83

Cultivation

Propagation In spring, separate the pulp of the ripe berry from the seed. Sow fresh, and place under protection at 60ºF (15ºC). Germination normally takes 1–2 months, but can take longer. Or take softwood cuttings in summer from non-flowering shoots. With both methods, pot up when well rooted, and grow on for two seasons before planting into a prepared site.

Site Plant in well-drained soil in full sun. Myrtle is quite hardy, but the wet will kill it quicker than cold. *M. communis* survives in temperatures of 14ºF (-10ºC). Variegated forms are less hardy surviving at 23ºF (-5ºC). In exposed sites, plant against a sheltered south- or west-facing wall. They grow well in containers, using a soil-based substrate. Do not pot on too often; myrtle prefers being potbound.

Maintenance Feed once in spring with well-rotted compost. Feed container-grown plants weekly during the growing season. Over-fed plants will not flower. In Mediterranean climates, trim myrtle in the fall. In colder climates, trim in spring.

Harvesting Pick fresh leaves throughout the year. Harvest fresh flowers as required in summer. Pick berries in late fall.

Uses Add leaves and berries to stews and soups. Use flowers as a garnish. In rural areas of Italy and Sardinia, cooking is flavored with the smoke of burning myrtle wood. Add myrtle leaves to the glowing coals of a barbecue to obtain a similar effect. Medicinally, the oil from the berries is used externally to alleviate acne. A leaf infusion is used to treat urinary infections.

Myrtus Myrtle MYRTACEAE

If I had to choose my all-time "Top 10" herbs, myrtle would feature in the list. The herb of "love" and dedicated to the goddess Venus, myrtle was grown around her temples – and Venus is often shown rising from the sea carrying a sprig of myrtle. Traditionally, brides carry a piece of myrtle in their bouquets as a symbol of love and constancy. Quite apart from its romantic history, myrtle looks wonderful grown in the garden or in containers. It smells fragrant and is an excellent culinary herb. It goes particularly well with barbecued food, to which it adds a distinctly Mediterranean flavor.

Myrtus communis subsp. *tarentina* 'Variegata'
VARIEGATED SMALL-LEAVED MYRTLE
Hardy, evergreen shrub. Height and spread up to 3ft (1m). Very attractive, fragrant white flowers with golden stamens appear in summer, followed by blue-black berries. The small, oval, light green and white variegated leaves are aromatic when crushed (though not as strong as *M. communis* 'Merion'). The leaves are the smallest of all the myrtles. Hardy to 23°F (-5°C). Do not over-water in winter.

Myrtus communis 'Merion'
MYRTLE MERION
Hardy, evergreen shrub. Height and spread up to 6ft (2m). It has very attractive, fragrant, small white flowers with golden stamens in summer, followed by blue-black berries. The oval, pointed, dark green leaves grow very close together, giving the shrub a very bushy appearance. The leaves are aromatic when crushed. This myrtle shrub has a very upright habit and is the least hardy of the evergreen species. The growing tips turn orange when the temperature drops below 32°F (0°C).

Myrtus communis

MYRTLE

Hardy evergreen shrub. Height and spread up to 10ft (3m). Very attractive, fragrant white flowers with golden stamens in summer, followed by blue-black berries. The oval, dark green leaves are aromatic when crushed and are a very good substitute for bay leaf in culinary dishes. This myrtle has the largest leaves and flowers of all the myrtles.

8IN (20CM)

Leaf *is oval and dark green, and very aromatic when crushed.*

Flower *is the largest of all the Myrtus species.*

Berry *is known as "mursins" in the Mideast, where it is used as a spice.*

Stem, *as it matures, develops a bark that was once used to tan leather.*

Cultivation

Propagation Sow seeds in early spring and place under protection at 65°F (18°C). Germination takes 1–2 weeks. In spring, propagate established plants by root division (page 57). Avoid bruising the roots when you dig them up or you will attract cats. In summer, take cuttings from non-flowering stems.

Site Plant in well-drained soil in sun or partial shade. Catnip will adapt to most soil conditions except clay or bog. *N. cataria* is a very good companion plant. Planted between brassicas, it will repel flea beetles, and will deter ants and aphids.

Maintenance Cut back hard after flowering to encourage a second flush of flowers and new growth. To protect a young plant from cats, turn a wire basket upside down over it and pin it to the ground. Encourage the plant to grow through the wire. This system allows your cat to eat some leaves without rolling in it.

Harvesting In spring, pick young leaves for culinary use. When the plant is in bud, pick leaves to dry for medicinal use.

Uses Young leaves have a slightly bitter, minty flavor and go well with soups and sauces. Medicinally, they are used to treat childhood ailments, such as colic, colds, and coughs. Catnip leaves can also be made into an ointment for the relief of piles. The leaves, when smoked, cause a mild euphoria, somewhat similar to marijuana.

Nepeta Catnip LAMIACEAE

This is a well-known feline aphrodisiac. Cats have been seen to decimate a plant as they roll about in ecstasy. On my farm, we named one of our cats after this herb, because as a kitten he chewed his way through many plants, lying on his back in hallucinatory heaven. Interestingly, it has a similar effect on humans and became a poor-man's substitute for cannabis. Medicinally, it has been successfully used to treat infections that afflict young children, like colic.

Nepeta cataria

CATNIP, CATMINT

Hardy, herbaceous perennial. Height 3ft (1m), spread 2ft (60cm). It produces clusters of pinkish-white tubular flowers in summer which are attractive to butterflies, especially the painted lady. The pungent, aromatic leaves are gray-green, toothed, and oval. The scent of this plant is said to repel rats, and when placed in bunches in chicken and duck coops, it acts as a deterrent.

Nepeta x *faassenii*

CATMINT

Hardy herbaceous perennial. Height and spread 18in (45cm). Clusters of small lavender-blue tubular flowers in summer. The oval gray leaves are toothed and have a pungent aroma. This species of catmint has less effect on cats and no known medicinal properties. It looks very attractive when grown in herbaceous beds or as an edging plant.

8IN (20CM)

Flowers are tubular and grow in clusters.

Stem is square, ridged, and slightly hairy.

Leaf is gray-green and pungent when crushed. Recent research has shown that the dried leaf is a deterrent to cockroaches.

Cultivation

Propagation In early spring, grow seeds under protection at 65°F (18°C). Germination usually takes 1–2 weeks, but it can take 3–4 weeks and may be erratic. Alternatively, sow seeds in late spring into prepared open ground, when the air temperature does not fall below 45°F (7°C) at night. Germination takes 2–3 weeks. In my opinion, sowing direct into open ground gives the best crop.

Site Plant in well-drained soil in a sunny position. A better crop is achieved in open ground rather than one grown in a container.

Maintenance A one-season crop. Prepare the site well prior to sowing. Do not feed with extra fertilizer once it has been planted.

Harvesting Collect the ripe seed pods and then crush and strain the contents to separate out the seeds. The seeds are either dried and then their oil extracted, or used whole or ground in medicine or in the kitchen.

Uses The seeds have a peppery aromatic flavor. Use in bread, cakes, sauces, curries, chutneys, and fish dishes. Medicinally, seeds are used in the treatment of respiratory conditions, allergies, fevers, flu, asthma, and emphysema. Research has shown that it inhibits certain forms of cancer. Sprinkling seeds in the folds of clothes acts as a moth and insect repellent. Commercially, the seeds are ground to make cooking oil.

Caution Do not take it medicinally during pregnancy.

Nigella Black cumin RANUNCULACEAE

A delicate and pretty herb, its black seeds were found in the Tomb of Tutankhamun. Cumin is mentioned in the Bible and has been used medicinally for thousands of years. It is also the "Muslim Miracle Herb" of which, according to an Arab proverb, it is said that "in the black seed is the medicine for every disease except death." Today, the seed of this herb is a popular spice in India, Egypt, and the Middle East. Do not confuse it with the garden plant love-in-a-mist (*Nigella damascena*); although they look similar, love-in-a-mist has no culinary or medicinal properties.

Nigella sativa
BLACK CUMIN, KALONJI
Half-hardy annual. Height 12in (30cm) and spread 9in (23cm). Small, pale blue to white flowers are produced in summer, followed by interesting horn-like seed pods, which contain black seeds. The gray-green leaves are finely serrated and divided.

Seed pods ripen to pale brown. They contain the black seeds that are used in cooking.

Flower is a very delicate pale gray.

Leaf is gray-green, very divided, and has little aroma.

5IN (12CM)

The Garden
PP. 21, 43, 49

Cultivation

Propagation Sow seeds in early spring. Cover with perlite or vermiculite (see page 45) and place under protection at 68°F (20°C). Keep watering to a minimum until germination takes place in 5–10 days. Once germinated, water sparingly to prevent seedlings from rotting. As the seedlings emerge, move the pots to a warm, light position and grow on. Plant out in the garden in a sheltered position, when all threat of frost has past. In warmer climates, with a minimum night temperature above 55°F (13°C), sow directly into a prepared site.

Site Plant in well-drained fertile soil in a sunny, warm site, which offers some shelter from the midday sun. It makes an ideal potted plant, especially in cool, temperate climates. Use a soil-based substrate. Basil is a good companion plant: it repels aphids, and fruit flies from other plants, as well as houseflies from the kitchen.

Maintenance
Mediterranean and Mexican basils are slightly hardier than the eastern basil and easier to grow outside in cooler climates. They are prone to attack from slugs, aphids, and red spider mite. Always pick the growing tips to encourage bushy growth.

Harvesting Pick leaves and flowering tops throughout the summer to use fresh or dry, or conserve in light olive oil (see page 88).

Uses Add fresh, torn leaves to salads, tomato, and pasta dishes. The flavor may be ruined if it cooks for too long. The leaves used fresh with cold food aid digestion. The juice of basil leaves rubbed onto skin repels mosquitoes.

Ocimum Basil LAMIACEAE

A pasta or tomato dish without the aroma and taste of basil is now quite naked, since it has become an everyday herb. It is best if you can grow your own – supermarket basil is grown as a salad crop and the plant only survives 3–5 days; it never sees the light of day or experiences the elements. Organically grown herbs raised in the garden have a much more pungent flavor, and when watered on a hot day, the aroma of the water drying on the leaf is fantastic. Basil has medicinal uses, too – in Elizabethan times, it was used as a snuff for colds, to clear the brain, and to soothe headaches.

Ocimum basilicum 'Cinnamon'
CINNAMON BASIL
Tender annual. Height 18in (45cm) and spread 12in (30cm). Clusters of small pink-mauve tubular flowers in summer. It has dark purple-brown stems and olive to green-brown, oval, pointed, and slightly serrated leaves that have a very spicy flavor. Cinnamon basil tastes particularly good in stir-fry dishes. It originates from Mexico.

Ocimum minimum 'Greek'
GREEK BASIL
Tender annual. Height 9in (23cm) and spread 6in (15cm). Clusters of small, white, tubular flowers are produced in summer. The leaves are small, green, oval, and pointed. In Greece, terracotta pots of this species of basil are placed on gate posts as a sign of welcome, or arranged on tables at mealtimes to keep away flies.

6IN (15CM)

Ocimum basilicum
SWEET BASIL, GENOVESE BASIL
Tender annual. Height 18in (45cm) and spread 12in (30cm).
Clusters of small, white tubular flowers appear in summer.
They have a lovely sweet classic basil flavor. The leaves are
green, oval, and pointed, and smell wonderful when crushed.
This is the variety of basil most commonly found in the
supermarkets and is the main type used in pesto sauce.

Leaf is smooth and highly
aromatic when crushed.

Ocimum basilicum 'Dark Opal'
DARK OPAL BASIL, PURPLE BASIL
Tender annual. Height 18in (45cm) and
spread 12in (30cm). It has clusters of small,
pink-mauve, tubular flowers in summer, light
purple stems, and dark purple, oval, pointed
leaves that have a very spicy warm flavor.
When added to rice and pastas, it provides a
stunning color contrast.

Stem is square in profile,
becoming woody with age.

Cultivation

Propagation Sow seeds in early spring. Cover with perlite or vermiculite (see page 45) and place under protection at 68°F (20°C), germination in 5–10 days. As these basils come from tropical climates, it is important to water in the morning, never at night, which in turn will help prevent the seedlings from damping off. Once the seedlings are large enough to handle, pot up and grow on as a potted plant. Plant in the garden or place the container outside only when the night temperature remains above 55°F (13°C).

Site Basil can only be grown in the garden in warm climates and even then needs shelter from midday sun.

Maintenance Only water in the morning. Keep picking the plant from the top to encourage it to bush out.

Harvesting Pick leaves and flowering tops throughout the summer to use fresh or to dry, or conserve in oil.

Uses In Thailand and other Asian countries, leaves are added to soups and fish dishes. The leaves are rarely used in Indian cooking. More often they are used to make herbal teas, combined with other herb seeds or simply with India tea leaves to make a refreshing drink. Medicinally, basil is used to treat bronchitis, colds, fevers, and stress. The juice of the leaves is used to alleviate skin complaints; the essential oil is used to treat ear infections by means of drops and rubbed onto the skin as an insect repellent. Research has shown that it has the ability to reduce blood sugar levels, and it is now being used in the treatment of some types of diabetes.

Ocimum Eastern basil LAMIACEAE

Our knowledge of culinary herbs like basil has widened with our increased interest in the cultures of countries such as India, Thailand, and Vietnam. I am particularly fascinated by the uses of basil in different societies. Holy basil (*O. tenuiflorum*), for example, is one of the sacred plants of India. This strongly flavored herb plays a key role in ceremonies of worship in thousands of homes and temples and in Hindu weddings, the parents of the bride present the groom with a basil leaf. The leaves are rarely used in Indian cooking – more often, they are mixed with Indian tea leaves to make a refreshing drink.

Ocimum basilicum 'Horapha Nanum'
THAI BASIL

Tender annual. Height 12in (30cm) and spread 8in (20cm). Clusters of small mulberry-purple tubular flowers appear in summer. The stem is dark purple to brown. The olive-green to purple leaves are oval in shape and slightly serrated. They have a hairy texture. The fresh leaves have a strong scent and flavor and are used in Thai and Vietnamese cooking.

Ocimum basilicum 'Siam Queen'
SIAM QUEEN BASIL

Tender annual. Height 12in (30cm) and spread 8in (20cm). Large clusters of small purple tubular flowers surrounded by mulberry-colored bracts in summer. It has a dark purple to brown stem, and olive-green to purple, oval, pointed, hairy, and slightly serrated leaves that have a pleasantly pungent scent and flavor. This is a cultivar of Thai basil that is easier to grow in temperate climates.

Seedhead *turns dark brown when fully ripe.*

Stem *is square and covered with fine hairs.*

Leaf *is very pungent and covered with very fine hairs.*

6IN (15CM)

Ocimum tenuiflorum

HOLY BASIL, TULSI

Tender annual. Height 12in (30cm) and spread 8in (20cm). Clusters of small pink-mauve tubular flowers appear in summer. The leaves are olive-green to brown-purple, oval, pointed, hairy, and slightly serrated, and have a very pungent scent and flavor.

Cultivation

Propagation Sow seeds in either spring or fall. Leave the seed uncovered by substrate and place it in a cold frame. Germination takes 3–4 weeks. If sowing in fall, pot up and winter the young plants in a cold frame before planting out. Or sow the seeds directly into prepared open ground in fall. Cover the soil with twigs to prevent birds from eating the seeds.

Site Plant in well-drained soil in a dry, sunny position. *O. biennis* is not suited to growing in containers because it is too tall. Shorter varieties are available, like *O. speciosa*, but it does not have medicinal properties.

Maintenance In the fall, cut back the flower heads before the seed pods open to prevent self-seeding. In winter, dig up the old roots of second-year growth of the biennials.

Harvesting Pick leaves to use fresh as required from spring until mid summer. Pick the flowers in bud or as they open throughout the summer. Dig up roots of the second-year's growth before seeds have set – they are at their best for medicinal use at this stage – in late summer. Collect seeds in early fall.

Uses Add fresh young leaves to salads. Cook mature leaves like spinach. The roots have an earthy, nutty flavor, and can be cooked like parsnips. Use seeds in baking. Medicinally, the seed oil is used to treat dry skin. The leaf and stem can be infused to make an astringent facial steam.

Caution Do not take evening primrose if you suffer from epilepsy.

Oenothera Evening primrose ONAGRACEAE

The potential of this herb is enormous because all parts of the plant are edible. Its value as a healing herb was recognized by Native Americans, who used it as a healing poultice for soothing itchy rashes and bites. The seeds contain a rich source of essential fatty acids, which in modern diets are often deficient. Oil extracted from the seeds of this plant is now used to treat medical conditions including chronic fatigue syndrome, premenstrual syndrome, hyperactivity in children, liver damage, and eczema.

Flower has four petals and is scented only in the evening when it opens.

4IN (10CM)

Oenothera biennis
EVENING PRIMROSE
Hardy biennial. Height in the second season reaches up to 4ft (1.2m) and spread 3ft (90cm). The yellow trumpet-shaped flowers are night-scented. The flowers appear in the second season and are followed by oval, downy pods containing masses of small seeds. The green leaves are lance-shaped.

Leaf is lance-shaped and textured.

The Garden
PP. 21, 43, 49, 66

Cultivation

Propagation First scarify the seed (see page 46). In early fall, sow fresh seeds and cover with coarse horticultural sand. Place under protection at 70°F (21°C) for 3–4 weeks. Then lower to 60°F (15°C). Germination takes 1–12 months. In summer, take cuttings from new growth, but do not let them dry out. It takes 4–8 weeks for them to root. In cool climates, grow all young plants in pots under protection (cold frame, cloche or greenhouse) for 4 years before planting out.

Site Plant in well-drained soil in full sun. It is a mix of wet and cold conditions that kill, not just cold. In arid, temperate, and cold climates grow as a container plant. Use a soil-based substrate.

Maintenance In Greece, I have seen olive plants grown as a hedge, which proves it can be clipped. Cut back in spring. To produce a good crop of fruit, do not let the plant dry out. Feed every fall with well-rotted manure or compost. Feed container-grown plants from spring until fall with liquid seaweed. Scale insect may attack container-grown plants.

Harvesting Pick leaves to use fresh as required. Pick fruit either when green or black, and treat (as described below) before eating.

Uses To make the fruit palatable, it has to be soaked in brine, salt, or oil prior to eating. The leaves can be infused and used as an antiseptic wash for cuts and grazes, or made into a tea to lower blood pressure and reduce nervous tension. The oil is good for circulatory diseases and helps improve digestion. Olive oil is one of the safest laxatives.

Olea Olive tree OLEACEAE

The olive tree, with its beautiful knarled bark and twisted trunk, is as old as the hills that it grows on. In the Old Testament, the dove returned to Noah's Ark with a sprig of olive in its beak, which showed that the flood waters were abating. It has been the symbol of peace for centuries. The Greeks and Romans valued the oil, and the winners of the Olympic Games were crowned with its leaves. Today, olive oil and the green and ripe black fruits remain a vital ingredient of the daily diet of Mediterranean people.

Leaf has a leathery texture, indicating that it does not need much water to survive.

Fruit starts off green and ripens to black. It cannot be eaten straight from the tree.

6IN (15CM)

Young, immature olive fruit follows flower.

Olea europea
OLIVE TREE
Evergreen tree. Height up to 30ft (10m). Numerous clusters of small creamy-white fragrant flowers in early summer, followed by green olive fruits that ripen to black. The oval gray-green leaves are leathery in texture with silvery undersides.

FOR USE IN **The Garden** 21, 43, 46, 53, 65

Cultivation

Propagation Mix the fine seed of *O. vulgare* with horticultural sand or flour to make it easier to handle. Sow in spring, but do not cover the seed. Place under protection at 68°F (20°C). Germination takes 10–20 days. The seedlings are prone to "damping off" so do not overwater. In summer, take cuttings from new growth. In warm climates, propagate established plants by division (see page 57) in spring or after flowering.

Site Plant in well-drained soil in a sunny position. The sun brings the aromatic oils up to the leaf surface and gives the plant its flavor and aroma. Oreganos attract bees and butterflies, so they are good companion plants, encouraging fertilization of vegetable crops. All oreganos grow successfully in containers using a soil-based substrate, mixed with extra sharp grit or sand.

Maintenance Cut back after flowering to encourage new growth, which will give added protection in winter. Feed once in spring, and once after cutting back, with liquid comfrey (see page 39).

Harvesting Pick leaves before flowering to use fresh or to dry. After the end of summer, cut back, and use the fresh leaves immediately; fresh leaf flavor deteriorates quickly in cold climates.

Uses For maximum flavor, use the herb dried in cooking. Oregano is a good antiseptic due to its high thymol oil content. It is used to treat respiratory conditions like bronchitis and asthma.

Caution Do not take medicinally during pregnancy. Do not take the essential oil internally.

Origanum Hardy oreganos LAMIACEAE

Oregano is a favorite in the kitchen. It combines particularly well with tomato dishes, pasta, meat (especially lamb), and fish. The heady aroma of this sun-loving herb fills the mountainous Mediterranean landscape, and it is credited with lifting people's spirits. The word oregano is derived from the Greek "oros" meaning mountain and "ganos" meaning joy and beauty, hence its full meaning "joy of the mountain." The ancient Greeks believed that wild oregano (*O. vulgare*) was a cure-all, including, as Aristotle suggested, an antidote for poison. Medicinally, it is probably one of the best antiseptics.

Origanum vulgare 'Acorn Bank'
OREGANO ACORN BANK

Hardy herbaceous perennial. Height and spread 18in (45cm). Clusters of tiny tubular pink flowers in summer. The golden-yellow leaves are oval and pointed in shape, and have a hairy texture and are aromatic. In winter, the leaves die back to form a mat on the ground. Protect the plant from full sun, since these golden leaves are prone to sun scorch. This variety is successfully grown from cuttings only.

Origanum x *onites*
FRENCH MARJORAM, FRENCH OREGANO

Hardy herbaceous perennial. Height and spread 18in (45cm). Clusters of tiny tubular pale pink flowers appear in summer. The oval leaves are green with a hint of gold. They have a hairy texture and are aromatic. Like other oreganos, they die back in winter to form a mat on the ground. This oregano has a light spicy flavor and tastes good with vegetable dishes. Grow from cuttings only.

Flower *has a classic herby flavor. Oregano flowers attract butterflies.*

Leaf *is very aromatic when crushed or eaten.*

Stem *is square and covered with fine hairs.*

4IN (10CM)

Origanum vulgare

OREGANO, WILD MARJORAM

Hardy, herbaceous perennial. Height and spread 18in (45cm). Clusters of tiny tubular mauve flowers appear in summer. The dark green hairy aromatic leaves die back to form a mat in winter. The vigor and flavor of this plant is affected by its planting site, and hours of sunshine.

Cultivation

Propagation See page 212 for details.

Site Half-hardy oreganos are ideal for rock gardens, which simulate their native stony landscape. Plant in well-drained soil in a sunny position. *O. majorana* is a good companion plant, since it deters aphids and is thought to improve the flavor of vegetables when planted between rows.

Maintenance See page 212 for details.

Harvesting See page 212 for details.

Uses *O. majorana* is the species of marjoram most commonly found on pizzas and added to dried herb mixtures. It is an ingredient in bouquet garni (see page 94). Medicinally, sweet marjoram tea helps ease bad colds, headaches, and insomnia, and has a calming effect on the nerves. Chewing the leaf will give temporary relief from toothache. It is also said to reduce sexual libido.

Caution Do not take the essential oil of *O. majorana* internally. Do not take origanums as a medicine when pregnant.

Origanum Half-hardy oreganos LAMIACEAE

I am often asked to explain why some members of the *Origanum* family are called oregano and others marjoram. What is the difference? Are their names interchangeable? The only species to include marjoram in its Latin name is *Origanum majorana* (known commonly as sweet marjoram), so logic would suggest that it is the only true marjoram. In the rest of Europe, however, this is not the case, and several edible oreganos are called marjoram, so perhaps the only way to be quite sure it to check the Latin name. Whichever common name you choose, *Origanum* species all look and smell wonderful. In cooking their flavor transforms an ordinary dish into a Mediterranean delight, and for personal wellbeing they act as a very good tonic.

Origanum dictamnus
CRETAN OREGANO, DITTANY OF CRETE

Half-hardy perennial shrub. Height up to 6in (15cm) and spread 16in (40cm). The tiny pink tubular flowers are surrounded by gray-green bracts that turn pink-purple in summer as they mature. The rounded, gray-green leaves are highly aromatic, and covered with soft wooly white down. The leaves have both culinary and medicinal uses.

FOR USE IN The Garden PP. 21, 43, 49, 53, 58, 62 The Kitchen PP. 85, 88, 94, 95 The Home PP. 100, 102, 109, 110, 111

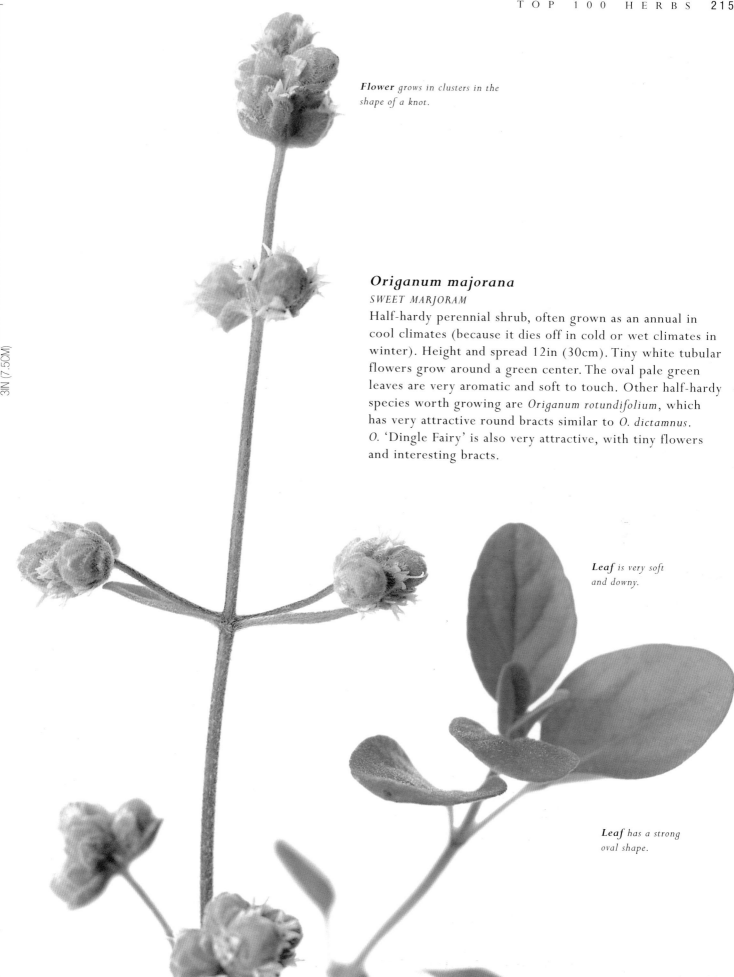

Flower grows in clusters in the shape of a knot.

Origanum majorana

SWEET MARJORAM

Half-hardy perennial shrub, often grown as an annual in cool climates (because it dies off in cold or wet climates in winter). Height and spread 12in (30cm). Tiny white tubular flowers grow around a green center. The oval pale green leaves are very aromatic and soft to touch. Other half-hardy species worth growing are *Origanum rotundifolium*, which has very attractive round bracts similar to *O. dictamnus*. *O.* 'Dingle Fairy' is also very attractive, with tiny flowers and interesting bracts.

Leaf is very soft and downy.

Leaf has a strong oval shape.

3IN (7.5CM)

Cultivation

Propagation These species can be propagated from seed. Sow in spring at 65°F (18°C) and place under protection. Germination takes 2–3 weeks and can be erratic. A more reliable method of propagation is to take cuttings in early summer from new growth. Under protection, cuttings will take 2–3 weeks to root.

Site In warm climates, when the night temperature does not fall below 48°F (9°C) plant in well-drained soil in a sunny position, sheltered form cold winds. In cold climates, plant in a pot and sink the pot in the garden for the growing season. Dig up the pot and bring it inside before the first frost. Scented pelargoniums also grow well as container plants, using a loam-based substrate.

Maintenance In cold climates, keep watering to a minimum in winter, and move potted plants to a frostfree environment. In spring, start watering slowly. For container-grown plants, water from the top, and let the water drain through. Do not leave the plant to sit in a saucer of water. Feed weekly with liquid comfrey (see page 39) from early spring until early fall. To maintain plant shape, nip out the growing tips. Scented pelargoniums are prone to disease, including black leg virus, gray mold, leaf gall, and rust – destroy infected plants.

Harvesting Pick leaves to use fresh or for drying in spring and summer.

Uses Rose-scented varieties can be used to flavor stewed apples and pears, as well as jellies and gelatins. See page 218 for other uses.

Pelargonium Scented pelargoniums GERANIACEAE

John Tradescant (d.1638), the botanist and gardener to Britain's King Charles I, introduced the scented pelargonium to the country from its native South Africa. This half-hardy plant grows well in containers and is happy in a sheltered site such as conservatory or on a kitchen windowsill. Unlike the true geranium, pelargoniums have relatively small, unscented flowers, but the fragrant leaves are present all year round and add flavor to desserts. They can also be used as natural air fresheners. Pelargoniums are very easy to hybridize, so each year plants with new leaf fragrances and flavors appear.

Pelargonium 'Chocolate Peppermint'
PELARGONIUM CHOCOLATE PEPPERMINT
Half-hardy, evergreen perennial. Height up to 24in (60cm) and spread 36in (1m). Clusters of very small white-pink flowers appear in summer. The green and brown variegated leaves are large, rounded, and shallow-lobed. They have a velvety texture and smell of peppermint with a hint of chocolate when rubbed or crushed.

Pelargonium 'Lady Plymouth'
PELARGONIUM LADY PLYMOUTH
Half-hardy evergreen perennial. Height and spread up to 24in (60cm). Clusters of small pink flowers appear in summer. The gray-green and cream variegated leaves are deeply cut and smell of a mixture of rose and peppermint when rubbed or crushed.

Pelargonium 'Attar of Roses'

PELARGONIUM ATTAR OF ROSES

Half-hardy evergreen perennial. Height up to
24in (60cm) and spread 12in (30cm).
Clusters of small, unscented pink flowers
appear in summer. The mid-green, three-lobed
leaves are covered with fine hairs and smell of
roses when rubbed or crushed.

Flowers grow in small clusters.

Leaf is covered with fine
hairs. It is highly scented
when crushed.

Stem has a velvety texture.

5IN (12.5CM)

Cultivation

Propagation See page 216 for details.

Site See page 216 for details.

Maintenance See page 216 for details.

Harvesting See page 216 for details.

Uses Infuse fresh leaves in milk, cream, and syrups for desserts, custards, and ice-cream or sherbets. When making cakes and pies, line the pan with the leaves. To make them lie flat in the pan, dip the leaves in hot water and shake dry. Add dried scented pelargonium leaves to pot-pourri or to cheesecloth bags to fragrance clothes and linens.

Pelargonium Fruit-scented pelargoniums GERANIACEAE

Simply by brushing past a pelargonium plant or rubbing the leaf between your fingertips, you can release a wonderful fruity fragrance. The variety of scents is astounding and ranges from intense lemon and peppermint to apples and sweet peaches. The Victorians favored pelargoniums as houseplants, and in the early nineteenth century, French perfume makers started to grow and harvest pelargonium plants on a large scale for perfume manufacture. Pelargonium leaves are still used to make geranium essential oil — an uplifting aromatherapy oil.

Pelargonium 'Apple Scented'
APPLE-SCENTED PELARGONIUM, APPLE GERANIUM

Half-hardy, evergreen perennial. Height up to 24in (60cm) and spread 36in (1m). Clusters of very small white flowers are produced in summer. The leaves are velvety, soft, and rounded with shallow lobes, and have an apple scent when rubbed or crushed. This pelargonium has a trailing habit and grows well in containers.

Pelargonium 'Atomic Snowflake'
PELARGONIUM ATOMIC SNOWFLAKE

Half-hardy, evergreen perennial. Height up to 24in (60cm) and spread 36in (1m). Clusters of small pink flowers appear in summer. The variegated green and silver-gray leaves are large, rounded, and shallow-lobed. They have an intense lemon fragrance when rubbed or crushed. This variety can be used to add a lemon flavoring to yellow cakes.

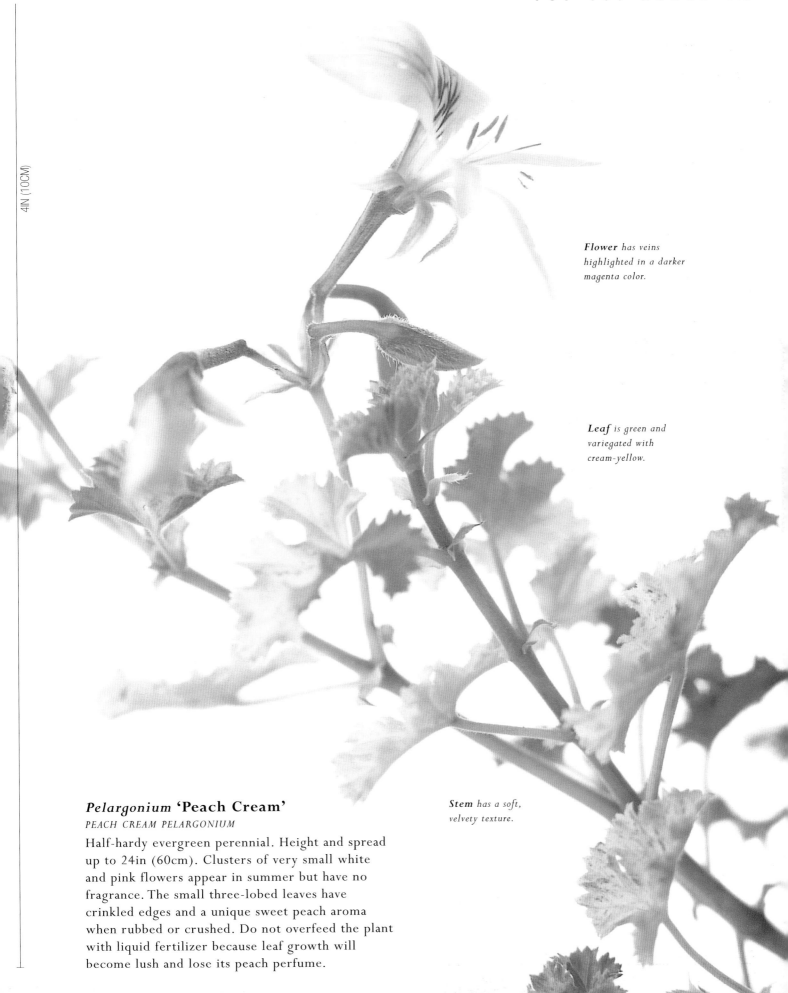

Flower *has veins highlighted in a darker magenta color.*

Leaf *is green and variegated with cream-yellow.*

Stem *has a soft, velvety texture.*

4IN (10CM)

Pelargonium 'Peach Cream'

PEACH CREAM PELARGONIUM

Half-hardy evergreen perennial. Height and spread up to 24in (60cm). Clusters of very small white and pink flowers appear in summer but have no fragrance. The small three-lobed leaves have crinkled edges and a unique sweet peach aroma when rubbed or crushed. Do not overfeed the plant with liquid fertilizer because leaf growth will become lush and lose its peach perfume.

Cultivation

Propagation Sow seeds in spring under protection at 68°F (20°C). Germination takes 1–2 weeks. Or sow in late spring in prepared open ground, when the night temperature does not fall below 45°F (8°C). In these conditions, it takes 14–20 days for germination to occur.

Site Plant in fertile, well-drained soil that has been dug the previous fall with well-rotted compost or leaf mold. Plant in the late spring in sun or partial shade. In arid climates, irrigation is necessary. Use a soil-based substrate when growing as a container plant.

Maintenance Pinch out growing tips to maintain the plant shape and to encourage bushy growth. Feed container plants weekly with liquid comfrey (see page 39). Remove caterpillars.

Harvesting Pick leaves to use fresh as required, and flowering tops in late summer. Harvest seeds in late fall.

Uses Purple shiso leaf is used as a natural dye for pickling vegetables and fruit like plums, and as flavoring in tea. The flowerheads are used as a seasoning for sushi. Green leaf shiso tastes of cumin with a hint of anise and cinnamon. In Japan, green leaf shiso is bought as a vegetable. The fresh leaves are used to wrap up rice, in salads, and tempura. The seed from this variety is used as a condiment. The flowering parts contain a substance even sweeter than sugar, and is used in Japanese confectionery.

Caution Can cause contact dermatitis.

Perilla Shiso LAMIACEAE

The first time I displayed purple shiso (*Perilla frutescens* var. *purpurascens*) at the Chelsea Flower Show, its striking appearance caused a storm of interest. Purple shiso is one of the few aromatic plants used in Japanese cuisine and is also an ancient ingredient of Chinese medicine. The common name "beefsteak plant" originated in the U.S., and refers to the size of the purple shiso's leaf, which looks like a large slice of raw beef. A useful culinary herb, the fresh leaf is excellent in stir-fry dishes and tempura.

Perilla frutescens var. *purpurascens*
PURPLE SHISO, BEEFSTEAK PLANT
Hardy annual. Height up to 4ft (1.2m) and spread 24in (60cm). It has deeply cut, dark purple leaves with crinkled bronzed edges, which are aromatic when crushed or eaten. It bears pink flowers in summer. There may be visible differences in plants raised from seed; the flower spikes can be red and the leaf surface smoother.

Flower grows in small clusters.

8IN (20CM)

Perilla frutescens var. *crispa*
GREEN SHISO, GREEN CUMIN
Hardy annual. Height up to 4ft (1.2m) and spread 24in (60cm). Leaves are bright green, but otherwise have the same appearance and aroma as purple shiso. It bears small white flowers in summer. In plants raised from seed, flowers may be cream and the leaves smooth.

Leaf flavor is a mixture of cumin and nutmeg with a hint of plums.

Cultivation

Propagation Take cuttings in spring until late summer. Also, because plant stems that come into contact with the soil take root easily, you can propagate Vietnamese coriander by simply cutting one of these stems with roots and potting it in a mix of bark and vermiculite. In spring until late summer, you can propagate established plants by division (see page 57).

Site This tropical plant will need protection when temperatures fall below 45°F (7°C) at night. In warm climates, plant in rich fertile soil in partial shade. It grows well as a potted plant in a soil-based substrate. A vigorous plant: repot twice a year to keep healthy.

Maintenance Because this plant is invasive, dig up and remove any surplus roots to keep it under control. In cool climates, it may disappear if you are reorganizing the garden, so take cuttings as insurance.

Harvesting Pick the leaves to use fresh as required throughout the growing season.

Uses The young leaf tastes like mild coriander (*Coriandrum sativum*). As it grows, it takes on a hint of lemon, and then mature leaves develop a strong peppery flavor that can dominate. Use as a fresh leaf condiment, at the end of cooking. Important in Vietnamese dishes, this herb is used in noodle soups (pho) prepared from vegetables, seafood, or meat, and also in stir-fried meat and vegetable dishes.

Caution Do not confuse this herb with the inedible *Persicaria bistorta*.

FOR USE IN

Persicaria Vietnamese coriander POLYGONACEAE

It is always interesting how new varieties of herb arrive at my farm – often by very circuitous routes. This plant was taken by some Vietnamese refugees to Australia, where it was given to a nurseryman, who in turn sent it to a friend in Britain who specialized in plants of the *Polygonaceae* family. He then gave it to me, knowing that I would be interested. In Australia, the essential oil produced by Vietnamese coriander, called "kesom oil," is undergoing research for its use as a natural food flavoring.

Persicaria odorata
VIETNAMESE CORIANDER, RAU RAM
Tender evergreen perennial. Height 18in (45cm) and spread indefinite. Attractive small creamy-white flowers appear in summer, though rarely in cultivated plants, or in cold climates. The green leaves are narrow and pointed, with a brown-maroon V-shaped marking near the base. The leaves are highly aromatic when crushed and have a very strong flavor.

8IN (20CM)

Leaf has a V-shaped marking near its base.

Stem is composed of many joints linked together by slightly bent "knots," which is typical of the Polygonaceae family.

The Garden
PP. 21, 43, 53, 55, 67, 68

Cultivation

Propagation The secret to growing parsley successfully is to keep the temperature consistent during germination and to keep the soil moist. Sow the seeds in early spring and place under protection at 65°F (18°C). Germination takes 2–4 weeks. Alternatively, sow the seeds in late spring in prepared open ground when the air temperature does not fall below 45°F (7°C) at night. Water the site well prior to sowing. Germination takes 2–4 weeks.

Site Plant in sun or partial shade in deep fertile soil that has been fed the previous fall with well-rotted manure. Ideally, the site should be sheltered from the sun.

Maintenance To deter carrot-root fly, plant either chives or garlic since their scent will discourage the fly. Or use horticultural fleece or a cloche to create a protective barrier over the crop, or improvise with a cut-off plastic bottle. Young parsley plants are also prone to slug attack. Sprinkle bran around the plants to protect your crop. Do not allow plants to dry out in summer. Feed weekly with liquid comfrey feed (see page 39).

Harvesting Pick fresh leaves as required during the growing season.

Uses Parsley leaves are a key ingredient in bouquet garni (see page 94), and are widely used in cooking. Medicinally, parsley leaves are strongly diuretic, and a hair rinse made from the seeds is effective for killing head lice. Infuse one teaspoon of crushed seeds for 10 minutes, strain, and use as a final rinse.

Caution Do not take medicinally if pregnant.

Petroselinum Parsley APIACEAE

This culinary delight and natural breath freshener is without doubt the most popular and well-known herb that I grow. It has been cultivated for thousands of years. The ancient Greeks associated parsley with death and so avoided eating it. Instead, they used it combined with rue (*Ruta graveolens*), see page 231, as an edging plant. The Romans used it to disguise strong odors, but believed that the seeds had to go the devil and back seven times before it would germinate. There are many recorded myths that are equally preoccupied with how to achieve successful germination of parsley seed. But if you follow the simple techniques outlined here, you will find that it is not as difficult to grow as past civilizations imagined.

Petroselinum crispum 'French'
FRENCH PARSLEY, FLAT-LEAFED PARSLEY
Hardy biennial. Height up to 24in (60cm) and spread 12in (30cm). Small creamy-white flowers grow in flat umbels in the summer of the second season. The mature leaves are flat, dark green, and divided with serrated edges. In my opinion, this species of flat-leaf parsley has a stronger flavor than curled-leaf varieties. It is lovely used in sauces and soups – or simply tear up the leaves and add to salads.

FOR USE IN

The Garden   The Kitchen
PP. 21, 43, 49, 62   PP. 84, 86, 88, 90, 91, 93, 94, 95

3IN (8CM)

Leaf *is bright green with serrated curly edges.*

Petroselinum crispum

PARSLEY

Hardy biennial. Height up to 16in (40cm) and spread 12in (30cm). Flat umbels of small creamy-white flowers appear in the summer of the second season. The bright green leaf has a fresh, mild flavor. The leaves have a higher vitamin C content than an orange.

Cultivation

Propagation In the fall, separate the seed from the flesh (see page 74) and either sow at once or the following spring (store seed in the refrigerator or in a cold, dry place). Pot up and cover with coarse horticultural sand and place in a cold frame. Germination takes 3–4 weeks. In winter, protect fall-sown seedlings in the cold frame. In either spring or fall, propagate established plants by division (see page 57), replanting in a well-prepared site.

Site Plant in fertile, moist soil, in sun or partial shade.

Maintenance To prevent the plant from producing berries and self-seeding, cut off the flowers just after flowering.

Harvesting Only pick fresh young leaves for cooking – mature leaves are toxic. In the fall, pick ripe berries to use medicinally or as a natural dye. For medicinal use, dig up the root of 2-year-old plants in the fall.

Uses The young leaves can be eaten like spinach, but must be boiled for 30 minutes in at least two changes of water before they are safe to eat. Eat with care. Medicinally, this herb should only be taken under professional supervision. It is used to treat chronic infections and as a poultice or ointment for fungal infections and scabies. A crimson textile dye can be made from ripe berries.

Caution Since the mature plant leaves and berries are toxic to humans, choose your site very carefully, and even though the cooked young leaves taste like spinach, never grow this plant in the vegetable garden.

Phytolacca Pokeroot PHYTOLACCACEAE

This herb is classed as a weed in the U.S. but in Europe it is valued as both a structural and ornamental garden plant. Herbalists use it with respect. Currently, it is being researched for its ability to stem the debilitating tropical disease bilharzia (carried by water snails) because the plant root is known to destroy snails. Traditionally, the young shoots of pokeroot were considered a wonderful culinary delicacy, but prepared incorrectly this plant is poisonous.

Berry is toxic to humans, but will attract birds to the garden.

8IN (20CM)

Flower is cup-shaped with a green center.

Phytolacca americana
POKEROOT, POKE BERRY

Hardy herbaceous perennial. Height and spread up to 5ft (1.5m). In summer, long clusters of small cup-shaped flowers with a hint of pink, white, and green appear. They are followed by poisonous black berries on bright pink stems. The mid-green leaves are lance-shaped, and in the fall, the leaf edges turn pink and orange.

Leaf is oval and lance-shaped. When mature, the crushed leaf releases an unpleasant odor.

The Garden

PP. 21, 43, 49, 58, 69

Cultivation

Propagation Sow seeds in early spring and place under protection at 68°F (20°C). Germination takes 1–2 weeks. Alternatively, sow into a prepared site in late summer, when the night temperature does not fall below 50°F (10°C).

Site Purslane will grow anywhere in light soil in temperate climates, but in cool and cold climates, sow each year in well-drained, fertile soil in a sunny site. Plant in soil that has been fed with well-rotted manure in the fall before planting – there is no need to feed again. It will grow in containers in a soil-based substrate mixed with a small amount of sharp grit, for extra drainage.

Maintenance Cover seedlings with horticultural fleece to deter pests like flea beetles and check regularly for slugs, who adore young plants. It does not need feeding, but water regularly to prevent the soil from drying out during summer months. However, avoid overwatering; this plant does not like to sit in water.

Harvesting Pick leaves, stems, and flower buds to use fresh throughout the growing season.

Uses The leaves, stems, and flower buds can be eaten raw in salads or cooked like a vegetable. It is a good source of vitamins A, B, and C, and calcium. In the Mideast, it is an ingredient of a traditional salad called fattoush. It is often pickled in vinegar. A natural diuretic, purslane is used to clear toxins from the body and lower fevers. It also helps build up the immune system.

Caution Do not take medicinally when pregnant.

FOR USE IN

Portulaca Purslane PORTULACACEAE

This herb has been grown for thousands of years as a vegetable and as a medicinal herb. It was popular in England in the reign of Elizabeth I, but it is no longer fashionable as a culinary herb in Britain, even though it is a popular salad herb in Europe. Research has shown that it contains a rich source of omega-3 fatty acids, which help to maintain a healthy heart and strengthen the immune system. Personally, I love the taste of this herb, and often eat fresh purslane leaves straight from the garden.

Portulaca oleracea

PURSLANE, PIG WEED

Hardy annual. Height up to 18in (45cm) and spread 24in (60cm). Its small yellow flowers open in the summer sun and close in the shade. It has thick, fleshy, spoon-shaped, mid-green leaves, which taste like a succulent version of snow peas.

6IN (15CM)

Leaves are fleshy, and the juice is soothing when applied to insect bites and burns. It also soothes eczema.

Stem is edible. Cut into bite-sized chunks to add crunch to salads.

The Garden   The Kitchen

PP 21, 43, 49, 62, 66   PP. 84

Cultivation

Propagation It is important to use fresh seed. Sow in late summer and place in a cold frame. Germination takes 2–3 weeks. Winter the young plants in the cold frame, planting out into a prepared site the following spring. It may not flower in the first season. In fall, propagate established plants by division (see page 57).

Site Plant in moist soil in semi-shade. In the wild, primroses thrive on west-facing banks, close to deciduous hedges and trees. Bear this natural habitat in mind when choosing a site in the garden. Primrose grow well in containers or as house plants, using a soil-based substrate. Outside, shelter the container from the midday sun; indoors keep it away from radiators.

Maintenance All primulas need to be divided in the fall to keep the plant healthy. Division also protects pot-grown plants from attack by vine weevil.

Harvesting In the fall, dig up the roots of 3–4-year-old plant to dry for medicinal use. In spring, pick flowers and leaves to use fresh in salads or to dry for medicinal use.

Uses Add flowers and young leaves to salads or desserts. Medicinally, the flowers, leaves, and roots are used to treat respiratory tract infections, insomnia, and anxiety. The flowers are used in infusion, ointments, and tinctures to treat minor wounds. Do not take medicinally when pregnant or on anti-coagulant drugs or if allergic to aspirin.

Caution All primulas can cause skin allergies or irritation when handled.

Primula Primrose PRIMULACEAE

This pretty yellow flower with its delicate scent marks the arrival of spring. It is the flower of my childhood: I used to pick tiny bunches of primroses from the garden at Easter, tie them up with yarn, and give them to my mother as a gift. Surprisingly, primroses are classified as an herb because the flowers possess useful medicinal properties. They were used to treat gout, respiratory tract infections, insomnia, and anxiety. The flowers and young leaves also have a good flavor and make an attractive addition to salads.

Primula vulgaris

PRIMROSE, FIRST ROSE

Hardy herbaceous perennial. Height and spread 6in (15cm). Sweetly scented pale yellow flowers with a deep yellow center appear in spring. The stems are covered with fine hairs. The mid-green oval-shaped leaves are textured. The primrose has become increasingly rare in the countryside. It is now illegal to dig up plants growing in the wild anywhere in Britain.

Leaf has a textured surface and the veins are visible.

3IN (7.5CM)

Flower grows singularly with four or five notched pale yellow petals with a darker center.

FOR USE IN

The Garden The Kitchen

PP. 21, 43, 49, 58, 64   PP. 83, 85

Prostanthera Australian mint bush LAMIACEAE

Cultivation

Propagation I have not known *Prostanthera* to set seed in Britain. After many trials, I have found it is best to propagate from cuttings taken from the current year's growth in late fall or winter. Once rooted, keep watering to a minimum, and winter it in a frostfree environment. Pot up in the spring and then grow on in pots, protecting young plants from winter frost for a further 2 years before planting out.

Site This alpine plant favors very free-draining soil and a sunny site. It prefers neutral to slightly acid soil. It grows well in containers using a peat-based substrate, mixed with extra grit for drainage.

Maintenance Do not overfeed this herb; otherwise, it will not flower — only feed container-grown plants once a month. Feed plants outside in the fall with leaf mold. It dislikes wet and damp conditions, so from fall on, cut down on watering, but do not let the substrate dry out. In early spring, slowly re-introduce weekly watering, depending on the weather. Container-grown plants are prone to sudden die-back. If a branch changes color from green to brown, cut it back to the main stem, and burn the diseased branches.

Harvesting Pick the leaves in summer for making infusions and oils.

Uses An essential oil from the leaves is used externally to alleviate tension and to release emotional exhaustion. Rub the oil into the temples to ease headaches. It can also be applied to the skin as a mosquito repellent. Mix a few drops with almond oil for massage.

This native Australian herb is quite stunning in flower, and I defy anyone not to want to try growing it in their garden. Medicinally, the leaves have been used to make an essential oil, which is beneficial for treating stress and tension, and the leaves have both antibacterial and antifungal properties. The fresh leaves also work as a decongestant. Simply place them in a bowl, pour boiling water over them, and inhale the steam. Australian mint bush remedies should only be used externally.

Prostanthera cuneata

AUSTRALIAN MINT BUSH, ALPINE MINT BUSH
Hardy evergreen shrub. Height 3ft (90cm) and spread 2ft (60cm). It has attractive white bell-shaped flowers with purple spots running down the flower's throat. Each flower occurs singularly, close to the end of a branch. The flowers appear from late spring until early summer. The small, dark green leaves are round with a wavy edge. When crushed, the leaves release a strong mint scent.

Leaf has a shiny, leatherlike texture.

Flower has distinct purple spots on the throat.

2IN (5CM)

FOR USE IN | The Garden

PP. 21, 43, 53

Cultivation

Propagation Sow seeds in early spring under protection at 70°F (21°C). Germination takes 1–2 weeks. After germination, do not over-water the seedlings because they are prone to "damping off" (see page 59). Or you can take cuttings of new growth in summer after flowering. Pot up when they are well rooted, and grow on under cold protection for one season before planting out. In spring or fall, rosemary can also be propagated by layering (see page 54). This is relatively simple since plants often have branches that droop down to the ground.

Site Plant in a warm, sunny site in well-drained, acid-free soil. This herb grows well in containers. Use a loam-based substrate and protect plants from wet or cold in winter.

Maintenance Rosemary can, in temperate climates, be grown successfully as a hedge. Cut back after flowering in late spring. This plant is prone to a die-back virus. Immediately cut the infected branch right off to the main stem, and burn, do not compost the branch. Act quickly, or the whole bush will die.

Harvesting Pick fresh leaves from this evergreen herb throughout the year.

Uses Rosemary leaf has many culinary uses. Medicinally, it alleviates hangovers and restores the memory. Rosemary aids recovery from long-term stress and chronic illness. The essential oil is a good insect repellent. Or, rub it onto the temples to alleviate headaches.

Caution The essential oil should only be taken externally. Excessive doses of rosemary leaf may cause convulsions.

Rosmarinus Rosemary LAMIACEAE

If I had to choose one culinary herb to take with me onto a desert island, it would be rosemary. It is one of the most versatile and useful herbs in the kitchen, in the home, and medicinally. It is associated with remembrance, and for hundreds of years, it was used to improve the memory. Currently, it is being tested in the treatment of senility. There are many lovely stories associated with it; one of my favorites is about the Virgin Mary, who is said to have thrown her blue cloak over a rosemary bush during her flight into Egypt, which turned its white flowers blue.

Rosmarinus officinalis 'Roseus'
PINK ROSEMARY
Hardy perennial evergreen. Height and spread 32in (80cm). Small pale pink flowers appear in early spring and last until early summer, with, occasionally, a second flush in early fall. It has short, needle-shaped, bright green leaves, with lighter undersides. These are highly aromatic when crushed.

Rosmarinus officinalis 'Aureus'
GOLDEN ROSEMARY, GILDED ROSEMARY
Hardy perennial evergreen. Height 32in (80cm) and spread 24in (60cm). Small very pale blue flowers appear in early spring and last until early summer. The highly aromatic leaves are short, thin, needle-shaped, and colored green splashed with gold. A slightly tender plant, you will need to protect it in temperatures below 28°F (-2°C).

FOR USE IN

The Garden   The Kitchen   The Home
PP. 21, 43, 49, 53, 55,   PP. 87, 88, 94, 95   PP. 100, 101, 102, 107,
64, 65   108, 109, 110, 112

Rosmarinus officinalis
ROSEMARY

Hardy perennial evergreen. Height and spread 3ft (1m). Small pale blue flowers appear in early spring and last until early summer, with, occasionally, a second flush in early fall. The short, needle-shaped, dark green leaves are highly aromatic. This is an important culinary and medicinal herb.

Leaf has a dark green shiny upper surface with a paler green underside.

8IN (20CM)

Rosmarinus officinalis **Prostratus Group**
PROSTRATE ROSEMARY

Hardy perennial evergreen. Height 12in (30cm) and spread 3ft (1m). Small light blue flowers appear in early spring and last until early summer, with, occasionally, a second flush in early fall. The leaves are short, needle-shaped, and dark green, and like other rosemary species are highly aromatic when crushed.

Flower tastes of sweet rosemary and is delicious with vegetable dishes.

Cultivation

Propagation Sow seeds in early spring and place under protection at 60°F (15°C). Germination takes 5–10 days. Alternatively, in late spring, sow seeds thinly into prepared open ground, when the air temperature does not fall below 45°F (7°C) at night. Germination takes 2–3 weeks. Thin seedlings to 12in (30cm) apart. Divide established plants in fall.

Site Plant in rich, fertile acid soil that has been fed with well-rotted manure in the fall before planting. Plants prefer sites shaded from the midday sun. French sorrel grows well in large containers. Use an ericaceous substrate and keep it out of the midday sun.

Maintenance The leaf flavor is best when the plant grows in cool soil. To prevent the leaves from becoming bitter in the summer months when the soil is warm, use a leaf or bark mulch (see page 37) to reduce soil temperature. Dry soil also impairs the leaf flavor, so keep the plants well watered. In the fall, feed around established plants with well-rotted manure. Feed container plants regularly throughout the growing season with liquid comfrey (see page 39). If plants become invasive, add lime to the soil to discourage growth.

Harvesting Pick leaves to use fresh throughout the growing season.

Uses Eating French sorrel in salads is thought to cleanse the blood and improve the hemoglobin content. Avoid overeating it while breast feeding, and do not take it if you have a tendency to develop kidney stones. The fresh leaves can also be used as a poultice to treat boils and acne.

Rumex French sorrel POLYGONACEAE

This sour but refreshing herb takes its name from the old French word "surelle" (meaning sour). The ancient Egyptians and Romans ate sorrel to counteract rich foods, and in fifteenth-century England, it was considered one of the finest vegetables. I am also of the opinion that it is a wonderful herb to use in hot and cold sauces and soups, while the young leaves can add a lemony or fresh apple flavor to summer salads.

Rumex scutatus
FRENCH SORREL, BUCKLER LEAF SORREL
Hardy herbaceous perennial. Height up to 18in (45cm) and spread 24in (60cm). It has small, inconspicuous green flowers that turn brown as seeds ripen. Its squat, shield-shaped leaves taste similar to crunchy green apples and can be eaten fresh or cooked. Crushed leaves are good for removing ink stains or rust marks from clothes and furniture.

3IN (7.5CM)

Flower bud is tinged red, but flowers are green.

Leaves are mid-green and shield-shaped.

Cultivation

Propagation Sow seeds in early spring and place under protection at 65°F (18°C). Germination takes 1–2 weeks. After germination, take care not to overwater because the seedlings are prone to "damping off" (see page 59). Take cuttings from new growth in late spring or early summer. Do not overwater; cuttings are prone to rot in damp conditions.

Site Plant in well-drained, poor soil. Choose a sunny position in the middle or back of a flowerbed where it will not be disturbed by passersby.

Maintenance Cut back to maintain the plant shape. Do this when the plant is dry, and wear gloves and cover your arms and legs to avoid being burned. Rue is prone to aphids, followed by a black sooty mold. Use horticultural soap, following manufacturer's instructions as soon as the pest appears on the plant. This soap will also control mold.

Harvesting Pick leaves to use fresh or to dry for medicinal use as required.

Uses This herb can be used in the kitchen, but is very bitter. A tastier culinary species is Egyptian rue *(Ruta chalapensis)*. Medicinally, rue was used for reducing blood pressure. It is still used in Mediterranean regions to stimulate the onset of menstruation. In homeopathy, rue is used to treat back pain, sciatica, strained muscles, tennis elbow, and eyestrain. In the home, dried rue will deter ants, and rue added to floral displays will deter flies.

Ruta Rue RUTACEAE

This herb has had some bad publicity because when the skin brushes against the leaves in certain weather conditions, it can cause phytol-photodermatitis (skin burn). However, rue is highly beneficial medicinally and is used in a number of homeopathic remedies. It also makes an attractive addition to the garden when planted in a carefully chosen site. To the Greeks and the Romans, it was considered the herb of grace, and all brides traditionally carried a sprig of rue in their wedding bouquet. It was also used as an antidote to snake venom and poisonous toadstools, and was thought to help preserve eyesight.

Ruta graveolens
RUE
Hardy evergreen shrub. Height and spread 24in (60cm). Small, yellow, waxy flowers with four or five petals in summer. The green-blue leaves are divided into small, rounded, oval lobes and have an unusual musky scent, which is hard to describe. To avoid skin burn, take care not to brush against the leaves when they are wet after rain or watering, or when they are in sunlight.

2IN (5CM)

Leaf is a rounded oval shape.

Leaf has an unusual, musky scent which acts as an effective fly deterrent.

Cultivation

Propagation Sow seeds in early spring, under cover at 65°F (18°C). Germination takes 1–2 weeks. Or sow seeds in late spring into open ground, when the air temperature at night remains above 45°F (7°C). Germination takes 2–3 weeks. Thin seedlings to 12in (30cm) apart. Protect young plants for the first winter. Take cuttings (see page 52) from perennial salvias in late spring to early summer. Propagate established woody plants by layering in either spring or fall (see page 54).

Site Plant in a warm sunny site in well-drained, acid-free soil. Hardy sages grow well in containers. Use a soil-based substrate and protect from wet or cold in winter.

Maintenance Prune lightly in spring to encourage young shoots for strong leaf flavor, and again after flowering in late summer. Clear away dead leaves from under the plant in spring to prevent mildew in damp weather. To sustain leaf flavor, replace the plant entirely every 4–7 years.

Harvesting Pick fresh leaves throughout the year. In spring (before the plant flowers), the leaves have a mild, warm flavor. After flowering, they have a stronger tannin flavor.

Uses Before cooking, quickly immerse sage leaves in hot water to bring the leaf oils to the surface and enhance the flavor. Sage is known to be antiseptic, astringent, carminative, antispasmodic, and a systemic antibiotic. It is used to treat sore throats, poor digestion, hormonal problems, and to stimulate the brain.

Uses Overuse of sage can have potentially toxic effects.

Salvia Sage LAMIACEAE

This Mediterranean herb has been in use for thousands of years. I never cease to be amazed by its healing and culinary properties. It was used to preserve meat, as an antiseptic, and as a cure for snakebite. Modern research has shown that it arrests the aging process, and it is being tested as a treatment for Alzheimer's. In addition, sage makes an attractive garden plant. The foliage presents a soft backdrop of gray-green, which sets off its pretty blue flowers in summer. Sage flowers are also very good for attracting butterflies and bees to the garden throughout the summer months.

Salvia officinalis Purpurascens Group
PURPLE SAGE, RED SAGE

Hardy perennial evergreen. Height and spread 28in (70cm). Grow from cuttings only. Mauve-blue flowers in summer. The aromatic oval leaves are a mix of purple-red-gray colors, and they have a soft texture. The leaves have a mild flavor and combine well with vegetable dishes, such as stuffed peppers and zucchini. Medicinally, purple sage makes a good antiseptic gargle for sore throats.

Salvia lavandulifolia
NARROW-LEAVED SAGE, SPANISH SAGE

Hardy perennial evergreen. Height and spread 18in (45cm). Grow from cuttings only. Attractive blue flowers appear in summer. The leaves are small, narrow, oval, textured, and highly aromatic, with an excellent strong culinary flavor. The leaves make a stimulating infusion. This sage is ideal for growing in containers.

FOR USE IN

The Garden	The Kitchen	The Home
PP. 21, 43, 49, 53, 55, 67	PP. 82, 88, 89, 90, 91, 94	PP. 102, 108, 109

Salvia officinalis

COMMON SAGE, GARDEN SAGE, SAWGE

Hardy perennial evergreen. Height and spread 2ft (60cm). It has highly aromatic, oval, green-gray textured leaves and mauve-blue flowers in summer. This is the standard culinary and medicinal sage. Types of sage with variegated leaves do not have such a strong flavor and are less potent medicinally.

Flower *petals form a protruding lower lip, which is characteristic of the Lamiaceae family.*

Leaf *is highly aromatic, velvet-textured, and feels raised to the touch.*

Stem *is square in profile – a distinguishing feature of this plant family.*

6IN (15CM)

Cultivation

Propagation Sow seeds in early spring under cover at 65°F (18°C). Germination takes 1–2 weeks. Or sow seeds in late spring into prepared open ground, when the air temperature remains above 45°F (7°C) at night. Germination takes 2–3 weeks. Thin seedlings to 8in (20cm) apart. *S. clevelandii* can only be grown from seed in warm climates. In late spring to early summer, you can take cuttings (see page 52) from the perennial species.

Site Plant in a warm, sunny site in well-drained, acid-free soil. Half-hardy salvias will only tolerate outdoor night temperatures above 50°F (10°C). They grow well in containers using a soil-based substrate. In winter, keep watering to a minimum since wet conditions kill them quicker than cold.

Maintenance Prune lightly in spring to encourage young shoots for a strong leaf flavor, and again after flowering in late summer. In the fall, collect the seeds from *S. viridis* and then remove this annual, digging over the patch. Before the first frost, lift half-hardy perennial salvia species, cut back flowering shoots, and pot up using a soil-based substrate. Protect in a glasshouse over the winter.

Harvesting Pick fresh leaves from evergreen sages as required. For drying, harvest leaves before flowering. Pick flowers as they open to use fresh or to dry.

Uses The cooking process destroys the flavor of aromatic sage leaves, so only add leaves to dishes right at the end. As leaf flavors are strong, only use a small amount to start with.

Salvia Aromatic sages LAMIACEAE

The genus *Salvia* includes over 900 species of aromatic annuals, biennials, and perennials, as well as evergreen shrubs. They are available in a choice of different colors and leaf fragrances, which gives them a special appeal. I am still amazed when crushing the leaf of Pineapple sage (*Salvia* 'Scarlet Pineapple') at how it smells so distinctly of fresh ripe pineapple. Many of the aromatic sages are winter hardy; those that are not are so beautiful that it is worth creating space in a conservatory or glasshouse to keep them in favorable conditions over the winter months.

Salvia clevelandii
JIM SAGE, CLEVELAND SAGE
Half-hardy shrub. Height up to 5ft (1.5m) and spread 3ft (90cm). Beautiful blue flowering spikes in summer. Oval, wrinkled green, slightly sticky aromatic leaves. The smell of this sage is the aroma of the California chaparral. Grow in very well-drained gravelly soil. Cut back one-third of growth in the fall, a further third in winter, leaving a third for the following season.

Salvia viridis syn. *S. horminum*
PAINTED SAGE, RED-TOPPED SAGE
Hardy annual. Height 18in (45cm), spread 8in (20cm). Small purple and white or pure white flowers, which are dominated by a series of colorful leaf bracts in shades of purple, pink, blue, and white that look like flower petals except that they are often marked with green veins. These colorful leaf bracts last all summer. The true green leaves are downy, rough-textured, and aromatic.

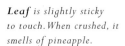

Leaf is slightly sticky to touch. When crushed, it smells of pineapple.

FOR USE IN   The Garden   The Kitchen
PP. 21, 43, 49, 53, 67   PP. 82, 83, 85

Salvia elegans 'Scarlet pineapple'

PINEAPPLE SAGE

Half-hardy perennial. Height 3ft (90cm), spread 2ft (60cm). Stunning trumpet-shaped red flowers appear from midsummer until early fall. The oval pointed green leaves have a slight red-brown tinge to the edges and a wonderful pineapple scent when crushed or rubbed between the fingertips.

Flower is narrow and trumpet-shaped with a protruding lower lip.

Salvia microphylla var. microphylla syn. S. grahamii

BLACKCURRANT-SCENTED SAGE

Half-hardy perennial evergreen. Height and spread up to 4ft (1.2m). Lovely raspberry-colored flowers with a characteristic lower lip that appear in late summer until early fall. Oval mid-green leaves smell of blackcurrants when rubbed between the fingertips.

5IN (12.5CM)

Cultivation

Propagation In late summer, separate the seed from the pulp and sow fresh. Cover the seed with coarse horticultural sand. In cold climates, place the potted seed outside to stratify it. Alternatively, mix the seed with sand in a glass jar and place in the refrigerator for 4 weeks before sowing. Germination takes 4–6 months. For the first winter, keep young plants in pots in a cold frame before planting out the following spring. Take cuttings from new growth in late summer.

Site Plant in fertile, moist soil in sun or dappled shade. Elder can grow up to 4ft (1.2m) in one season.

Maintenance To maintain a good shape and to keep rapid growth in check, prune hard back every three years during the fall. Elder is not suitable for growing in containers because it becomes too large.

Harvesting Pick the flowers in the spring just before they open fully. Gather berries in early fall.

Uses Fresh flowers are used to make elderflower cordial (see page 83). Medicinally, the flowers are used to treat coughs, colds, allergies, and arthritis. They are also used in skin lotions. The berries are mildly laxative and should only be eaten cooked in sauces, syrups, and pies. Elder spray is effective against aphids, caterpillars, carrot-root fly, and root maggots. Simmer 1ib (500g) leaves in 1 quart (1 liter) of water for 30 minutes, strain then dilute with another quart (liter) of water. (Do not use pan for food.) Apply by spray. All plant parts contain colored pigment and can be used as natural plant dyes.

Sambucus Elder CAPRIFOLIACEAE

This herb was once regarded as one of the most magically powerful of plants and offered protection against evil spirits. It is a truly useful herb – all parts of the plant have been exploited to make everything from delicious wine to a musical instrument. Elderflower has many culinary and medicinal uses, and current research shows that it can aid recovery from colds and flu. The berries are also a good source of vitamin A and C, but require cooking before eating to avoid stomach upsets. The leaves have a rather unpleasant scent when crushed and are poisonous, but they can be used in the organic garden to make a potent caterpillar or fly repellent.

Flower grows in large, flat clusters and has a sweet perfume.

Berry must be cooked before eating. It is a good source of vitamins A and C.

8IN (20CM)

Sambucus nigra
ELDER, COMMON ELDER, BLACK ELDER
Hardy deciduous shrub. Height up to 20ft (6m). Attractive, flat heads of lightly scented, creamy-white, star-shaped flowers appear in the summer and are followed by masses of small, round, black fruits. Its large leaves are made up of green saw-edged leaflets.

Leaves are large and serrated.

FOR USE IN

The Garden	The Kitchen	The Home
PP. 21, 43, 49, 53, 55	PP. 83, 91, 92	PP. 107, 108

Cultivation

Propagation Sow fresh seeds in the fall. Cover with perlite or vermiculite (see page 45), and place in a cold frame. Germination takes 2–3 weeks. Winter young plants in a cold frame. Alternatively, sow seeds in early spring, cover with perlite or vermiculite, and place under protection at 65°F (18°C). Germination takes 2–4 weeks. Divide established plants in the fall, replanting in a prepared outdoor site.

Site Plant in well-drained soil in sun or partial shade. In traditional herb gardens, salad burnet was often mixed with thyme and planted next to paths to perfume the air. This is a good system to follow, since paths give easy access to the plant, especially in winter. Alternatively, grow salad burnet in containers close to the house using a soil-based substrate.

Maintenance In hot weather, the leaves become bitter as the sun brings tannin to the surface. Trim the bush to keep it compact, and to inhibit flowering. Cutting back will also promote new, tender growth. For plants in containers, water regularly in the growing season, and feed once a week with liquid comfrey (see page 39).

Harvesting Pick the fresh young leaves as required.

Uses Salad burnet, as its name suggests, tastes good in salads. The leaf has a nutty, dry cucumber flavor, which also works well in sauces for broiled or poached fish. The young leaves can also be used in winter dishes as a substitute for parsley when it is out of season. Medicinally, chewing young salad burnet leaves aids digestion.

Sanguisorba Salad burnet ROSACEAE

Traditionally this pretty herb was infused in a drinking cup of wine or beer as a cure for gout and rheumatism. The soft green leaves are deceptive because salad burnet is an evergreen plant that survives winter conditions. Even in hard winters, salad burnet leaves will only die back for a short time before reappearing in early spring. This hardy nature makes salad burnet a useful herb to grow in the kitchen garden. It can be harvested throughout the winter when most other green salad leaves have died back.

4IN (10CM)

Flower head is shaped like a thimble. The flower is like a tiny powderpuff.

Leaves are toothed. Young leaves taste of cool cucumber.

Sanguisorba minor (syn. Poterium sanguisorba)

SALAD BURNET, PIMPERNEL
Hardy evergreen perennial. Height up to 24in (60cm) and spread 12in (30cm). Tiny magenta flowers appear in summer with compact, thimble-shaped heads. The flowering stalks stand out above the gray-green tooth-edged leaves. In summer, the mature leaves become very bitter to taste. Cut hard back to encourage new growth of the sweeter young leaves.

Cultivation

Propagation Sow seed in the fall in standard seed substrate mixed with horticultural sand and place in a cold frame. Germination takes 4–6 months. Grow on in a cold frame for 2 years before planting out. Take stem cuttings from new non-flowering growth in late summer. Winter young plants in a cold frame before planting out the following spring. In late summer, mature woody stems can be propagated by layering (see page 54). Cut off the flowers before you start the process.

Site Plant in well-drained soil in a sunny position. Avoid nutrient-rich soils for best results. Plant individual plants 24in (45cm) apart and hedge plants at 15in (38cm) intervals. Lavenders cotton grows well in containers. Use soil-based substrate. Feed once a week only during the growing season with a liquid seaweed fertilizer.

Maintenance Lavender cotton plants can be clipped to shape in spring after flowering. In spring, cut out dead wood from established plants. In late summer, cut off the flowers to prevent the plant from becoming woody. In cold climates, do not cut back lavender cotton in the fall because frost and damp will take hold and destroy the plant.

Harvesting Pick leaves for drying from spring until just before flowering in summer. In late summer, harvest small bunches of flowering stems for drying.

Uses An effective anti-inflammatory. Crushed leaves rubbed on insect bites will ease the pain.

Santolina Lavender cotton ASTERACEAE

This silver-leafed herb is both useful and attractive in the herb garden. Medicinally, it was used by Arabian people as an eyewash, but today it is used in the home as an insect and moth repellent. Some sources suggest that its aroma can also help to keep cats out of the flowerbeds, but after testing this, I can honestly say that it does not work. It is useful in herb garden design as an edging plant or as a dividing hedge within a larger bed, and is a suitable candidate for a dry or Mediterranean-type gravel garden.

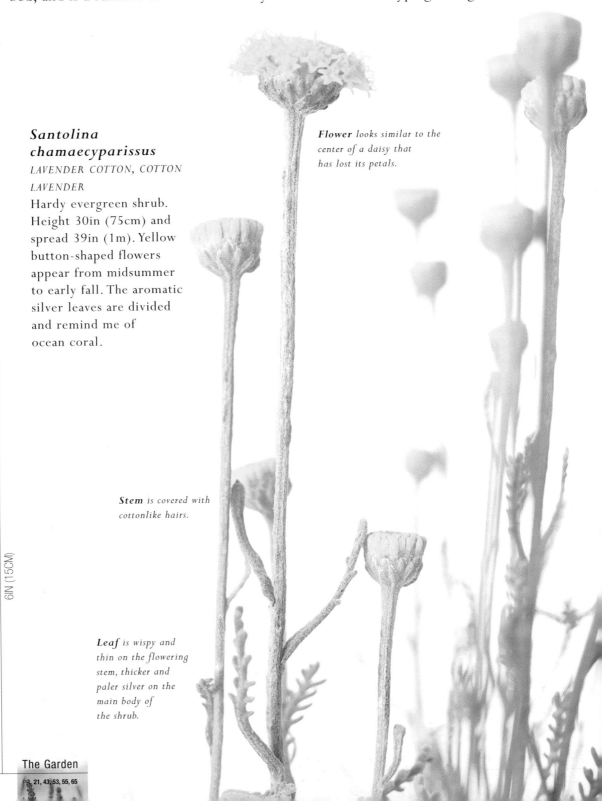

Santolina chamaecyparissus
LAVENDER COTTON, COTTON LAVENDER
Hardy evergreen shrub. Height 30in (75cm) and spread 39in (1m). Yellow button-shaped flowers appear from midsummer to early fall. The aromatic silver leaves are divided and remind me of ocean coral.

Flower looks similar to the center of a daisy that has lost its petals.

Stem is covered with cottonlike hairs.

Leaf is wispy and thin on the flowering stem, thicker and paler silver on the main body of the shrub.

6IN (15CM)

Cultivation

Propagation In my experience, it is far easier to grow soapwort from stem cuttings or by division than from seed – it takes a long time for the seed to germinate, and success is not always guaranteed. Take cuttings at the stem joint in late spring to early summer. Divide established plants in fall after cutting back.

Site This plant will tolerate any soil in a sunny position, but if the soil is too rich in nutrients, soapwort growth will be too rapid and difficult to control. Avoid planting soapwort near fish ponds because the plant has creeping rhizomes that excrete a poison in wet soil which is harmful to fish. Dwarf species like *Saponaria ocymoides* are better suited to containers because they are small.

Maintenance Cut back after flowering to clear up the garden and prevent self-seeding. Cutting back will also encourage new growth and, in mild winters, a second flowering. In fall, dig up any invasive roots.

Harvesting Pick fresh leaves as required throughout the growing season.

Uses Soapwort is used as a treatment for dry itchy skin conditions and as an anti-inflammatory. Mildly poisonous, it should only be used medicinally when prescribed by a qualified herbalist. In the home, it is used in both skin- and haircare products, particularly for those with sensitive skins. Simmer a handful of leaves for 7 minutes, strain, and add to a bath to treat dry, itchy skin. Soapwort also makes a good cleaning product for delicate silk garments and upholstery.

Saponaria Soapwort CARYOPHYLLACEAE

As its name suggests, a natural lather can be made from the leaves, stem, and roots of this herb. When boiled in water, the plant releases saponins and produces a slippery substance that has the power to lift grease and dirt. Interestingly, soapwort was once used in the wool industry for cleaning new wool, and in Britain, colonies of soapwort plants can still be found growing close to old mills. It is still used by museum conservators to lift surface dirt gently from fragile antique textiles and paintings.

Flower has five petals and grows in clusters.

Saponaria officinalis
SOAPWORT, BOUNCING BET
Hardy herbaceous perennial. Height up to 3ft (1m), spread 2ft (60cm) or more. Compact clusters of small pretty pink or white lightly scented flowers are borne in summer until early fall. The smooth leaves taper to a point.

6IN (15CM)

Stem is notched.

Leaf is soft and smooth to the touch.

Cultivation

Propagation Sow seeds in early spring and place under protection at 68°F (20°C). Germination takes 1–2 weeks. Once germinated, do not overwater because seedlings are prone to "damping off." Take cuttings of perennial savorys in summer from new stem growth. Once rooted, pot and grow on in a cold frame. Plant out the following spring into a well-prepared site.

Site Plant in a sunny position in well-drained, poor soil that has not been fed the previous fall. Perennial savorys grow well in containers. Use a soil-based substrate, mixed with equal parts of coarse horticultural grit. Place the container in a sunny, dry, sheltered position.

Maintenance Cut back perennial savorys after flowering. Keep picking summer savory from the top to maintain leaf supply for as long as possible. Do not feed garden plants with compost or liquid fertilizer. For container plants, feed once a week with a liquid seaweed fertilizer during the growing season.

Harvesting Pick leaves to dry and use fresh before flowering.

Uses Fresh savory leaves have a sweet aroma and pungent flavor and can be used as a substitute for black pepper in cooking, though the flavor becomes less pungent when the herb is boiled for any length of time. Medicinally, species of savory have properties similar to thyme, rosemary, and oregano; they are antibacterial, antifungal, and antiseptic.

Caution Do not take medicinally during pregnancy.

Satureja Savory LAMIACEAE

Like the Romans who used it to flavor food, I use savory liberally in cooking to add a spicy taste to meat and fish dishes. Good specimens for the herb garden include: pink savory (*Satureja thymbra*) from the Mideast, which has pale purple flowers and a spicy flavor; lemon savory (*S. biflora*) from Africa, which has a spicy lemon taste; and winter savory (*S. montana),* which has a peppery taste and is a successful low edging plant.

Satureja hortensis
SUMMER SAVORY, BEAN HERB

Half-hardy annual. Height 12in (30cm) and spread 8in (20cm). Small white flowers tinged with mauve appear in summer. The aromatic leaves are oval, pointed, and green. A favorite in Europe and America, it is known as the bean herb, because when it is used with bean dishes, it helps prevent flatulence.

Satureja douglasii
YERBA BUENA

Half-hardy evergreen perennial. Height 4in (10cm) and spread indefinite, since it trails and creeps. Small tubular white to lavender flowers grow where the leaves join the stem. The leaves are small, oval, and mint scented. This California herb has very strong minty but spicy flavored leaves and can be used sparingly to make an herbal tea that is used medicinally to reduce fevers.

The Garden | The Kitchen
PP. 21, 43, 49, 53, 55, 62, 67 | PP. 84, 87, 89, 93, 94, 95

Satureja montana

WINTER SAVORY

Hardy semi-evergreen perennial. Height 12in (30cm) and spread 8in (20cm). Small, white with a hint of pink-mauve flowers. The leaves are dark green, linear, and very aromatic. This herb is more pungent than summer savory, with a peppery undertone. It is ideal for flavoring vegetable stews and bean or legume dishes. Macerated leaves can be rubbed on wasp and bee stings to ease the pain.

Flower is tubular, with two protruding lower lips typical of the Lamiaceae family, and can vary in color from white to very pale pink or purple on the same plant.

Leaf is narrow, oval, and pointed.

6IN (15CM)

Stem becomes woody with age.

242

Cultivation

Propagation Sow fresh seeds in the fall and place in a cold frame. Germination takes 3–4 weeks. Winter young plants in a cold frame. If there is no germination during this time, place the seed tray outside so the seeds can be stratified by the cold weather. In warm climates, place the seeds in the refrigerator for 4 weeks to stratify seeds. Germination can take a further 5–7 months. It can flower in the first season from seed. Take root cuttings from the rhizomes in spring (see page 56), or stem cuttings in summer from nonflowering shoots. Divide established plants in the fall.

Site Plant in poor, moisture-retentive soil in sun or semi-shade. Virginia skullcap will adapt to most soil types with the exception of acid and waterlogged soils. This plant is not suited for container growing because the rhizomes tend to rot if they are unable to spread out.

Maintenance After collecting seeds, cut back to promote new growth. In the fall, dig up any plants that have started to spread. Divide established plants every third year to maintain a healthy plant. Do not feed; a nutrient-rich soil will cause soft growth and excessive root spread.

Harvesting Pick leaves and flowers for drying in summer for medicinal use only.

Uses This is an important medicinal herb, *S. lateriflora* has similar but stronger properties compared to *S. galericulata*, which looks similar but is shorter. Both are used to treat insomnia, stress, and muscular tension.

Caution This is not a culinary herb. It should not be taken during pregnancy.

FOR USE IN

Scutellaria Virginia skullcap LAMIACEAE

Its common name "skullcap" is said to have originated from the shape of the flower, which was thought to resemble the helmets worn by Roman soldiers. It was used by Native Americans to treat women's menstrual problems, and in the eighteenth century, it was thought to be a cure for rabies, although this has been disproved. Personally, I grow this herb because it is very attractive in the garden. The seeds are not only a good source of bird food, they also make a delightful sound in a light breeze.

Scutellaria lateriflora
VIRGINIA SKULLCAP
Hardy herbaceous perennial. Height 24in (60cm) and spread 12in (30cm), or more. The small bicolored flowers are dark blue-purple on the upper lip and pale mauve on the lower. They blossom in summer, and the flowers are followed by small, pale beige round seeds. The oval mid-green leaves have a crinkled texture.

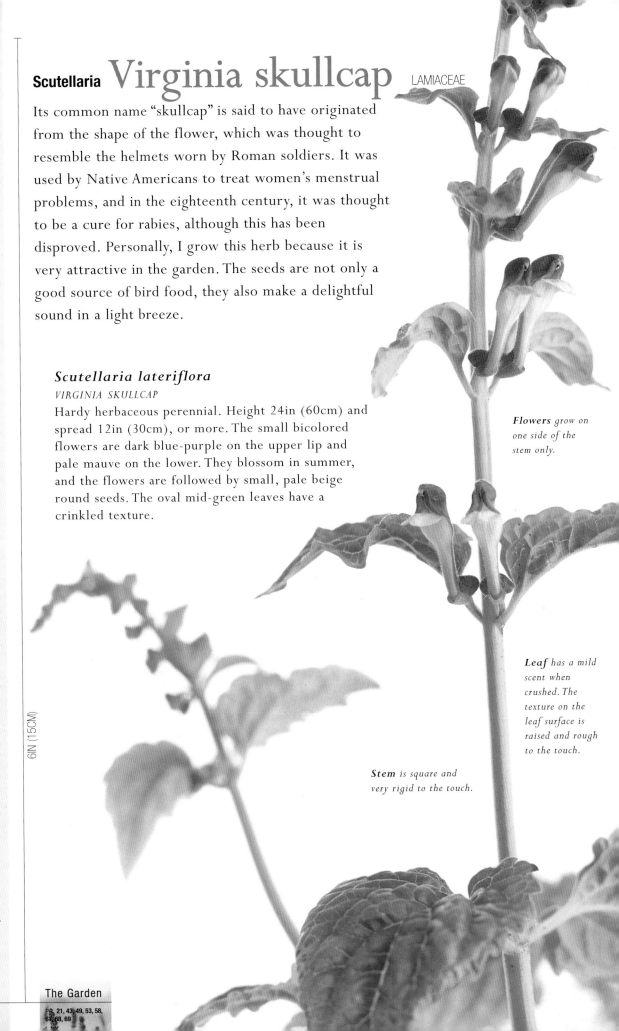

Flowers grow on one side of the stem only.

6IN (15CM)

Leaf has a mild scent when crushed. The texture on the leaf surface is raised and rough to the touch.

Stem is square and very rigid to the touch.

The Garden
21, 43, 49, 53, 58, 67, 68, 69

Cultivation

Propagation Sow fresh seeds in spring or summer. Because they are very fine, mix with the finest sand or flour. Water from the bottom or with a fine spray, and cover the container with glass to keep the seed warm. Place in a frostfree environment like a cold frame. Germination takes 1–6 months. Once this happens, remove the glass and cover with fine sand. All houseleeks produce offsets that cluster around the base of the parent plant. In spring each offset starts its own root system. Either pot up each individual, or plant each one directly into the ground.

Site Houseleeks grow happily in very little soil since they have very short roots. Plant either in wall crevices, rock gardens, or in between paving stones. For growing in containers, use a soil-based substrate mixed equally with sharp horticultural grit to improve drainage.

Maintenance In the fall, if the plant has become invasive, remove offsets and pot them to produce a new stock of young plants as insurance against a bad winter. Pests like vine weevils attack pot-grown houseleeks, so check the roots each fall for infestation and repot if necessary.

Harvesting Pick leaves to use fresh throughout the growing season.

Uses Apply the saplike gel directly to nettle stings and minor burns. Make an infusion from the leaves to treat bronchitis. To remove a corn, cut a leaf in half, bind the fleshy side to the corn for a few hours, then soak the foot in water. Try to scrape the corn off gently. Repeat as necessary.

Sempervivum Houseleek CRASSULACEAE

This herb is an old family favorite. When my son was growing up, I encouraged him to keep houseleek leaves in his pockets to rub on nettle stings and cuts, since they have gently healing properties similar to *Aloe vera* (however, the two plants are not related). Historically, houseleeks were grown on the roofs of houses since it was believed that they would protect a thatched roof from fire and the occupants from witchcraft. They are also useful for removing corns.

Sempervivum tectorum
HOUSELEEK
Hardy evergreen succulent. Height 6in (15cm) when in flower and spread 8in (20cm). Pink star-shaped flowers appear in summer, though they can take several years to flower. When broken in half, the succulent leaves release a sappy gel, which can be applied to minor burns, insect bites, or nettle stings. Plant in a container or in a niche in a garden wall. Each offshoot around the base of the mother plant has its own integral root system.

7IN (17.5CM)

Leaves are succulent, oval, and gray-green with darker tips.

FOR USE IN

The Garden	The Home
21, 43, 49, 58, 64	PP. 104, 109

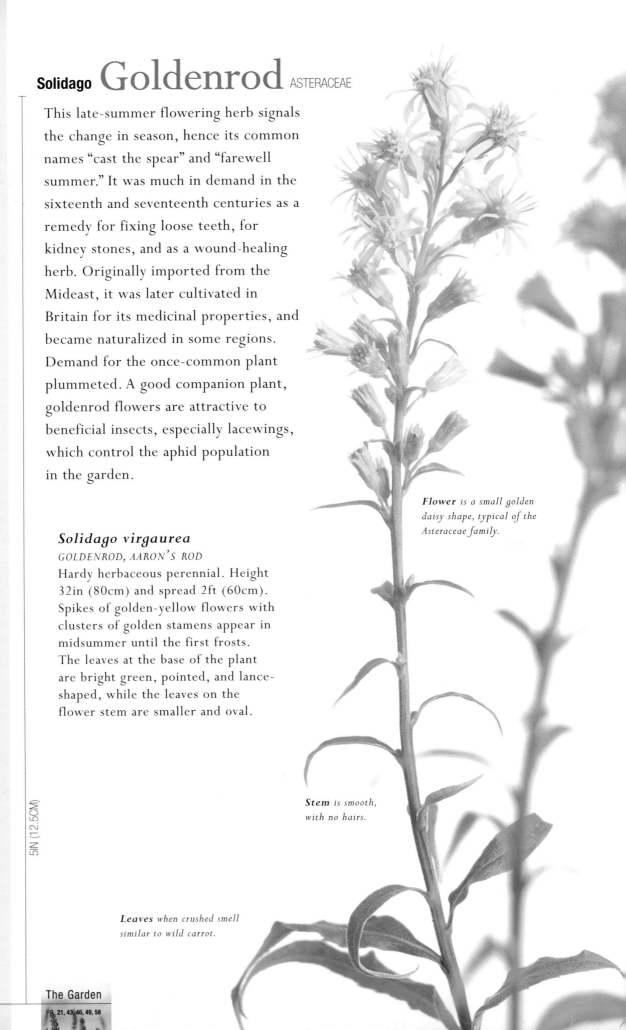

Cultivation

Propagation The seeds need stratification to germinate (see page 46). Sow fresh in the fall and place the container outside to expose it to winter weather. In warm climates place seed in the refrigerator for 4 weeks, then sow and place outside. Germination takes 4–6 months. Take root cuttings in spring. Divide established plants in the fall, replanting in a well-prepared site.

Site Goldenrod will grow in most soils, with the exception of rich soils. It favors a moisture-retentive soil in a sunny position. It can be grown in containers, but use a soil-based substrate mixed in equal parts with fine bark that is low in nutrients.

Maintenance Lift the roots and replant every other year to prevent matting and invasive spreading. Repot container-grown plants every fall to prevent the roots from rotting. In addition to attracting beneficial insects, it also attracts the tortrix moth, whose caterpillars roll themselves up in the leaves. The only organic way to get rid of this pest is to use an elder leaf wash (see page 236) or hand-pick them off.

Harvesting Pick leaves and flowering tops just before the flowers are fully opened to dry for medicinal use.

Uses It is used medicinally to treat urinary infections, skin diseases, kidney stones, wounds, insect bites, and external skin ulcers. The leaves and flowers are also used to make a yellow plant dye for textiles.

Solidago # Goldenrod ASTERACEAE

This late-summer flowering herb signals the change in season, hence its common names "cast the spear" and "farewell summer." It was much in demand in the sixteenth and seventeenth centuries as a remedy for fixing loose teeth, for kidney stones, and as a wound-healing herb. Originally imported from the Mideast, it was later cultivated in Britain for its medicinal properties, and became naturalized in some regions. Demand for the once-common plant plummeted. A good companion plant, goldenrod flowers are attractive to beneficial insects, especially lacewings, which control the aphid population in the garden.

Solidago virgaurea
GOLDENROD, AARON'S ROD
Hardy herbaceous perennial. Height 32in (80cm) and spread 2ft (60cm). Spikes of golden-yellow flowers with clusters of golden stamens appear in midsummer until the first frosts. The leaves at the base of the plant are bright green, pointed, and lance-shaped, while the leaves on the flower stem are smaller and oval.

Flower is a small golden daisy shape, typical of the Asteraceae family.

Stem is smooth, with no hairs.

Leaves when crushed smell similar to wild carrot.

5IN (12.5CM)

Cultivation

Propagation Sow seeds when fresh in early fall. Place in a cold frame. Germination takes 2–4 weeks, but can be longer. Winter young plants in the cold frame before planting out the following spring. Or sow directly into the planting position in the fall. Cover lightly with leaf mold (see page 37). Mark the area where you have sown. Germination occurs the next spring. Divide established plants in spring or fall. Replant 12in (30cm) apart.

Site This herb tolerates most situations. For preference, plant in fertile soil in sun or partial shade. Another favored site is at the edge of deciduous woodland. I have also grown it to great effect in a container mixed with other wildflowers, using a loam-based substrate.

Maintenance This plant needs little maintenance. In early fall, save the seed before cutting back the flowers. In dry soils, mulch with a layer of leaf mold (see page 37).

Harvesting Collect the leaves for drying in late spring before the plant flowers. Pick flowers for drying just as they open. Gather fresh leaves before and after flowering.

Uses Betony is used in Europe to treat diarrhea, cystitis, and liver and gall bladder infections. A weak infusion makes a refreshing cup of tea, which also treats headaches.

A final hair rinse made from an infusion of the leaves darkens gray hair. All parts of the plant can be used as a yellow plant dye for textiles.

Stachys Betony LAMIACEAE

This attractive flower is a worthwhile addition to any herb garden. Even though it is a wild plant, it has adapted to the cultivated garden, giving a colorful display in the summer and attracting butterflies and bees. On the occasions when I have exhibited betony at flower shows, it has always drawn the crowds. Medicinally, it was claimed that it could cure over 47 different ailments. Today, it is taken for nervous disorders. The root, however, is toxic, and it should never be self administered.

Flower attracts insects.

Flower grows at the top of the stem in dense whorls, which form short spikes.

8IN (20CM)

Stachys officinalis
BETONY
Hardy herbaceous perennial. Height 24in (60cm) and spread 10in (25cm). Dense spikes of pink or purple flowers appear throughout summer. The dark green oval leaves have scalloped edges. The leaf surface is perforated with glands that contain a bitter aromatic oil.

Leaf is rough to the touch and has a scalloped edge.

The Garden
PP. 21, 43, 49, 58

Cultivation

Propagation Sow seeds in the fall and place in a cold frame. Germination takes 3–20 weeks, but is very erratic. The easiest method is root cuttings taken in spring (see page 56). Established plants can be divided in the fall. Any piece of root that is left in the soil will root and create another plant.

Site Comfrey prefers a moist soil in sun or partial shade. It is ideal for clay, though it will tolerate all but arid conditions. Choose the position in the garden with care. *S. officinale* will self-seed erratically, and because of its very long taproot, it is nearly impossible to move once established. Comfrey can be grown in large containers. A trash can with drainage holes is ideal. Use garden loam with 10 percent coarse horticultural grit added.

Maintenance Comfrey sometimes suffers from rust (see page 194) and powdery mildew. With both diseases, cut the plant down to the ground and burn the contaminated leaves. When growing comfrey for leaf harvest, do not allow the plant to dry out in summer.

Harvesting Cut the leaves before flowering from early summer until fall to provide foliage for the liquid fertilizer (see page 39). Each plant is able to provide four leaf harvests per season. In the fall, dig up second-year growth roots for drying.

Uses Medicinally it is used externally for cuts, as a compress, and to treat varicose veins. It can also be used for curing septic sores on animals, and as an animal feed. A golden yellow textile dye can be made from the leaves.

Symphytum Comfrey BORAGINACEAE

This invasive plant may be considered a weed by many, but the nutrients it contains are useful to the organic gardener. The leaves are naturally high in protein, potash, and potassium, and make a wonderful mulch or liquid feed (see page 39) without having to resort to chemically manufactured products. Medicinally, its potential for healing external wounds and broken bones is unchallenged, hence its common names "knitbone" and "boneset." Currently one of its key constituents, allantoin, which stimulates the growth of new cells, is undergoing research. Do not take comfrey internally unless it has been prescribed by a qualified herbalist. Skin contact can also cause dermatitis, so wear gloves when picking for composting or medicinal use.

Symphytum x *uplandicum*
RUSSIAN COMFREY

Hardy herbaceous perennial. Height and spread 3ft (1m). It produces clusters of pink, purple, and blue flowers in summer and it has green lance-shaped leaves covered with fine, slightly prickly hairs. A cross between *S. officinale* and *S. asperum*, it does not self-seed, but has the same nutrient-rich foliage properties as *S. officinale*.

FOR USE IN

The Garden	The Home
PP. 21, 43, 58, 67	PP. 105, 106

5IN (12.5CM)

Symphytum officinale
COMFREY, KNITBONE
Hardy herbaceous perennial.
Height and spread 3ft (1m).
Clusters of white, purple, or pink
flowers appear in summer. The
leaves are green, lance-shaped,
and hairy. Young fresh leaves and
shoots can be eaten like spinach,
and are a rich source of
vitamin B12.

Leaf *is covered
with bristly hairs.
It decreases in size
the higher it grows
up the stem.*

Flower *grows in one-sided clusters
along a curving hairy stem.*

Root *is fibrous with
a blackish exterior.
Internally it is
fleshy, juicy,
and white.*

Cultivation

Propagation Sow in early spring under cover at 68°F (20°C). Germination takes 14–21 days. Or sow in late spring into prepared open ground when the air temperature does not fall below 50°F (10°C) at night. Germination takes 2–4 weeks. Take cuttings of perennial varieties from non-flowering stems in summer. Winter young plants in a frostfree environment.

Site Plant in well-drained fertile soil in a sunny position. Mexican marigold is ideal for interplanting in the vegetable garden – it not only repels soil nematodes, but also slugs and aphids. *T. lucida* is a tender perennial that grows well in pots. Winter in a frostfree environment and use a soil-based substrate mixed with ⅓ coarse horticultural grit.

Maintenance In early summer, pinch out or cut back the growing tips of young plants to promote bushy growth. Deadhead flowers to prolong flowering.

Harvesting Pick flowers for drying in summer. Harvest leaves in summer to use fresh or to dry. If protected from frost, the leaves of *T. lucida* can be picked up until midwinter.

Uses Medicinally, *T. patula* is a diuretic and improves digestion. Externally, it relieves sore eyes and rheumatism. The yellow pigment in the fresh or dried flowers has been used to dye textiles. *T. lucida* grows in winter in cool climates under protection and so is a good substitute for *Artemisia dracunculus*. Leaves can also be burned as an insect repellent. Medicinally, *T. lucida* treats diarrhea, indigestion, and feverishness. It is used externally to remove ticks.

Tagetes Mexican marigolds ASTERACEAE

The following marigolds are from the *Tagetes* genus, rather than the *Calendula* genus (see page 140), with which they are sometimes confused. This family contains 56 species and includes the lesser-known perennial species and the popular annual bedding plants, known as Mexican, French, or African marigolds, which all originated in Central and South America and were used as medicinal and ritual plants. I have chosen two Mexican marigolds that I find invaluable in an organic herb garden. They are the wild Mexican marigold (*Tagetes patula*), which is good for pest control, and *Tagetes lucida, a* perennial marigold whose fresh leaves have a flavor similar to French tarragon (*Artemisia dracunculus* see page 137), hence its common name, winter tarragon.

Tagetes lucida
WINTER TARRAGON, SWEET MACE
Tender herbaceous perennial. Height 32in (80cm) in warm climates only and spread 18in (45cm). Yellow flowers appear in late summer. The mid-green leaves are narrow and toothed. They have a strong aniseed scent and similar flavor to tarragon. In cool climates, this herb dies back in early spring, reappearing in early summer.

The Garden

21, 43, 49, 53, 58, 67

Flower *is typical of the Asteraceae family. The daisylike petals can vary in color from golden yellow through to brown.*

4IN (10CM)

Leaf *shape is typical of Tagetes species.*

Leaf *is highly aromatic with a pungent scent.*

Tagetes patula

WILD MEXICAN MARIGOLD, FRENCH MARIGOLD

Half hardy annual. Height 4ft (1.2m) and spread 18in (45cm). Clusters of single yellow flowers appear in midsummer until the first autumn frosts. The mid-green leaves are deeply divided and lightly toothed. This species is a good companion plant as it deters nematodes in the soil and repels aphids from ripening tomatoes.

Cultivation

Propagation Sow seeds in spring and place in a cold frame. Do not cover. Germination takes 2–4 weeks. Plant out when the seedlings are large enough to handle. Divide established plants in the fall or spring, replanting in a prepared site. Plant *T. cinerariifolium* 12in (30cm) apart and *T. balsamita* at 24in (60cm) intervals.

Site Plant in well-drained, fertile soil in a sunny position. Both species are drought tolerant and will adapt to most soils and conditions. However, if planted in shade, they are unlikely to flower. Both grow well in containers. Use a soil-based substrate and feed once a month throughout the growing season with liquid seaweed.

Maintenance Deadhead regularly to promote new flower growth. Divide established plants every few years to keep them healthy and to prevent them from becoming too invasive. Do not feed with nutrients which will encourage soft growth and disease.

Harvesting Pick the leaves of *T. balsamita* before flowering to use fresh or to dry. Pick the flowerheads of *T. cinerariifolium* just as they open and dry on a fabric frame (see page 73). Store dried flowers in a dark glass jar out of direct sunlight.

Uses Wearing gloves, sprinkle the powdered flowers of *T. cinerariifolium* around the doors to repel ants. *T. balsamita* was used for brewing ale.

Tanacetum Silver tanacetums ASTERACEAE

Tanacetums are members of the daisy (Asteraceae) family and thrive in the herb garden or herbaceous bed. Silver leaves distinguish the silver tanacetums. Like many ancient herbs, they grow very successfully and become invasive, which is perhaps one reason why they have managed to survive for so long. Pyrethrum, a well-known and useful insecticide, is made from the dried flowers of *Tanacetum cinerariifolium*. It acts by paralyzing the nervous system of insects. It is illegal in the European Union to use pyrethrum in spray form because insecticide sprays can also kill beneficial insects. However, it is nontoxic to mammals. Wear gloves when handling; the flower can cause a minor skin rash.

Tanacetum balsamita
ALECOST, COSTMARY
Hardy herbaceous perennial. Height 3ft (1m) when in flower and spread 18in (45cm). In cold climates it can be grown from cuttings only. Clusters of small, white, yellow-eyed daisy flowers appear from mid- to late summer. The soft, aromatic, silver-gray-green leaves grow in large, oval rosettes. Rub a fresh leaf on a bee sting or a fly bite to relieve the pain.

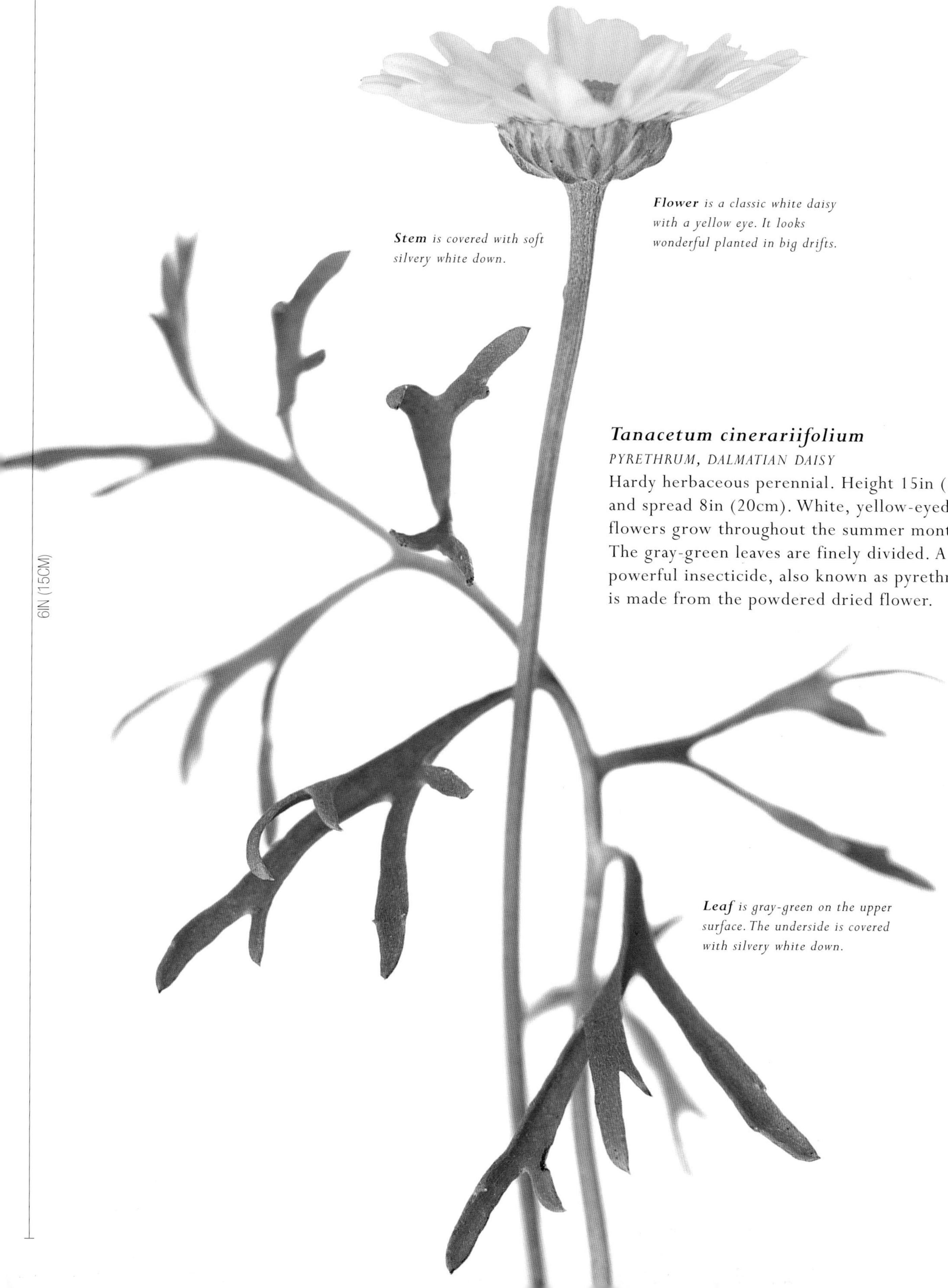

Stem is covered with soft
silvery white down.

Flower is a classic white daisy
with a yellow eye. It looks
wonderful planted in big drifts.

6IN (15CM)

Tanacetum cinerariifolium

PYRETHRUM, DALMATIAN DAISY

Hardy herbaceous perennial. Height 15in (37cm)
and spread 8in (20cm). White, yellow-eyed daisy
flowers grow throughout the summer months.
The gray-green leaves are finely divided. A
powerful insecticide, also known as pyrethrum,
is made from the powdered dried flower.

Leaf is gray-green on the upper
surface. The underside is covered
with silvery white down.

Cultivation

Propagation Sow seeds in the fall or spring and place in a cold frame. Do not cover. Germination takes 2–4 weeks. For fall sowings, winter in a cold frame. Divide established plants in fall or spring. Do not leave any root of *T. vulgare* behind as it will spread. Replant into a prepared site. Plant *T. parthenium* 12in (30cm) apart and *T. vulgare* at 24in (60cm) intervals.

Site Plant in well-drained fertile soil in a sunny position. Both species are drought tolerant but may not flower in shade. Tansy is unsuitable for small sites because it is invasive.

Maintenance Deadhead regularly to promote new flowers, and to prevent *T. parthenium* from self-seeding. Divide established plants every few years. Cut back in fall. Do not feed.

Harvesting Pick the leaves of *T. parthenium* before flowering, to use fresh or to dry. Pick the flower heads of *T. vulgare* as the flower opens to dry.

Uses *T. parthenium* is a known remedy for certain types of migraines. Eat 2–3 fresh leaves with a slice of bread as they are very bitter. A decoction made from the leaves is also a good household disinfectant. *T. vulgare* can only be used medicinally by a qualified herbalist. To deter pet fleas, rub the fresh leaves into your pet's coat. The dried leaves and flowers repel ants and mice.

Caution Do not take any tanacetum during pregnancy. Eating fresh leaves may cause mouth ulcers. Only take tansy medicinally under supervision.

Tanacetum Green tanacetums ASTERACEAE

Old survey maps of the land surrounding my farm refer to it as "clay fields" – a soil type not ideally suited to growing herbs because of its poor drainage. Herbs like feverfew (*T. parthenium*) and tansy (*T. vulgare*) have adapted and flourish in these conditions, but because the soil is heavy, their roots cannot become as invasive as they would in lighter soil, making them much easier to control. As with other species of *Tanacetum*, green tanacetum plants are rich in oils, making the fresh and dried leaves and flowers invaluable in the home as a source of a natural disinfectant and as a fly and flea repellent.

Tanacetum vulgare
TANSY

Hardy herbaceous perennial, Height up to 4ft (1.2m) and spread indefinite. Clusters of yellow, buttonlike flowers appear from summer until late fall. The dark green, feathery-looking leaves have toothed edges. Dried bunches of aromatic tansy make effective fly repellents in the home.

Tanacetum parthenium

FEVERFEW

Hardy herbaceous perennial. Height up to 48in (1.2m) and spread 18in (45cm). It has clusters of small, white, yellow-eyed daisy flowers from early summer until the first frosts. The leaf is mid-green, lobed, and divided with lightly serrated edges.

Flower *is daisylike with white petals and a yellow center. It grows in loose clusters.*

Leaf *is lobed with serrated edges. It contains parthenolide, which helps prevent migraines.*

Leaf *is very bitter to taste.*

7IN (17.5CM)

Cultivation

Propagation Sow seeds in the fall, using a loam-based seed substrate mixed in equal parts with coarse horticultural sand. Place outside for the winter. The seeds need stratification to germinate (see page 46). In warm climates, place in a refrigerator for one month prior to sowing. Germination takes 4–6 months. When large enough to handle, plant out into a prepared site 8in (20cm) apart. A simpler method of propagation is to take cuttings in summer from new growth. Winter young plants in a cold frame, planting out the following spring. Divide established plants in the fall, replanting in a prepared site.

Site Plant in well-drained, slightly alkaline soil in a sunny position. This species tolerates temperatures as low as -20°F (-29°C) but it dislikes wet conditions. *T. x lucidrys* makes an ideal hedge. Plant 6in (15cm) apart. Germanders make good container plants, especially *T. x lucidrys*.

Maintenance When grown as a hedge, clip in spring and fall to maintain shape. If you do not cut back in the spring, it will produce pink flowers in late summer. After this, cut back fairly hard to encourage lower growth.

Harvesting Cut leaves when the plant is in flower for drying or for use in medicinal infusions.

Uses Rarely used in medicine, there is interest in it as an aid to weight loss. It is still used in the flavoring of liquors.

Caution Do not take internally unless under professional guidance.

Teucrium Germanders LAMIACEAE

There has been a lot of confusion over species of *Teucrium*, and when purchasing plants for medicinal use, it is important to establish their correct identification. The species found growing wild, in walls and rock crevices, is wall germander (*T. chamaedrys*). The leaf resembles an oak-tree leaf, giving rise to its common name "small oak." It is this species that is used to treat digestive disorders. Hedge germander (*T. x lucidrys*) grows in knot gardens as an edging plant. It has darker, shinier green leaves than *T. chamaedrys*.

Teucrium x lucidrys
HEDGE GERMANDER
Hardy evergreen shrub. Height 18in (45cm) and spread 8in (20cm). Grown from cuttings only. Pink flowers bloom from midsummer until early fall. The aromatic, lightly toothed leaves have a shiny upper surface and a matte underside. In Elizabethan times this shrub was a popular edging plant, for which it is ideally suited today.

6IN (15CM)

Teucrium chamaedrys L.
WALL GERMANDER
Hardy herbaceous perennial. Height and spread 10in (25cm). Pink flowers appear in midsummer until early fall. The aromatic, matte green leaves are oval, pointed, toothed, and lobed.

Leaf has a pleasantly spicy smell when rubbed.

Stem is square in section.

Flower is rose-colored, with a large protruding lower petal, and grows in groups of 3 or 6.

Cultivation

Propagation see page 254 for details.

Site Plant in any but water-logged soil. It adapts happily to well prepared clay soil in sun or partial shade. I have grown both wood sages very successfully in containers using a loam-based substrate. Feed only twice during the growing season with comfrey liquid feed (see page 39). Overfeeding produces too lush a growth making the plant prone to disease.

Maintenance Cut back after flowering to produce new growth in the fall. Divide established plants every third year to maintain them and also, in light soils to stop them becoming invasive.

Harvesting Pick the leaves either side of flowering to use fresh for medicinal use or to dry. For culinary uses pick in spring before the leaves become tough.

Uses The leaves can be added to salads but be cautious – they are bitter.

Teucrium Wood sage LAMIACEAE

This natural woodland plant is ideally suited to damp areas of the garden, where it offers a subtle display of pale green and white in summer. The cultivated form, with its crinkled leaves, is often remarked upon by people, and they either love it or hate it. It had the common name "hind heal," from the belief that the hind (female deer) will eat it when sick or wounded. It grows wild in Jersey in the Channel Islands, where it was used as an alternative to hops in beermaking.

Teucrium scorodonia
WOOD SAGE

Hardy herbaceous perennial. Height 24in (60cm) and spread 10in (24cm). Pale greenish-white flowers are borne in summer. The soft green, heart-shaped leaves have finely toothed edges. This natural woodland plant can be grown to great effect in a mixed herb garden. The leaves give texture and the flowers a subtle hue.

Flower when fully open has a lower petal that hangs down, making it look rather like a beard.

Stems become thin and rigid as the plant grows.

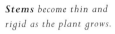

8IN (20CM)

Leaf is soft with a textured upper surface. When crushed, it has a musty smell, and it is bitter to taste.

Teucrium scorodonia 'Crispum'
CURLY WOOD SAGE

Hardy herbaceous perennial. Height 14in (35cm) and spread 12in (30cm). Pale greenish-white flowers are borne in summer. It has soft, green heart-shaped leaves, with very ruffled crinkled edges, which can have a reddish tinge in the fall. This herb was much used by Gertrude Jekyll, a famous British plantswoman, who recognized its esthetic value.

Cultivation

Propagation Sow the seed in spring. Because the seed is so small, mix it with fine horticultural sand or flour to make it easier to handle. Do not cover. Place under protection at 60°F (20°C). Germination takes 5–10 days. Keep watering to a minimum, because the seedlings are prone to "damping off." Always water from the bottom. Take cuttings from new growth before flowering in late spring. Winter late cuttings in a cold frame. Divide established plants in spring in cold, wet climates; in warm, hot, dry climates divide in the fall.

Site Plant in well-drained soil in a sunny position. Thymes do not like wet winters or sitting in water. Make sure the soil has adequate drainage. To improve drainage, dig in extra horticultural grit. To grow in containers, use a soil-based substrate.

Maintenance In spring, lightly prune all upright and mounding thymes to encourage young shoots for strong leaf flavor, and again after flowering in late summer to prevent the plants from becoming woody.

Harvesting This evergreen herb can be picked all year round. For making herb oil (see page 88) or drying, pick sprigs just before flowering.

Uses Upright thymes are the classic thymes used in bouquet garni (see page 94). Added to cooking, they aid digestion and help break down fatty foods. They also have strong antiseptic properties. An infusion or tea makes an excellent remedy for sore throats and hangovers.

Caution Do not take thyme medicinally when pregnant.

Thymus Upright thymes LAMIACEAE

The classic culinary thyme has an upright habit, making it easier to pick than the spreading or mounding thymes. The leaves of this group can vary in scent and flavor from the classic thyme to the more exotic spicy orange. In their natural environment, they grow at the edges of paths in rockeries and on escarpments — habitats that can be easily recreated in the garden. They also make a lovely edging for a path. Current research has shown that *Thymus vulgaris* helps to arrest the aging process and is very beneficial in the treatment of stomach ulcers.

Thymus x *citriodorus* 'Silver Queen'
SILVER QUEEN THYME

Hardy evergreen perennial. Height 10in (25cm) and spread 18in (45cm). Terminal clusters of small pink flowers appear in summer. The leaves are small, oval, and gray variegated with silver. They have a strong lemon scent when rubbed between the fingertips or used in cooking, and this thyme combines particularly well with chicken and fish dishes.

Thymus 'Fragrantissimus'
ORANGE-SCENTED THYME

Hardy evergreen perennial. Height 12in (30cm) and spread 18in (45cm). Terminal clusters of pale pink, almost white flowers appear in summer. The small, narrow, oval, gray-green leaves have a spicy orange scent. This thyme also has a delightful warm flavor, which not only tastes good with meat and vegetables, but wonderful with some sweet dishes.

FOR USE IN

The Garden	The Kitchen	The Home
PP. 21, 43, 49, 53, 55, 64, 67	PP. 87, 88, 89, 90, 91, 94, 95	PP. 100, 101, 102, 108, 110

Flower *is small and tubular with a hanging lower petal.*

Stem *is ridged to the touch. Young growth is green; mature growth brown.*

Leaf *is small, oval, pointed, and highly aromatic, with classic thyme scent.*

1IN (2.5CM)

Thymus vulgaris 'Compactus'

COMPACT THYME

Hardy evergreen perennial. Height and spread 12in (30cm). Terminal clusters of small, pale pink flowers appear in summer. The dark green leaves are aromatic with the strong classic thyme aroma. This thyme is identical to *T. vulgaris* in flavor and medicinal properties. The only difference is its neater growing habit.

Cultivation

Propagation See page 256 for details.

Site To create a thyme path, prepare the site well before planting. Choose a sunny position. Thymes will not survive in shade, especially in wet climates. Dig the area over, removing all weeds. If the soil is heavy or cold, add plenty of extra sharp horticultural grit. Lay a permeable membrane over the soil to inhibit weeds, while allowing rainwater to seep through to the soil. Cut slits in the membrane and plant the thyme plants through it, spacing them at 6in (15cm) intervals. Once planted, cover the membrane with washed grit or fine gravel. right up to the "necks" of the plants, laying the green plant growth over the grit.

Maintenance See page 256 for details.

Harvesting See page 256 for details.

Uses See page 256 and page 260 for details.

Thymus Creeping thymes LAMIACEAE

There is nothing more romantic than coming across a bank covered in creeping thyme or walking across ground overrun with these aromatic plants, which release their delicous fragrance as they are crushed underfoot. Their creeping habit and robust leaves make them ideally suited to path or lawn surfaces. The right growing conditions are particularly important for creeping thymes; they originate in the Mediterranean and need a sunny, well-drained site. Their creeping habit can, however, make it difficult to pick enough for culinary use.

Thymus serpyllum
CREEPING THYME, WILD THYME

Hardy evergreen perennial. Height 3in (7cm), spread 36in (1m). Terminal clusters of small pink, mauve, or purple flowers appear in summer. It has small, oval, hairy, dark green, aromatic leaves. This thyme has strong medicinal properties and makes a potent natural antiseptic for use in the home.

Thymus 'Coccineus'
CREEPING RED THYME

Hardy evergreen perennial. Height 3in (7cm) and spread 36in (1m). Terminal clusters of small magenta flowers appear in summer. The flowers attract bees and butterflies. The leaves are small, oval, hairy, dark green, and aromatic. This species can be grown successfully as part of a thyme walk.

FOR USE IN

The Garden
PP. 21, 43, 49, 53, 55, 58, 67

The Home
PP. 100, 101, 102, 108, 110

5IN (12CM)

Thymus pulegioides
BROAD-LEAVED THYME, MOTHER OF THYME
Hardy evergreen perennial. Height 10in
(25cm) and spread 18in (45cm). Small
terminal clusters of mauve flowers appear
in summer. The dark green leaves are small,
rounded, and aromatic. It produces much
leaf with an excellent culinary flavor. Grow
over a wall feature or along the edge
of a flowerbed.

Flower *grows in terminal clusters
blooming throughout the summer.*

Stem *is green when showing new
growth, turning brown
with maturity.*

Leaf *is rounded and
highly aromatic.*

Thymus serpyllum '**Minimus**'
MINIMUS THYME
Hardy evergreen perennial. Height ½in (1cm) and spread 6in
(15cm). It has very short-stemmed pink flowers in summer, but
will only flower in sunny, well-drained sites. Its dark green
leaves form a mat on the ground. This tight-growing thyme
is able to withstand being trampled underfoot.

Cultivation

Propagation See page 256 for details.

Site See page 256 for details. Mounding thymes are ideal for growing in containers. Use a soil-based substrate with extra drainage in the base of the container. Do not upgrade the pot size too often – all species of mounding thyme prefer to be slightly potbound.

Maintenance In spring, clear away dead leaves from under the plant to prevent mildew in damp weather. Like all thymes, replace the plants entirely every 4–7 years to maintain leaf flavor.

Harvesting See page 256 for details.

Uses Mounding thymes fall between upright and creeping in terms of their properties and taste. They can be used in cooking in the same way as upright thymes. They also offer interesting thyme flavors that make lovely dressings or marinades. Medicinally, mounding thymes have milder properties than *T. vulgaris*, but all *T. vulgaris* species are useful as a gargle for sore throats.

Thymus Mounding thymes LAMIACEAE

The ancient Greeks used thyme in their baths and burned it like incense in temples – not only did it smell good, but it was also a fumigator, which they thought banished "venomous creatures." Mounding thymes have beautiful flowing shapes. They are ideal for containers, and their rounded profiles work well when planted in a garden of mixed thymes where they offer a fuller, more three-dimensional shape to the design of the garden than either creeping or upright thyme species. They are also suited to growing in lawns, as they are short enough to walk on. The flavor is milder than the upright thymes.

Thymus 'Peter Davis'
PETER DAVIS THYME

Hardy evergreen perennial. Height 6in (15cm) and spread 8in (20cm). This is an early-flowering thyme. Round clusters of very small pink flowers form in the first months of summer. The gray-green leaves are very small but richly aromatic. After flowering, it is essential to cut back this species to prevent the stems from becoming woody.

Thymus vulgaris 'Snow White'
COMPACT WHITE-FLOWERING THYME

Hardy evergreen perennial. Height 6in (15cm) and spread 8in (20cm). Small clusters of tiny white flowers appear in summer. The leaves are mid-green and very small. This thyme has an upright but predominantly mounding habit. I find it excellent for cooking with fresh summer vegetables. The leaf flavor complements egg dishes because the taste is smoother and milder than *T. vulgaris*.

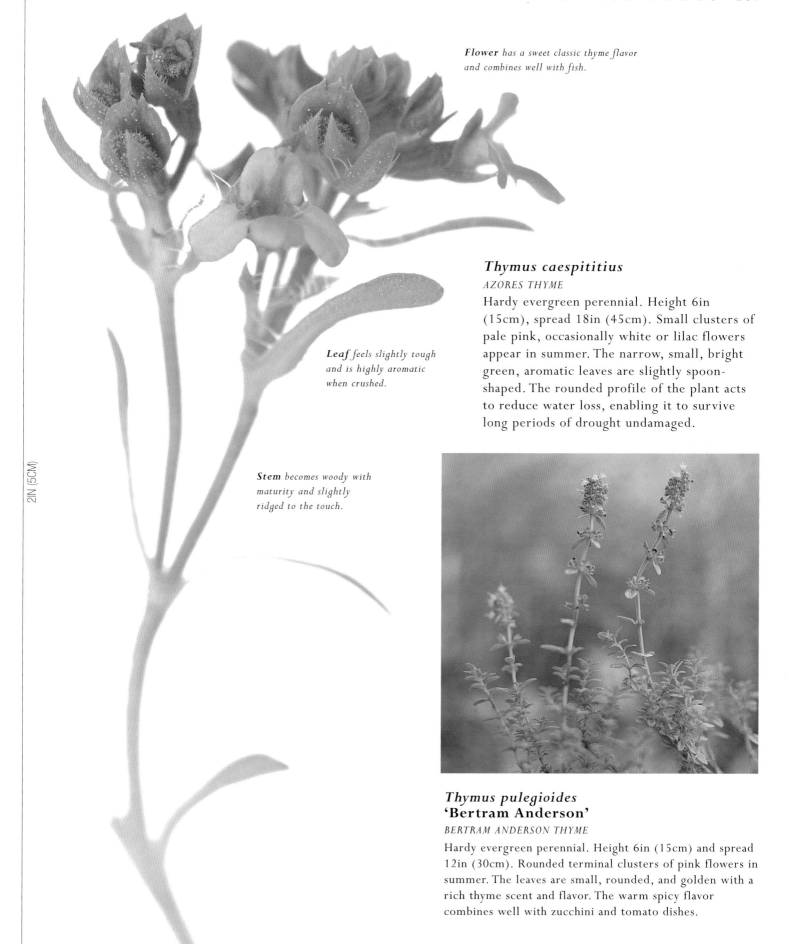

Flower has a sweet classic thyme flavor and combines well with fish.

Leaf feels slightly tough and is highly aromatic when crushed.

Stem becomes woody with maturity and slightly ridged to the touch.

2IN (5CM)

Thymus caespititius
AZORES THYME

Hardy evergreen perennial. Height 6in (15cm), spread 18in (45cm). Small clusters of pale pink, occasionally white or lilac flowers appear in summer. The narrow, small, bright green, aromatic leaves are slightly spoon-shaped. The rounded profile of the plant acts to reduce water loss, enabling it to survive long periods of drought undamaged.

Thymus pulegioides 'Bertram Anderson'
BERTRAM ANDERSON THYME

Hardy evergreen perennial. Height 6in (15cm) and spread 12in (30cm). Rounded terminal clusters of pink flowers in summer. The leaves are small, rounded, and golden with a rich thyme scent and flavor. The warm spicy flavor combines well with zucchini and tomato dishes.

Cultivation

Propagation Sow annual varieties in pots in early spring and place under protection. Germination takes 10–20 days. Or sow the seeds into prepared ground 8in (20cm) apart, when the air temperature does not fall below 48°F (9°C). Germination takes 14–21 days. Unlike the annual, sow *T. speciosum* in fall and place in a cold frame. Germination takes 3–4 weeks. If nothing happens, place outside for the winter. Germination can take as long as 2 years.

Site Plant in well-drained soil in sun or partial shade. If the soil is too rich, there will be too much foliage and little flower. They grow well in containers. Be stingy with the nutrients in the substrate. Dilute with ⅓ bark or coir.

Maintenance Deadhead regularly to maintain flowering. Pick off seeds as they form to inhibit self-seeding. Water throughout the summer months. Nasturtium is renowned for attracting aphids and the caterpillars of the cabbage white butterfly. If the infestation is light, wash off; if severe, cut right back.

Harvesting Use fresh, picking flowers, leaves, and seeds as required.

Uses The seeds, leaves, and flowers all have a piquant taste and can be eaten in salads. Chopped leaves give a peppery flavor. Seeds can be pickled and used as an alternative to capers. Medicinally, all parts of the plant are antibiotic. The leaves contain vitamin C and iron, as well as an antiseptic substance, which is most potent before the plant flowers. Nasturtiums are thought good for the skin.

Tropaeolum Nasturtium TROPAEOLACEAE

Common nasturtium (*Tropaeolum majus*) is a valuable summer annual with its wonderfully bright and brazen flowers. It is a familiar sight in many gardens, but is rarely acknowledged as the useful culinary and medicinal herb that it is. It was introduced into Europe from Peru in the sixteenth century and was first known as Indian cress (*Nasturtium indicum*), because of the peppery watercresslike flavor of the leaves. The practice of eating fresh petals and using them in tea originated in the Orient. There are now many more varieties, including those with variegated leaves and multicolored flowers.

Tropaeolum speciosum
FLAME NASTURTIUM, SCOTTISH FLAME FLOWER
Hardy perennial climber. Height up to 10ft (3m) and spread indefinite. In summer, scarlet flowers appear, followed by bright blue fruits. The leaves are green and lobed. Plant the roots in shade, so they do not dry out in hot summers. The plant flowers in 3–5 years if grown from seed.

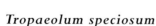

Tropaeolum majus 'Empress of India'

NASTURTIUM EMPRESS OF INDIA

Half-hardy annual. Height 8in (20cm) and spread 12in (30cm). It has dark red, helmet-shaped flowers with a long nectar spur that last throughout summer until the first frosts. The mid-green leaves are round with distinct veins. A good companion plant, it deters wooly aphids from apple trees.

Flower is shaped like a metal helmet, with a long nectar spur protruding from the rear.

Stem is succulent when broken.

Leaf has distinct veins running into a center point.

6IN (15CM)

Cultivation

Propagation Either leave the berries on the bush until spring and sow fresh, or pick when ripe and store in a cold, dry place in a tray in a single layer until spring. Sow, and place under protection at 60°F (15°C). Germination takes 1–2 months, but can take longer. Take softwood cuttings in summer from non-flowering shoots. For both propagation methods, pot up when the roots are established and grow on in a container for 2 seasons, before planting into a prepared site.

Site Plant in well-drained acid soil in full sun. Wet conditions will damage the plant quicker than cold. On an exposed, windy site, plant against a south- or west-facing wall. In warm climates grow it as a low hedge. It can also be grown in containers. Use an ericaceous substrate. Do not upgrade the pot size – it prefers being potbound.

Maintenance Feed only once in spring with well-rotted compost. In containers, feed weekly during the growing season. Overfed plants will not flower. In warm climates, trim the plant in the fall to maintain its shape; in colder climates trim in spring.

Harvesting Pick fresh leaves as required through the year. Harvest fresh flowers in summer. By late fall the berries will be ripe and ready to eat.

Uses The leaves can be used to make a spicy tea, or to add a warm spicy flavor to stews and casseroles. In Chile, the seeds are roasted and used as a coffee substitute. The berries can be eaten raw or cooked. They become more tart in flavor when cooked.

Ugni Chilean guava MYRTACEAE

I grow hundreds of different herbs. All are wonderful, but occasionally there is one that becomes a particular favorite. This is one of those. Chilean guava is characterized by its charming shell pink flowers, followed by lush dark red fruit in the fall. The fruit tastes of wild strawberries and was apparently a great favorite of Queen Victoria, who requested that jam be made from the sweet berries.

Ugni molinae

CHILEAN GUAVA

Hardy evergreen shrub. Height up to 8ft (2.5m) and spread 5ft (1.5m). Pretty pale pink flowers appear in summer, followed by round fruit, which ripen to a very dark red. The small dark green leaves are leathery in texture and aromatic. In the fall, they may turn a slightly copper color.

Fruit *ripens to dark red. It should be just soft to the touch before eating.*

2IN (5CM)

Leaf *is shiny on the upper surface, matte on the underside.*

Flowers *are pale pink, cup-shaped, and hang down.*

FOR USE IN **The Garden**
PS. 21, 43, 53

Cultivation

Propagation Sow seeds in spring and place in a cold frame. Germination takes 3–4 weeks. Plant out 24in (60cm) apart, when large enough to handle. Alternatively, sow into prepared open ground in late spring. Leave uncovered, when the air temperature is above 48°F (9°C). Divide established plants in the fall and replant in a well-prepared site.

Site Choose the site carefully to avoid having to move the plant later; the scent of broken roots will attract cats. Plant in sun or partial shade, but keep the roots cool and damp in summer. It will grow well next to a pond. Valerian is a good companion plant for vegetables because the roots stimulate phosphorus and earthworm activity. Valerian also grows well in a large container placed in partial shade. Use a soil-based substrate and water regularly to keep the soil moist.

Maintenance Cut back after flowering to prevent self-seeding. Place the leaves on the compost heap – they are rich in minerals.

Harvesting Dig up the roots of a second- or third-year plant for drying.

Uses Historically, this medicinal herb has been used as a sedative and relaxant. The roots, prepared into tablet, powder, capsule, or tincture form, are a safe, non-addictive relaxant that reduces anxiety and promotes sleep. In the garden, spray an infusion of the root onto the topsoil to attract earthworms.

Valeriana Valerian VALERIANACEAE

The scent of the flowers is deliciously fragrant, but the fresh root, when dug up, has a pungent odor. Cats, however, find the smell of the root even more seductive than catnip (*Nepeta cataria*), as do rats, so valerian root can be used as an enticing bait in rat traps as a chemical-free alternative to poison. Medicinally, valerian is a well-known sedative and, combined with other herbs, makes a good remedy for insomnia and restlessness. Do not take for an extended period or during pregnancy.

Valeriana officinalis

VALERIAN, ALL HEAL
Hardy herbaceous perennial. Height up to 4ft (1.2m) and spread 3ft (1m). In summer, it has clusters of small, sweetly scented white flowers that are often tinged pink. The mid-green leaves are deeply divided and toothed at the edges. In spring the new leaf growth has an attractive bronze tinge.

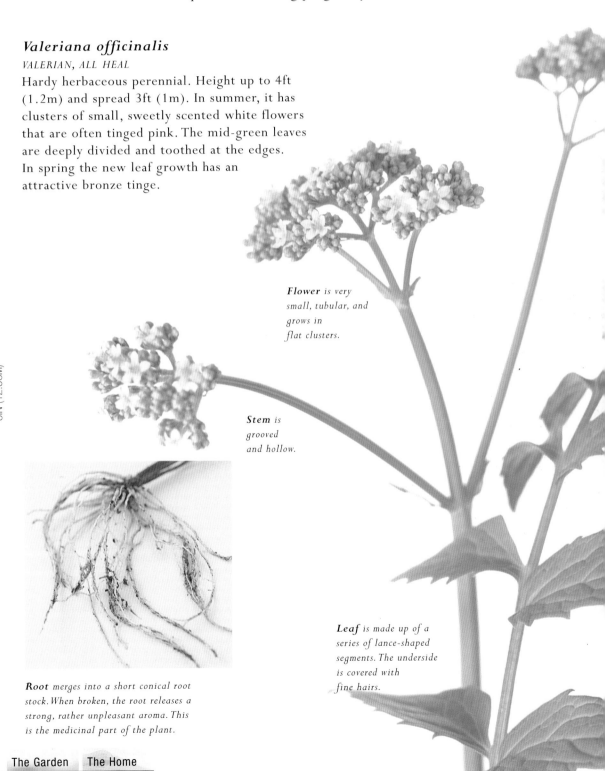

5IN (12.5CM)

Flower is very small, tubular, and grows in flat clusters.

Stem is grooved and hollow.

Leaf is made up of a series of lance-shaped segments. The underside is covered with fine hairs.

Root merges into a short conical root stock. When broken, the root releases a strong, rather unpleasant aroma. This is the medicinal part of the plant.

FOR USE IN

The Garden   The Home
PP. 21, 43, 49, 58   PP. 110, 113

Cultivation

Propagation The seeds of this herb need stratification before germination (see page 46). In cold climates, sow the seed into a pot and place outside for the winter. Germination takes 4–6 months. In warm climates, first place the seeds in the refrigerator for one month to stratify them, then sow in a pot or tray and place outside. Germination is erratic, so be patient. Once large enough to handle, leave the seedlings in pots outside and then plant out 12in (30cm) apart. Divide established plants in the fall or spring, replanting into a prepared site.

Site Plant in any well-drained soil in sun or partial shade. Vervain plants will adapt to clay soils. To increase its visual impact, plant in groups against a dark backdrop like a hedge to help to show off the flowers. It will grow in containers, using a soil-based substrate.

Maintenance Cut back after flowering to prevent self-seeding. To maintain healthy leaf growth, divide established plants in the fall or spring every third year.

Harvesting Fresh vervain leaves can be harvested throughout the growing season. For drying, harvest the flowers in summer.

Uses An important medicinal herb, it is used by Western and Chinese herbalists to treat nervous exhaustion, headaches, and liver and urinary tract infections. It is can be administered as a medicinal tea, but it is very bitter.

Caution Do not take during pregnancy.

Verbena Vervain VERBENACEAE

Although the flowers of this insignificant-looking herb have no fragrance, and it is bitter to taste, vervain contains important medicinal properties. The ancient Greeks attributed magical properties to it and wore amulets made from vervain flowers and leaves to protect themselves against demons and disease. In contemporary society, it is used as an effective natural remedy to relieve nervous tension and anxiety. Do not confuse vervain (*Verbena officinalis*) with lemon verbena (*Aloysia triphylla*) see page 127.

Verbena officinalis
VERVAIN, HERB OF GRACE
Hardy herbaceous perennial. Height up to 36in (90cm) and spread 12in (30cm). Tiny terminal clusters of very pale lilac flowers appear in summer. Its green leaves are often deeply divided into lobes with curved teeth.

2.5IN (5CM)

Flower grows in small clusters at the end of wandlike, flowering stems.

Flowers appear progressively up the stem.

Cultivation

Propagation Sow seeds in the fall. Do not cover, with substrate and place in a cold frame for the winter. Germination will occur by the following spring. Once large enough to handle, plant out 6in (15cm) apart. Divide established plants in the fall, replanting in a prepared site.

Site Violas are self-seeding and adapt to most soil type, but they dislike waterlogged sites. They favor sun or partial shade. They grow well in containers, on their own or with other herbs. Use a soil-based substrate.

Maintenance Deadhead flowers and pinch out growing tips to maintain flowering throughout the season. Cut back in the fall to encourage new growth and to help the plant survive the winter months.

Harvesting Pick fresh flowers throughout the season. In summer, pick the flowering parts for use in infusions or for drying.

Uses Medicinally, violas are used as a detoxifying herb to treat arthritis, whooping cough, bronchitis, and skin diseases. An infusion made from the flowers, leaves, and stems will soothe itchy skin. An infusion of the flowers only has long been prescribed for mending a broken heart. It is also beneficial when added to a bath for easing aches and pains. A cold infusion of the flowers, leaves, and stems is diluted in drinking water and given to racing pigeons to help them fly faster.

Caution High doses can cause nausea and vomiting.

Viola Viola VIOLACEAE

These small wild pansies with their cheerful faces always turn to face the sun. Violas were made famous by Shakespeare in *A Midsummer Night's Dream*, and many references are made to violas in romantic literature and poetry since they were used to make love potions.

Viola tricolor

HEART'S EASE, WILD PANSY

Hardy perennial that is often grown as an annual, since it produces the most flowers in the first year. Height and spread 15in (38cm). Small, tricolored, pansylike flowers with blue, yellow, white, purple, and black petals. They flower throughout the summer until the first frosts. The leaves are heart-shaped or oval with toothed edgings. The flowers are edible and look attractive added to salad dishes.

Flower petals are purple or paler violet marked with dark purple spots or lines.

4IN (10CM)

Leaf becomes narrower and smaller higher up the flowering stem.

Viola odorata

SWEET VIOLET

Hardy perennial. Height 6in (15cm) and spread 12in (30cm). White, dark purple, and occasionally yellow sweetly scented flowers appear from late winter until mid-spring. The leaves are often a broad heart shape.

Index

Numbers in **bold** indicate major references. Numbers in *italic* refer to illustrations and/or their captions.

N

Herb Gardens to Visit

Agecroft Hall, 4305 Sulgrave Rd, Richmond, VA 23221-3256. 804-353-4241. Elizabethan garden, knot garden, medicinal, culinary, and fragrant herbs.

Atlanta Botanical Garden, Piedmont Park at the Prado, Atlanta, GA 30357. 404-876-5859. A knot and herb garden with fragrance plants.

W. J. Beal Botanical Garden, Michigan State University, 412 Olds Hall, East Lansing, MI 48824-1047. 517-355-9582. A botanical collection of herbs.

Brooklyn Botanic Garden, 1000 Washington Ave., Brooklyn, NY 11225-1099. 718-622-4433. Herb gardens with a knot garden and specialty gardens.

Caprilands Herb Farm, 5354 Silver Street, Coventry, CT 06238. 203-742-7244. A charming herb farm, surrounding an eighteenth-century farmhouse, with a Silver Garden, Saint's Garden, and more.

Chicago Botanic Garden, Lake Cook Rd., Glencoe, IL 60022. 708-835-5440. Formal and informal herb gardens with a knot garden, and culinary, and dye collections.

Cleveland Botanical Garden, 11030 East Boulevard, Cleveland, OH 44106. 216-721-1600. A great herb garden design, cared for by The Herb Society of America. It has a knot garden, historic roses, and dye, culinary, and fragrance gardens.

The Cloisters, Metropolitan Museum of Art Medieval Herb Garden, Fort Tryon Park, New York, NY 10040. 212-233-3700. Recreation of a monastic garden.

Colonial Williamsburg, Williamsburg, VA 23185. 804-220-7645. Williamsburg has a series of gardens, many of which contain colonial herbs.

Cornell Plantations, Robison York State Herb Garden, 1 Plantation Rd., Ithaca, NY 14850-2799. 607-255-3020. A series of herb gardens, with a broad range of native herbs.

Dallas Civic Garden Center, P.O. Box 26194, Dallas, TX 75226. 214-428-7476. A Shakespearean garden, rose garden, and an herb and fragrance garden with Braille labels.

Devonian Botanic Garden, University of Alberta, Edmonton, AB T6G 2E1, Canada. 403-987-3054. An herb garden with a variety of culinary, medicinal, and economic herbs.

J. Paul Getty Museum, 17985 Pacific Coast Hwy., Malibu, CA 90265-5799. 213-458-2003. Herbs appropriate to ancient Rome, set in gardens of a recreated Roman villa garden.

Hancock Shaker Village, Rt. 20, Hancock, MA 01237. 413-441-0188. Herbs that were grown, used, and sold by the Shaker community, in a farm setting.

The Herbfarm, 32804 Issaquah-Fall City Rd., Fall City, WA 98024. 206-784-2222. A series of theme gardens featuring many varieties of herbs.

Huntington Botanical Gardens, 1151 Oxford Rd., San Marino, CA 91108. 818-405-2100. An extensive collection of herbs planted in a series of specialty gardens.

Longwood Gardens, P.O. Box 501, Kennett Square, PA 19348-0501. 215-388-6741. A formal herb garden, children's garden, and idea garden.

Matthaei Botanical Garden, The University of Michigan, 1800 N. Dixboro Rd., Ann Arbor, MI 48105. 313-998-7061. A traditional herb garden that includes a knot garden and broad range of herbs.

Michigan 4-H Children's Garden, 4700 South Hagadorn Rd., East Lansing, MI 48823. 517-353-6692. A series of innovative children's gardens.

Missouri Botanical Garden, P.O. Box 299, St. Louis, MO 63166. 314-577-5111. A fenced formal garden with a variety of ornamental and culinary herbs.

Montreal Botanical Garden, 4101 Sherbrooke Street East, Montreal, QC H1X 2B2, Canada. 514-872-1400. Extensive collections of economic plants and herbs in their outdoor and conservatory gardens.

The National Herb Garden, U.S. National Arboretum, 3501 New York Avenue, N.E., Washington, DC 20002. 202-245-2726. A project of The Herb Society of America. Features a knot garden, historic rose garden, and ten specialty gardens.

New York Botanical Garden, Bronx, NY 10458-5126. 212-220-8700. This garden features knot gardens done with clipped boxwood and planting beds of ornamental herbs.

Royal Botanical Gardens, 680 Plains Road West, Burlington, ON L7T 8H4, Canada. 905-527-1158. A large garden with a teaching garden for children that includes herbs and extensive collections of roses.

University of British Columbia (UBC) Botanical Garden, 6804 Southwest Marine Drive, Vancouver, BC V6T 1Z4, Canada. 604-822-9666. Recreation of a 16th-century European physic garden.

University of California at Davis Arboretum, Davis, CA 95616. 916-752-2498. Medicinal plants, specialty gardens, and culinary herbs.

University of Minnesota Landscape Arboretum, 3675 Arboretum Drive, Chanhassen, MN 55317. 612-443-2460. A small knot garden, and collections of historic, medicinal, and fragrant herbs.

University of Washington Medicinal Herb Garden, University of Washington, Seattle, WA 98195. 206-543-1126. A medicinal herb garden.

VanDusen Botanical Garden, 5251 Oak Street, Vancouver, BC V6M 4H1, Canada. 604-878-9274. A 55-acre garden, including an Elizabethan maze, with more than 6,500 plants from six continents.

Books for Further Reading

Akerele, O., Heywood, V., and Synge, H. (eds.), *The Conservation of Medicinal Plants* (Cambridge, 1991)

Bensky, D. and Gamble, A., *Chinese Materia Medica* (Seattle, Washington, 1993)

Bown, D., *Fine Herbs* (London, 1988; as *Ornamental Herbs for Your Garden*, London, 1993)

Bown, D., *Eyewitness Garden Handbooks: Garden Herbs* (New York, 1998)

Bremness, L., *Eyewitness Handbooks: Herbs* (London, 1994)

Chevallier, A., *The Encyclopedia of Medicinal Plants* (London, 1996, 2001)

Culpeper's *Complete Herbal* (Ware, 1995)

Davidow, J., *Infusions of Healing* (New York, 1999)

Duke, J., *A Handbook of Northeastern Indian Medicinal Plants* (Lincoln, Massachusetts, 1986)

Duke, J., *The Green Pharmacy* (Emmaus, Pennsylvania, 1997)

Duke, J. and Vasquez, R., *Amazonian Ethnobotanical Dictionary* (Boca Raton, Florida, 1994)

Evans, W. C., *Trease and Evans' Pharmacognosy* (London, 13th ed., 1989)

Facciola, S., *Cornucopia II – A Source Book of Edible Plants* (Vista, California, 1998)

Foster, S. and Duke, J., *Field Guide to Eastern/Central Medicinal Plants* (Boston, Massachusetts, 1990)

Foster, S. and Yue, C., *Herbal Emissaries* (Rochester, Vermont, 1992)

Frawley, D. and Lad, V., *The Yoga of Herbs: An Ayurvedic Guide to Herbal Medicine* (Santa Fe, New Mexico, 1986)

Genders, R., *Scented Flora of the World* (St Albans, 1978)

Grieve, M., *A Modern Herbal* (London, 1931; ed. C. F. Leyel, London, 1976, 1988)

Griggs, B., *New Green Pharmacy* (London, 1981, 1997)

Iwu, M., *A Handbook of African Medicinal Plants* (Boca Raton, Florida, 1990)

Krochmal, A. and C., *A Field Guide to Medicinal Plants* (New York, 1973)

Lassak, E.V. and McCarthy, T., *Australian Medicinal Plants* (Kew, Victoria, 1997)

Lehane, B., *The Power of Plants* (London, 1977)

Mabberley, D. J., *The Plant-Book* (Cambridge, 1997)

Miller, A. G. and Morris, M., *Plants of Dhofar* (Diwan of the Royal Court Sultanate of Oman, 1988)

Moore, M., *Medicinal Plants of the Desert and Canyon West* (Santa Fe, New Mexico, 1989)

Moore, M., *Medicinal Plants of the Pacific West* (Santa Fe, New Mexico, 1993)

Morton, J. F., *Herbs and Spices* (New York, 1976)

Murray, M. T., *The Healing Power of Herbs* (Rocklin, California, 1992, 1995)

Nadkarni, K. M., *Indian Materia Medica* (Bombay, 1908, 1996)

Ody, P., *The Herb Society's Complete Medicinal Herbal* (London, 1993)

Ortiz, E. L., *The Encyclopedia of Herbs, Spices, and Flavourings* (London, 1992)

Phillips, R. and Foy, N., *Herbs* (London, 1990)

Roberts, M., *Indigenous Healing Plants* (Johannesburg, 1990)

Rohde, E. S., *The Old English Herbals* (New York, 1971)

Schultes, R. E. and Raffauf, R. F., *The Healing Forest* (Portland, Oregon, 1990)

Stobart, T., *Herbs, Spices and Flavourings* (London, 1970)

Taylor, L., *Herbal Secrets of the Rainforest* (Rocklin, California, 1998)

The Revolutionary Health Committee of Hunan Province, *A Barefoot Doctor's Manual* (London, 1978)

Tierra, M., *Planetary Herbology* (Santa Fe, New Mexico, 1988)

Tyler, V. E., *The Honest Herbal* (Binghamton, New York, 1993)

Tyler, V. E., *Herbs of Choice* (Binghamton, New York, 1994)

Van Wyk, B-E., van Oudtshoorn, B., and Gericke, N., *Medicinal Plants of South Africa* (Pretoria, 1997)

Weiss, R. F., *Herbal Medicine* (Beaconsfield, 1988)

Woodward, M. (ed.), *Gerard's Herbal* (London, 1994)

Wren, R. C., *Potter's New Cyclopedia of Botanical Drugs and Preparations* (Saffron Walden, 1988)

ALSO RECOMMENDED:
HerbalGram. Published quarterly by the American Botanical Council and the Herb Research Foundation, P.O. Box 144345, Austin, TX 78714-4345, USA.
Herbs, Journal of The Herb Society. Published quarterly by The Herb Society, Deddington Hill Farm, Warmington, Banbury, Oxon OX17 1XB. +44-1295-692000.

Acknowledgements

This book would not have been possible without Mac's love and support, William's constant companionship, Hampton's boundless energy, and not forgetting Hannah and Alistair's continuous encouragement.

I would like to thank Julie, Dan, Jill and Paul for keeping the farming going while I was writing.

Bella Pringle and Robin Rout for producing a beautifully designed book and Craig Knowles, Tim Winter and Sarah Cuttle for their photographs.

To Guy Ackloque and Emma and Anton Buckoke for allowing the team to photograph in their beautiful gardens and to Chelsea Physic Garden and the Royal Botanic Gardens Kew.

To Jane and Christopher Goodger for the loan of their house for photography, to Toby for his modeling, and to Chester, Lemon and Shula. Special thanks to Ed the dog, and his hamster chum for their petcare modelling.

To John Barford for providing emergency supplies of well-rotted manure and to Jim at Almondsbury Garden Center for gardening equipment.

Also, to Formica UK Ltd for colored backgrounds on which to photograph the herbs.

To Jamie Oliver for his support and enthusiasm for using fresh herbs in cooking.

To Anthea for her support and to all the team at Dorling Kindersley for their encouragement.

PHOTOGRAPHY CREDITS

Craig Knowles
Pages 1–6, 11, 12, 14 *third from right*, 16, 19, 20, 22–3, 24 (top left), 27 *except bottom left*, 28–9, 35, 36–9, 42, 44–5 *except 44 bottom left*, 46–59, 62–9, 71–77, 81, 95 *bottom*, 99, 105, 113 *top, bottom right*, 118–267 *except 141 inset, 146 top, 159 inset, 190 inset*, and *255 inset*.

Tim Winter
Pages 78–9, 80, 82–94, 95 *top*, 96–7, 98, 100–104, 106–112, 113 *bottom left*.

Sarah Cuttle
Pages 8–9, 10, 14 *except third from right*, 15, 17, 18, 24 *except top left*, 26, 27 *bottom left*, 34, 40–41, 60–61, 70, 114–115, 116.

Jekka McVicar
Page 190 *inset*.

Harry Smith Collection
Pages 141 *inset*, 159 *inset*.

John Glover,
The Garden Picture Library
Page 146 t*op*.

Jerry Pavia,
The Garden Picture Library
Page 255 *inset*.